Endorsements

The diaspora studies in recent decades have garnered increasing interest among evangelicals worldwide due to the extensive migration of people. This migration has attracted the interest of Christian mission thinkers and practitioners alike, who have been exploring various venues for engaging these displaced people worldwide. Dr. Sadiri Joy Tira and his team have been relentlessly attempting to produce valuable resources to enable the global church to engage with the diaspora people missionally and ministerially. *Tides of Opportunity: Missiological Experiences and Engagement in Global Migration*, is one such valuable resource that certainly has the potential to help us understand the importance of taking diaspora missiology seriously. This book draws stories, experiences, insights, and implications from the writings of those with significant exposure and experience with the diaspora people from around the world. Insights from this book are bound to compel the traditional mission academicians and practitioners to think afresh about mission and ministry among people on the move. This book is a significant contribution to understanding and practicing diaspora missiology.

Atul Y. Aghamkar, PhD
Director, National Center for Urban Transformation
Former Professor and Head of the Department of Missiology,
South Asia Institute of Advanced Christian Studies, Bangalore, India

This fine collection of essays brings together a rich compendium of studies and resources for anyone wishing to understand and engage with contemporary trends and practical approaches to mission in the multiplicity of emerging diaspora communities around the world. The field is rapidly changing, and the movement of peoples in our complex, global mosaic challenges us to pray, think, reflect, and respond practically to the opportunities this movement presents for all who take seriously our Lord's mandate to "make disciples of all nations." Dr. Sadiri Joy Tira and his colleagues have blessed us with a great gift, a snapshot of how God is at work, and how we are called to participate in the mission of God today.

Richard Harvey, PhD
All Nations Christian College, UK
Senior Researcher, Jews for Jesus

The collective experience and wisdom that shaped *Tides of Opportunity* represents the best of evangelical diaspora missiology. A hallmark of the scholarship that shapes this volume is its determination to resource diaspora ministries and the many women and men who serve people on the move in the name of Christ. I am delighted to commend this new volume from the team of authors and editors, led by Dr. Sadiri Joy Tira, who have yet again crafted a remarkable resource.

Rev. Darrell Jackson
Associate Professor, Whitley College, University of Divinity, Melbourne

Books of this nature tend to look only backward at the past contributions of missiological giants. But the robust collection here seems to agree that a bold forward march into the future of global mission is needed. The readers of this volume, *Tides of Opportunity: Missiological Experiences and Engagement in Global Migration*, will enjoy the occasional glance over the shoulders of the giants to discern their thoughts about missions and migration. But, again and again, we find our heroes waving us on forward—urging us to keep blazing the trail ahead until the kingdom fully comes.

Rev. Hon. Cody Lorance
Co-CEO, Endiro Coffee; Trade Representative of the President of Uganda
Honorary Consul for the Republic of Uganda in the USA

Tides of Opportunity takes the sustained effort to develop diaspora missiology one giant step forward by arguing that challenging migration and devastating human displacements are God's purposeful design to fulfill his mission. Reading this book can be a powerful spiritual experience as the authors urge mission academics and practitioners to take a divine perspective on the tides of human movements.

Julie C. Ma, PhD
Professor of Mission and Intercultural Studies, Oral Roberts University

Global migration opens for us big opportunities for missions. It is a necessity for us to study these migrations and learn how we can respond and engage with them biblically and humanely. Great movements of people show us that the Lord is bringing people out of countries where the gospel is hard to access. *Tides of Opportunity: Missiological Experiences and Engagement in Global Migration* offers us a variety of experiences learned firsthand by brilliant and godly authors and will be a great tool for mission leaders, churches, and Christian individuals. Let us learn from them! May we learn to embrace the opportunity to be used by God to minister to these migrants. Let us passionately treat the migrants as our mission field.

Timothy K. Park, PhD
Senior Professor of Asian Missions, Fuller Theological Seminary

On November 15, 2022, the world population reached a staggering 8 billion! Almost 80 percent were newly born in Asia, and they will not stay put! More people will move away from their "birth or present" country than any other time in human history. The wave is growing in height, size, and sheer immensity. Meanwhile, our Father continues his God-sized rescue operation to save humanity. The future must be seen through a new lens; the day of exclusive male, pale, and getting frail Western-dominant ministry is gone. The church needs to grow in cultural intelligence and competency in engaging and empowering multiethnic, multicultural, hybrid Christian communities in order to meet the rising wave of God's scattered people. When you digest the contents of *Tides of Opportunity: Missiological Experiences and Engagement in Global Migration*, your game will change.

Rev. Warren Reeve, DMin
Founder, Missional International Church Network
Pastor, Martin Luther King Église, Greater Paris, France

This compendium of mission writings will serve as a significant resource for any Christian who wants to be informed and engaged in what God is doing in the midst of global migration. This book is not for the hobby reader—the authors go deep in their global research, missional insights, and cultural perspectives. The principles presented call for rigorous thinking and determined response from the reader. The themes examined range broadly from the vast stream of global diasporic trends, to the salvific impact of mother-child relationships. Although each article in this book is unique in its perspective, the authors speak with one voice to call the church to understand their times and to see how God is at work among his people from every nation and in every nation.

Sandra Ryan
Global Mission Pastor, The Peoples' Church, Toronto

This volume has led me to three reflections on diaspora missiology. First, it is an important discipline that continues to grow and develop. Dr. Sadiri Joy Tira and the contributors to this volume present new data and new ideas as to how we approach diaspora missions. Second, this volume presents both the global scale of diaspora and the local voices through stories and examples. It is necessary for academics and practitioners to be informed of the magnitude of missional opportunities brought by diaspora missions and yet to be moved with the personal stories of how viable this ministry is. Last, the book has been true to the nature of diaspora—which is liminality—by discussing crucial issues like identity, hybridity, prostitution, human trafficking, exploitation, and injustices.

Juliet Lee Uytanlet, PhD
Former Lausanne Catalyst on Diasporas (2016–2018)
Author, *The Hybrid Tsinoys*

Global migration and the growth of diaspora communities in and from every continent are among the most visible and urgent missional challenges to the global church—including the church within some of those very diasporas. So a book of this scale and diversity is a most valuable contribution to our missional thinking, strategy, and engagement in what God is doing in the midst of these phenomena.

Rev. Chris Wright, PhD
Global Ambassador, Langham Partnership
Chief Architect of the Cape Town 2010 Commitment Call to Action,
Lausanne Movement

Diaspora is the motif of both the Old and New Testaments, as God reveals himself to humanity and unveils his plan to bring redemption to all creation. God continues to act in and through the diaspora people. The unique challenges that people on the move face open their hearts to the message of the gospel and prepare them to be God's instrument of blessing. This book presents fine essays on recent world trends on diaspora missiology and passionate accounts to voice the pain of those suffering during their journeys. This book inspires us to live on mission, as God's people on the move, proclaiming the salvation of Jesus Christ to all nations.

Rev. Jura Yanagihara, PhD
President, Alliance World Fellowship

This volume is a veritable smorgasbord of stories, statistics, and Scripture about global diasporas today. It beautifully overlays these elements into a stunning picture of the current state of human migration. This is essential reading for anyone hoping to glean valuable insights into the move of God in his beloved people and what this means for our world's immediate future.

Allen Yeh, DPhil
Professor of Intercultural Studies and Missiology, Biola University

Tides of Opportunity

Missiological Experiences
and Engagement in Global Migration

Editor
Sadiri Joy Tira

Associate Editors
Damples Dulcero-Baclagon
Lorajoy Tira-Dimangondayao

visit us at missionbooks.org

Tides of Opportunity: Missiological Experiences and Engagement in Global Migration
© 2024 by Sadiri Joy Tira. All Rights Reserved.

Chapter 2 by Steve Ybarrola, and chapter 4 by Thomas Harvey, were originally published by Lifechange Publishing Inc. and Jaffray Center for Global Initiatives, 2013 under the title *The Human Tidal Wave*. Registered at the National Library of the Philippines. Used by permission.

No part of this book may be reproduced, stored in a retrieval system, or transmitted in any form or by any means—electronic, mechanical, photocopy, recording, or otherwise—without prior written permission from the publisher, except brief quotations used in connection with reviews. This manuscript may not be entered into AI, even for AI training. For permission, email permissions@wclbooks.com. For corrections, email editor@wclbooks.com.

William Carey Publishing (WCP) publishes resources to shape and advance the missiological conversation in the world. We publish a broad range of thought-provoking books and do not necessarily endorse all opinions set forth here or in works referenced within this book.

The URLs included in this workbook are provided for personal use only and are current as of the date of publication, but the publisher disclaims any obligation to update them after publication.

Scripture quotations marked NIV are taken from the Holy Bible, New International Version®, NIV®. Copyright © 1973, 1978, 1984, 2011 by Biblica, Inc.™ Used by permission of Zondervan. All rights reserved worldwide. www.zondervan.com. The "NIV" and "New International Version" are trademarks registered in the United States Patent and Trademark Office by Biblica, Inc.™

Scripture quotations marked ESV are taken from the ESV® Bible (The Holy Bible, English Standard Version®), Copyright © 2001 by Crossway, a publishing ministry of Good News Publishers. Used by permission. All rights reserved.

Published by William Carey Publishing
10 W. Dry Creek Cir
Littleton, CO 80120 | www.missionbooks.org

William Carey Publishing is a ministry of Frontier Ventures
Pasadena, CA | www.frontierventures.org

Cover and Interior Designer: Mike Riester

ISBNs: 978-1-64508-478-5 (paperback)
          978-1-64508-480-8 (epub)

Printed Worldwide

28 27 26 25 24   1 2 3 4 5   IN

Library of Congress Control Number: 2024933911

Dedication

This book is dedicated to my family and my friend Stanley Douglas Birdsall.

This book project was conceived after my cruel stroke in the summer of 2020. The medical team informed me that I am now in a new journey. My family: wife, children, and grandchildren came to the hospital to pray and wipe my tears. I experienced God's gentle touch. He was merciful and gracious to extend my life, in fact he snatched me from the gate of death to what is now my new life! After the great Physician healed my brain (hemorrhage), I committed to write my unfinished two book projects. This book is one of the two volumes.

Lourdes, Lorajoy, Dennis, Santiago, and Isabel; Tonyvic, Zenavid, Sophie, and Bishop, you inspired me to live.

Rev. Dr. S. Douglas Birdsall, honorary Chairman of the Lausanne Movement representing hundreds of friends whom I consider my "cloud of witnesses," and my "inner circle" of co-pilgrims who are praying, cheering, and walking with me during the stormy and dark days. You never cease to assure me that I am loved and cared for.

This book will outlive me. But may this book inform, instruct, and inspire the global mission leaders and future, younger kingdom workers, like you (my children and grandchildren).

Your co-pilgrim,
Joy, Dad, and Grandpa

Prayer for Migrants

Oh God, Creator, sustainer of life and helper of the pilgrims. "Lord, you have been our dwelling place throughout all generations" (Psalm 90:1).

I come before you, in the name of Jesus Christ, the Great High Priest who is able to sympathize for all our needs. Thank you, spirit of the living God for your tender mercies and for directing my prayers to the highest glory of the triune God.

I do not fully understand the flight of humans; they are mysterious and too deep to fathom.

Today, I specifically pray for the diasporas, the scattered people in our borderless world. Too many of them are like grains scattered in the vast field, in the world you created.

Some of them are left with no choice but to leave their homeland because of the forces of nature that have washed away their properties and destroyed their homes. While others flee the terrors of war and conflict, still others leave for the betterment of their lives and advancement of their careers. For reasons I do not know, these scattered people are now separated from their families, isolated from their communities, confused and lonely in a foreign land.

I pray for the homeless and uprooted refugees … have mercy Lord,

The children caught in the middle of wars and conflict … protect them, Father.

The women trafficked and sold into the sex industry …
Preserve them Almighty God and destroy the work of the enemy.

The economic migrants … Who are abused by their earthly masters, maltreated and cheated for their labor … compassionate God provide for them.

The international students who are future leaders of their native-land, grant them, Master, their hearts' desires for academic excellence.

The seafarers and fishermen working and living in high seas protect them from pirates and send your angels to surround their boats and ships.

The scientists in the space labs and in both poles, North and South, God of comfort, comfort them and their loved ones awaiting their swift return.

The armies and navies in the battlefield and on the seas, may they be peace makers. Shield them, our God.

The newly landed immigrants, Lord, may they plant roots in their adopted country and be moored in Christian community.

Oh God, now I commit the millions of migrants. May they find peace, strength, and joy in Christ Jesus as they travel on in our borderless world.

This is my prayer, in the name of our Lord Jesus Christ, the friend of the migrants and pilgrims. Amen.

Sadiri Joy Tira

Contents

Foreword by *Michael Oh* — xi

Preface by *Sadiri Joy Tira* — xiii

Introduction by *Damples Dulcero-Baclagon* — xv

Part I: Understanding the Realities of Tides of Opportunity in Global Migration

1 Global Gateway Cities in Canada as Diaspora Epicenter — 3
  Christopher Carr

2 Diasporas and Multiculturalism: Social Imaginaries, Liminality, and Cultural Identity | *Steven Ybarrola* — 15

3 La Mamá as Missionary to the Next Generation: A Case Study of a US Latina Immigrant Mother and Her Influence on the Religious Identity Formation of Her Gen Z Daughter — 31
  Rebekah Clapp

4 Pluralism, Multiculturalism, and Diaspora Mission: Discovering the Relevance of Apostolic Mission Today — 45
  Thomas Alan Harvey

5 Religious Pluralism in the Twenty-First Century Global Diaspora: A Case of Canadian Pluralistic Communities and the Evangelical Response | *Sadiri Joy Tira* — 63

6 Ethnic and Cultural Hybridity: Jewish-Gentile Intermarriage in North America | *Tuvya Zaretsky* — 75

Part II: Responding and Engaging the Tides of Opportunity in Global Migration

7 Models of Diaspora Communities for Missiological Application — 91
  Jason Richard Tan

8 Rural Migration and Diaspora Missions | *Matt Cook* — 117

9 Embracing the Refugees in Canada through Hospitality — 135
  Craig C. Kraft

10 Understanding and Ministering to Survivors of Sex Trafficking — 149
  Valerie Geer

11 Examining Ourselves: Working for Freedom in a World of Exploitation and Trafficking | *Marion L. S. Carson* — 163

12 Missional Transnationals: Coming Full Circle — 171
  Sadiri Joy Tira

13 Rooted in Spirituality, Committed to Missions: My Tribute to the Late Dr. Thomas Wang — 175
  Juno Wang

Appendix A: Resources and Tools for Diaspora Missions: Annotated
   Bibliography 187
Appendix B: The Seoul Declaration on Diaspora Missiology 195
Acknowledgments 197
About the Editors and Contributors 199

Foreword

I grew up loving the ocean. I can spend hours looking at the water, and my love for the ocean has deepened (literally) in the past few years as I have earned my scuba diving license. I grew up watching waves, and my eyes would light up as I saw a potentially big wave on the horizon. This is not as easy as you might think—the difference between a truly huge wave and a wave that you thought was big is very slight.

Human migration will be a huge wave. It is already a sizable wave, and it could reach as many as one billion people by 2050!

What does that mean for us?

We need to learn that this huge wave has turned into a tide—a tide of opportunity to understand migrants brought by God to our doorsteps. Gaining that understanding is why you need to read this book, *Tides of Opportunity: Missiological Experiences and Engagement in Global Migration*. You need to learn from those who really know the waves and the tides. Those people are the contributors to this book—foremost my friend Dr. Sadiri Joy Tira.

I still remember Joy running down the walkway in the main meeting space of our venue in Bangalore, India in 2013. It was the site of my installation as the new leader of the Lausanne Movement. Joy gave me a book which was the first edition of this wonderful work freshly off the press. The huge smile on his face showed the passion that he has in his heart for this critical issue.

We were together again in Manila, Philippines for the 2015 Global Diaspora Forum which was, in many ways, the extended fruit of this volume. Human migration is personal for Joy. It's personal to him as a Filipino thinker and leader who migrated to Canada and from there traveled around the world. And it's personal for me too.

Long before I was a third culture kid learning to navigate life as a second-generation Korean-American, and eventually living and serving in Japan as a missionary myself, my own family was living out the opportunities and challenges that are reflected in this book.

My father, as a young boy growing up under the Japanese occupation of Korea, spent the years before the eventual end of World War II in Manchuria where my grandfather was a migrant worker doing forestry under Japanese rule. My great aunt was married off at a young age to avoid becoming a victim of human trafficking as a "comfort woman" of the Japanese army.

My father and mother left Korea, at one point among the ten poorest nations on earth, to migrate to America where they pursued the American dream. In many ways, that dream was fulfilled though not without cost. My family and I lived through some of the realities described in this book.

This volume is also meaningful to the Lausanne Movement.

Joy not only served as the founding catalyst for Lausanne's diaspora global issue network, he helped the global movement to see the wave that was approaching. In the early days the wave seemed so small, it was almost imperceptible. But Joy kept pointing and teaching us and challenging us. Now it's upon us, and we are better prepared for today and the future because of the diligence of Joy and his co-laborers.

Read this book. Study it. Pray through it. Share it.

The wave continues to build. And we must be prepared.

MICHAEL OH, PhD
Global Executive Director/CEO, Lausanne Movement

Preface

Two announcements are mind boggling to me: On November 15, 2022, the UN declared the world population surpassed eight billion. Two days later, Canadian media outlets announced that Canada will receive five hundred thousand new immigrants per year by 2025. These announcements are not just numbers, but humans and migrants—a huge wave! What are the implications of these facts for the global church?

Migration and the massive scattering or "diasporas of people" are as widespread as waves reaching the shores. As I write, close to ten million Ukrainians have fled their homeland, and thousands of Russians, mostly men, are running away from the war-torn Eurasian region. Since January 2020, millions have scrambled to escape from the COVID-19 pandemic that resulted in millions of infected people. The World Health Organization (WHO) reported that the pandemic disrupted all nations and all seven continents. Global poverty and hunger, as well as global warming, also referred to as climate change, are uprooting and dislocating nations. Racial and cultural violence and political chaos are causing political disorder.

In the late modern period, we are experiencing immense human suffering, but in the midst of this pain, two passages from Scripture remind me of God's sovereignty. The Lord Jesus Christ himself said, "The gates of hell shall not prevail against it" (Matt 16:18 KJV). Then, according to the psalmist, "God is our refuge and strength, an ever-present help in trouble. Therefore, we will not fear, though the earth gives way and the mountains fall into the heart of the sea, though its water roar and foam and the mountains quake with their surging" (Ps 46: 1–3). He says, "Be still, and know that I am God" (Ps 46:10).

The global church must not lose hope in the midst of suffering, turmoil, hunger, violence, and the threat of perilous days.

The book *Human Tidal Wave* was originally published as a "bridge" to connect the diaspora missiology materials *Scattered to Gather: Embracing the Global Trend of Diaspora* presented during the Lausanne Congress on World Evangelization III held in Cape Town, South Africa from October 16–25, 2010, to the Global Diaspora Forum held on March 24–28, 2015, in Metro Manila, Philippines. That book was originally published in 2013 to keep up the momentum of diaspora missions that was evidently embraced by the global church during the Cape Town conference in 2010. The result of the Global Diaspora Forum (2015) was the publication of *Scattered and Gathered: A Global Compendium of Diaspora Missiology*.

Many regional events have taken place in the last decade, and more books have been published. The global church is now being ushered into the next quarter of the twenty-first century. Human migration, or waves of migration are accelerating and growing, impacting world evangelization. How will the global church respond to the issues presented by migration in the twenty-five years to come? The so-called "human tidal wave" has resulted in "tides of opportunities" to advance the kingdom of God and the growth of the global church.

In this new book entitled, *Tides of Opportunity: Missiological Experiences and Engagement in Global Migration* contributors re-address current global events. Several multi-disciplinary researchers, mission practitioners, and specialists collaborate to address the issues of global migration, including the push and pull, or voluntary and involuntary factors, and diasporic consequences—urban and rural immigration, multiculturalism, pluralism, transnationalism, and racial and cultural hybridity. Human geographers, historians, sociologists, anthropologists, environmental experts, and theologians are predicting not only regional but larger global waves in the next twenty-five years. Therefore, missiologists, mission strategists, ministry coaches, academics, and agency church leaders must prepare their students and local congregations to embrace and engage the "tides of opportunities."

In this resource, mission practitioners respond with justice and compassion to global crises of homeless, naked, hungry, and broken refugees and to the victims of labor injustices and abuses—particularly the victims of human trafficking. Finally, the writers examine how we can learn from the old mission practitioners like the Moravians. The Christian mission practitioners of the twenty-first century can learn from the old Moravian movement who practiced "glocal missions."

I hope that this volume is not only for the academics and mission leaders but will find its way to ordinary migrant workers who are witnesses of Jesus Christ right in their homes and respective communities.

Jochebed (Exod 2:9–10), the Hebrew "migrant, refugee mother," introduced her children to the true God. She specifically developed the religious and spiritual life of her son Moses. Consequently, her son became the great Hebrew leader in the foreign land of Egypt. Let there be more Jochebeds and Moseses among the immigrant peoples.

Soli Deo Gloria
SADIRI JOY TIRA, DMiss, DMin
Edmonton, Alberta, Canada

Introduction

When it comes to global migration, the Philippines has a lot of stories to tell. Its beginning came from several waves of migration of people from all over Asia and the West. So this archipelago made of 7,641 islands is a mixture of people who settled and lived harmoniously to become the melting pot of cultures in South East Asia.

At the end of World War I, White Russians came to the Philippines to flee from the Red Russians. In 1934, before World War II began, President Manuel L. Quezon, the Commonwealth President allowed the Jewish refugees to escape to our country from Nazi persecution and offered them sanctuary in Mindanao. In 1980, the Philippines hosted Vietnamese refugees to prepare and process for their relocation to Western countries. If a country like the Philippines can welcome refugees to its territories and care for their needs, a church can do it more out of God's unlimited love.

Human migration is not a new thing. Every country has its own story to tell about migration. Even the Bible is teeming with stories about migration. Elimelech and Naomi went to Moab together with their sons, and later Ruth, the Moabitess migrated to Judah to accompany Naomi on her return (Ruth 1). Joseph to Egypt, Moses to Midian, and Joseph and Mary with the baby Jesus to Egypt. These are migration stories that speak of God's will for people to move toward his direction.

This book, *Tides of Opportunity: Missiological Experiences and Engagement in Global Migration*, also contains stories about people moving from their home country to a host country. It opens the window for us to see a world of people's movements and mobility. As in the ancient times of the Bible, God is moving the Naomis to seek greener pastures, Josephs to be migrant workers, Moseses to run for safety, and Josephs and Marys to follow God's direction. The Lord is working to bring people to the ends of the world.

Every chapter of this book contains the author's engagements with missions among the migrants. On top of these missiological engagements are stories of rich experiences of the writers ministering with migrants and refugees who left their countries and settled in host countries. From this book readers will learn about:

1. Voluntary and Involuntary Migration
2. Urbanization
3. Multiculturalization

4. Pluralization
5. Racial Hybridity
6. Hospitality and Ministry for Refugees

This volume also explains some of the reasons why and how migration happens and what happens after migrants are settled in.

Reading this book made me realize the importance and urgency of how we look at the global movements of people as part of our move toward the Great Commission. Dr. Sadiri Joy Tira in chapter 5, from his paper "Religious Pluralism in the Context of the Twenty-First Century Global Diaspora," urges the churches to be trained in intercultural competence to engage people with different faiths, worldviews, cultures, and family backgrounds. He urges Christians to open their church buildings for interfaith dialogue and to provide a space where people come to learn more about Christianity. The people of God must embrace God-appointed diversity. May churches respond to this call!

And to the churches who responded to the call of urgency and engaged with a ministry to the migrants, Dr. Craig Kraft (chapter 9, "Embracing the Broken, Dislocated, Homeless Refugees in Canada through Hospitality") has this to say as encouragement: based on his case study, those who "demonstrated the critical importance of biblical hospitality in the life of a local church and in missional engagement with refugees, indicated improved vitality, stronger community, and intentional mission as a result of their reciprocal hospitality with the Syrian people. Refugee ministry is an effective method for revitalizing churches and making disciples." This example proves that God will bless those who reach out, welcome, and minister to the migrants. As doing so has always been a part of his plan and purpose.

How do we reach out? Dr. Kraft further shared:

> Knowing who lives next door is a big step toward recognizing their needs and finding opportunities for connections. We don't have to sponsor a refugee to be hospitable. We can show hospitality to people who are already here in our neighborhoods. As we have seen in Scripture, hospitality was not just for the foreigner or stranger, but also the widows, orphans, prisoners, and the sick. There are people in every neighborhood who need to experience God's hospitality through the local church. My fifth recommendation for churches and followers of Christ is to repent of our fear and pride and pray that God will give us a vision for what hospitality must look like in our immediate context. One size does not fit all. Each church must discern

Introduction

what God has called it to do in its own community. There will be contextual expressions of hospitality in each community that will be unique from other communities across Canada or around the world.[1]

We hope that this book will be a challenge to churches and their leaders to open up to a new way of friendship and lovingkindness toward migrants. Our desire is for mission organizations and missionaries to seek ways to be theologically aligned in their engagements with migration and missions to migrants. And we hope Christian families and individuals will learn to open up their arms and reach out to their cross-cultural neighbors in their communities. Let us think about being borderless! Our next-door neighbor should not be seen as being yellow or brown, but being a person loved by God, who must therefore be loved by us as our brothers or sisters. Let us engage ourselves with the affairs of the migrants!

In the 1990s, the medical schools of the Philippines accepted and welcomed Iranian students who were scholars of the Shah of Iran. More than a thousand of them enrolled to study medicine for over four years in Metro Manila. Since our church is located near one of those medical schools, many Iranian students were seen in the vicinity. Our church never once looked at them or made friends with them. The church did not see them as people we could share the Lord Jesus Christ with. They were looked upon with suspicion and fear. Our church did not welcome foreign students and failed to provide them help in times of need, or brotherly love in times of loneliness. We missed the opportunity for them to believe in the Lord Jesus Christ and bring him in their hearts when they returned to Iran. We have failed the Lord in this, and I pray no other church will do the same!

Our challenge now is put into words by Dr. Juno Wang from chapter 13 ("Rooted in Spirituality, Committed to Missions"):

> What is God communicating to us through the rising tides of opportunities? Loving those from the diasporas, whether similar to us or not, requires us to draw upon the Spirit's power. It frees us from our comfort zones, disobedience, fear, limitations, and all forms of weakness. With humility and obedience, we place our trust in the Lord to enact His will through us by His grace and might. Our spirituality must be deeply rooted, and our commitment to diaspora missions resolute, as we strive to reach every non-believer across the globe.[2]

---

1 See chapter 9, page 146, of this book.
2 See chapter 13, page 183, of this book.

My hope is that those who read this book will learn to be ready to seize the opportunity when migrants move into their communities and that their arms will be open to welcome them as the Lord brings them to the ends of the world and to the end of this age!

In the words of Dr. Valerie Geer in chapter 10 ("Understanding and Ministering to Survivors of Sex Trafficking"):

> My concluding prayer is that the Holy Spirit will lead you as you engage in contextualized ministry ... I hope that some of the resources, information, and perspectives shared in this chapter will be both foundational and useful for my fellow co-laborers in the gospel of Jesus Christ in today's world.[3]

Let us join Dr. Geer in her prayers for the migrants, refugees, sexually exploited, and those millions who are being moved by God to hear the gospel and settle in God's saving grace.

DAMPLES DULCERO-BACLAGON
Managing Editor, *Asian Missions Advance*

---

3 See chapter 10, page 161, of this book.

Part I: Understanding the Realities of Tides of Opportunity in Global Migration

Chapter 1
Global Gateway Cities in Canada as Diaspora Epicenter

Christopher Carr

The Bible is full of stories, starting with Genesis, that show the sovereignty of God at work as he moves the chess pieces of human history to position individuals, families, clans, and sometimes entire people groups in new geographic locations to expose them to the good news of his kingdom and invite them into it. The Old and New Testaments abound with examples of people group migrations resulting in diasporas, both willing and forced. These migrations and displacements have led directly to urbanization and a phenomenon that we in Canada call *global gateway cities*.

The gateway phenomenon is not a historic anomaly, but rather a recovered understanding of Scripture, church history, and the contemporary *motus Dei*. Those of us serving with Global Gates Network of Canada (GGNC) want to share an overview of both the broad and specific elements of the missiological reality known as gateways and its strategic mission importance. This chapter focuses on the phenomenon, missiological definition, and meaning of global gateway cities in Canada and around the globe.

A New Era

Due to the increasing presence of diaspora least-reached people groups (LPGs) in urban gateways, we face quite a different mission landscape in the coming quarter of the twenty-first century than the one we knew as we ended the twentieth century. Modern immigrants symbolize a new era in pioneer missions—one in which today's migration, transnationalism, globalization, glocalization, ethnoburbs, and urbanization present unprecedented opportunities for Christians to take the gospel to the ends of the earth via gateways.

The global gateway city concept is far more expansive and far-reaching missionally than the previous global city paradigm and has wider and deeper missiological implications. Further, whereas the megacity concept came to us from economic, social, and political scientists, *gateway* is GGNC's best term missiologically and linguistically in our current globalizing and glocalizing hybrid world paradigm.

Today, according to the Joshua Project,[1] at least 41.6 percent of the world's peoples remain unreached by the gospel. Nowhere is there a greater concentration of unreached (and least-reached) peoples than in Canadian gateway cities. GGNC is focusing on the unengaged and least-reached in these cities who have been neglected or written off as too difficult to reach. We seek to make disciples and start churches among peoples without a witness. When the church is established, we want to help them multiply a movement of disciples building more churches that will transform their community with the gospel here in Canada and to the ends of the earth.

Global Gateway Cities

Global gateway cities derive their definition and value from their relationship to "reaching the ends of the earth." They are a means and not an end.

"The ends of the earth" is a theological term that comes from Acts 1:8, "you shall be my witnesses in Jerusalem, Judea, Samaria, and to the ends of the earth." Here, "the ends of the earth" refers not so much to geographical designation as to those peoples who had not yet received the gospel, and to whom Christ was sending his disciples.

As Matthew Barrett states:

> One of the essential aspects of God's nature is that he doesn't need anything to support his existence (Acts 17:24–25). If a perfectly self-sufficient, satisfied, wise, and good God has chosen to create, then he must have a purpose for doing so. In this way, divine creation presupposes divine mission. As Scripture reveals, the mission of God involves sharing and increasing the knowledge of himself within his creation. This knowledge of God is most fully revealed in the sending of the Son in the incarnation (John 1:1–18). God's self-revelation then continues in the sending of the Holy Spirit to fill the church (John 14:15–26). Furthermore, Jesus describes the relationship between the sending mission of God and the sending of his disciples when he says, "As the Father has sent me, even so I am sending you" (John 20:21). God's trinitarian nature, then, grounds our concept of mission as he calls us into his own purpose: to share the knowledge of the triune God to the ends of the earth.[2]

Translated into the twenty-first century then, "the ends of the earth" refers to the world's least-reached people groups, particularly those language communities and populations who have yet to receive the good

---

1 Joshua Project, "Global Summary."
2 Barrett, "Is the Trinity Optional?"

news of Christ's salvation. It is for the sake of reaching these least-reached, unevangelized populations that GGNC is on mission. Therefore, it is in relation to reaching these least-reached ethnolinguistic people groups that the term *global gateway cities* must be understood.

With the object of global gateway cities clearly defined as "the ends of the earth," we now turn our attention to these three words: *global*, *gateway*, and *city/cities*.

Global

Global is not merely about size but also composition. For this reason, we limit our list of global gateway cities to those that contain a substantial population of least-reached peoples. Typically our metric is a city/metro area containing at least one million people. However, tier two Canadian gateways (metros such as Winnipeg, Hamilton, Quebec City, Halifax, London, and the Kitchener-Waterloo-Cambridge-Guelph corridor) have populations of less than a million.

Gateway

There are two key aspects to the term *gateway*. First, being a gateway is about having access and ability to move about freely and openly. A city may have a large number of "ends-of-the-earth" people groups within it, but if that city is itself closed or highly restricted from gospel witness, then it is hardly a gateway. Second, "gateway" conveys the relationship back to the people groups' communities of origin. These relationships are nurtured by individuals traveling back to their homes to visit family and friends, vacation, conduct business, or represent some branch of the government for trade, commerce, or diplomacy. Such relationships are also nurtured and empowered in real-time via social media, messaging, and video calling. Increasing numbers of diaspora immigrants and refugees are using Canadian channels for inviting and sponsoring family members into open, accessible gateways. However, diaspora ethnic groups that are generations away from their places of origin with no ongoing relationship back to their places of origin are not very effective gateway communities.

City

Finally, the word *city* is important, not only because GGNC is primarily an urban mission organization, but also because cities are where we have the highest concentrations of the least-reached, "ends of the earth" people groups that we are seeking to reach. In our current Acts 17:26–27 *"kairos"* season, it is the size of the least-reached populations, rather than mere categories of ethnolinguistic composition existing within a given gateway setting, or mere existence of people groups, that takes precedence. A handful of diaspora individuals in a suburb or small town lack the gravity (according to GGNC's vision) to warrant a full-time GGNC missionary engagement. Though we can't give serious organizational attention in such contexts, we rejoice that the Lord calls many local churches and sister mission organizations to focus some of their efforts and resources to such settings.

People Movements to Cities

Globally, over 272 million people currently live away from their home country,[3] but the numbers are even larger when you add the children of immigrants, those who lived abroad and then returned home, and those who have internally migrated within their own countries. GGNC is focusing on a newly recovered era of mission (in reality, an ancient one) aimed at reaching a world already connected through global diaspora relationships, by ministering initially in our tier one gateways of Metro Vancouver (comprised of twenty-one municipalities, one electoral area, and one Treaty First Nation), Calgary, Edmonton, Greater Toronto Area, Ottawa, and Montreal.

Luke's record of Paul's visit to Athens in Acts 17 is crucial for GGNC and its understanding of diaspora dynamics especially in relation to Canadian gateways. Of first importance is Paul's mention of how God has created us all (people groups, nations, Gentiles) from one blood (v. 26) and has defined where and for what seasons of time we would "live and move" (v. 28) on the entire planet. God decides when a people group, through what we might typically view as political, social, economic, meteorological, religious, and other reasons, will live in certain locales and when events will result in their migration to a new place. In looking at the entirety of the Bible and its plethora of people group migration evidence, it is clear to us that God himself is orchestrating such dynamics for his kingdom mission purpose. Yes, individuals, married couples, nuclear families, and extended families immigrate to new geographic locations (in our context, Canadian gateways) because of political repression, religious persecution, a failing economy, better opportunities for their kids and grandkids, etc. But could it be that God is bringing such individuals and people groups into Canadian gateway cities for more than just a "better life"? It seems to us that God is intentionally orchestrating such people group migration movements so that people seek him, though they may be quite unconscious as to the ultimate goal of their

---

3 United Nations, "World Urbanization Prospects."

searching out a new geographic space in which to bring stability and new opportunities to their families.

When they do move, these people are often moving to the city. Unfortunately, while the world goes urban, mission endeavors have largely remained rural in much of the world. Missionaries often live in cities but focus their efforts in rural areas which they perceive to be more open to the gospel. However, over 4.4 billion people as of early 2021 are already living in cities. That number makes up 56.2 percent of the world population (as of November 2020 per the World Economic Forum) and is estimated to surpass 68 percent by 2050. The urban population of the world has grown rapidly from only 751 million in 1950.[4] GGNC is focusing on what the world is becoming—an urban world!

People Movement to Canada

In the context of urbanization, Canada is on track to welcome record numbers of new immigrants between 2022 and 2024. Despite the pandemic, Canada recorded its highest-ever immigration numbers in 2021 with over 405,000 people becoming permanent residents. For 2022, Canada released a revised target of over 432,000 immigrants and even higher numbers in 2023 and 2024. These numbers may seem highly specific, but each target is based on the Canadian government's Immigration Levels Plan 2022–2024.[5]

GGNC has identified six tier one Canadian gateway cities: Vancouver/Abbotsford lower mainland, Calgary, Edmonton, the Greater Toronto Area (GTA; includes the cities of Brampton, Richmond Hill, Mississauga, Newmarket, Markham, Vaughan, Milton, Oakville, Burlington, Scarborough, Etobicoke, York, North York, East York), Ottawa-Gatineau, and Montreal.

Each qualifying Canadian gateway city must meet the following requirements: (1) have five or more qualifying unreached people groups that each have a population greater than five thousand in that gateway city; and (2) have an overall population close to or greater than one million.[6]

A Kairos Moment

As a primary destination for global immigration, Canada has become the global epicenter for diaspora people group migration into our gateway cities. God is dropping a kingdom mission gift into our laps; will we recognize it and seize the day? Will we move in obedience to mobilize and train more Jesus-

---

[4] United Nations, "World Urbanization Prospects."
[5] Robitaille, "How Many Immigrants?"
[6] Global Gates Canada, "Canadian Gateway Cities."

followers? Will we share the good news and make disciples of individuals from the least-reached people groups who continue to surge into Canadian gateways, all at the invitation of Canada's secular government? We do not know how long this window and season of opportunity will remain open to us. For now, it appears that for at least several more years the Canadian government aims to allow upwards of 450,000 immigrants and refugees to insure the ongoing demographic and economic stability of the country, due to the ageing population of North American Caucasians like myself, who will increasingly move into minority Canadian population status in coming years.[7]

Paul presciently appeals to this season of opportunity in his choice of Greek word for *time* in Acts 17:26; it is not *chronos* (χρονος) time, but rather, *kairos* (καιρος) time, which is not linear like *chronos* time, moving into the future with regularity, sequence, and unbrokenness as a clearly measured, specific amount of time. *Kairos* time is here (often quite unexpectedly or even spontaneously) for a season and then gone. It is a "fitting" time; *kairos* is used in Mark 1:15; Galatians 4:4; and over eighty other places in the New Testament.

Do we truly understand and grasp the missiological moment in which we are living in Canadian gateway cities and the critical opportunity God is putting in front of us?

It is most urgent that Christians in North America cease viewing immigrants and refugees primarily through economic, social, and especially political filters, rather than through biblical and missiological lenses as participants in God's gracious *motus Dei* kingdom mission movement. When we follow the former and ignore the latter, the diaspora refugee and immigrant neighbor, her struggles and hopes, becomes invisible, as noted by Carroll and Bacote.[8] When we follow only the former, Christians fail to live up to the spirit of what Carroll and Bacote see as an additional Reformation *sola* to the marks of the church in the world, namely, a *sola hospitalitate dei* (God's hospitality alone).[9]

When we see the diaspora in gateways through the filter of the *Motus Dei*, we accept and rejoice that God himself is bringing to us the immigrant and refugee for his kingdom mission purpose. The next great evangelistic movements of God in Canada and North America likely will originate from within and flow through diaspora LPGs in Canadian gateway cities, hence our sense of anticipation and urgency.

---

7 Ibbitson, "Politics of 2036."
8 Carroll and Bacote, *Global Migration and Christian*, 4.
9 Carroll and Bacote, 5.

Case Study: Toronto

The Greater Toronto Area (GTA) has more than 250 nationalities and 170 languages represented within its geography[10] and is the most multi-ethnic and multicultural gateway metro in the world. While not all global cities are necessarily (or even ontologically) gateway cities, the gateway cities GGNC has defined, including the GTA, are global cities. As CIC News noted in May 2022:

> The unmitigated size of the Greater Toronto Area is a challenge for mission efforts among diaspora LPGs, especially in light of COVID-19 and the attendant restrictions at provincial and municipal levels, which contributed to further urbanized migration and the maturing and/or creation of ethnoburbs. During especially heavy rush-hour traffic, it easily can take two hours or more (if driving) to traverse the metro. This has time, distance, travel, human resource, and cost implications for planning and implementing evangelism and training events, strategic planning and team meetings, defining event and meeting locations, etc.[11]

In late 2020, GGNC missionary Seth Beebe shared with the author his concerns about some of the difficulties of diaspora gateway mission:

> The greatest challenges in Toronto with sustainable ministry seem to be the transitional nature of the lifestyles of people in the city. As you move into the city and engage newcomers (international students, refugees, or migrant/skilled workers), especially in the center of Toronto rather than in suburban areas, there is a high transition rate of people from living in one place to another, of changing jobs with their assimilation process, and general time constraint issues with people taking public transportation. I believe church formation becomes more fluid in such a context. Disciple-making and discipleship relationships are more secure. People cannot always commit to the same groups throughout the year due to the many transitions of the city. A model of evangelism, follow-up, long-term evangelism, short- and long-term discipleship, and reproducible church formation are all impacted and need to be adjusted. The only other option would be to restrict these movements or demand for a more institutional kind of

---

10 Ryan, "How Multicultural Is Toronto?"
11 Robitaille, "How Many Immigrants?"

gathering, where people are forced to choose to come to a specific location or choose another ministry.[12]

In Canadian gateway cities with burgeoning and ever-growing international student and diaspora populations that are transitory, we typically have a two- or three-year window of opportunity to connect with people before they return to their country of origin. This fact is especially true if they are not seeking permanent residency status. We do as much as we can to connect them to Jesus and train them for evangelism and disciple-making. This is often the best we can do given the hybrid/vaporous nature of large gateways such as Montreal, Vancouver, the GTA, etc. But if new immigrants, refugees, and international students remain in the gateway or a suburb of it and settle down, prospects for multiplying disciples can skyrocket. Because of the hybridity of relationships within a gateway setting like the GTA, at times cross-cultural mission practitioners struggle with the temptations of attractionalism and extractionalism, rather than focusing more on incarnation and representation of the good news and the kingdom, knowing that often the time they have with international LPG students, as well as an increasing number of new immigrants, may well be short.

WIGTAKE: What's It Going to Take?

WIGTAKE: this stands for "What's It Going to Take?" This question embodies the spirit of partnership, collaboration, intentional networking, and kingdom-minded thinking necessary to motivate and to mobilize the entire body of Christ into the Lord's mission. No one church, denomination, confession, network, convention, sending agency, organization, or group of people can accomplish the multiplicative evangelism, disciple-making, and church-planting efforts needed to address the lostness of LPGs in gateway cities such as those in Canada. We must find ways to increase and exponentially multiply concerted efforts together in this regard and not concern ourselves with who gets the credit or attention outside of God alone. This level of collaboration has been seen in Canada before.

Many are unaware that Canada has a rich history of evangelism/mission especially due to the Bible school/college/institute movement of the 1880s–1940s.

Bruce Guenther stated in 1993:

> Since the start of the first Bible school in Canada in 1885, Protestant groups have initiated more than 140 such institutions

---

12 Seth Beebe, email to the author, November 9, 2020.

throughout the country. Like their American counterparts, these schools typically offered a Bible-centered, intensely practical, lay-oriented program of post-secondary theological training, and have scattered thousands of church workers, pastors, missionaries and evangelists to every corner of Canada and the world. A conservative estimate indicates that at least 200,000 people have spent at least one academic term at a Canadian Bible school or college. (This figure does not include the many who frequently attended weekend teaching conferences organized by these schools, or those who were influenced by reading the literature published by these schools, or those who regularly listened to radio broadcasts aired by these schools, or those who were significantly influenced by alumni from these schools.) The Bible school movement has been a significant factor in the remarkable growth experienced by evangelical Protestant groups in Canada during the twentieth century.[13]

Of those two hundred thousand Bible school participants, it is estimated that more than sixty thousand of them scattered missionally as a different kind of diaspora across Canada, North America, and to the ends of the earth from the 1880s to the 1940s with both a nation-specific and an LPG focus.[14] Only the London, England metro area had a higher number of people sent into mission during the same time period. Jesus-followers in Canada will be incredibly remiss if we fail to understand the convergence of similar new factors in our contemporary era in which *Motus Dei* is setting the stage to reach the ends of the earth from Canada as the epicenter of and for diaspora mission. God invites us to join him with our minds, hearts, and wills through prayer, personal involvement, and financial support as we grow in our understanding of the recovered gateway paradigm.

---

13 Bruce, "Bible School Movement," 135–74.
14 Carr, "Paul's Letter," 134.

Gateway Cities with Significant Diaspora Populations

There are a multiplicity of gateway cities with significant diaspora presence. For example, in 2007 the Greater Toronto Area (GTA) and Vancouver represented Canada on a list of the twenty-five global locales having the highest number of immigrants, with immigrants making up at least 9.5 percent of each locale's population of over one million. The diaspora immigration numbers for both the GTA and Montreal have increased rapidly over the last few years, meaning Montreal is by now a clear candidate to be on the list in the near future if not included already. The list of cities, starting with highest percentage of diaspora immigrants in 2007, included Dubai, the Greater Toronto Area, Muscat, Hong Kong, Vancouver, Jeddah, Miami, Tel Aviv-Yafo, San Jose, Los Angeles, Singapore, Auckland, Perth, Riyadh, Sydney, Jerusalem, Mecca, San Francisco, Melbourne, Amsterdam, Medina, New York City, Frankfurt, Tbilisi, and London.

I include the list below[15] to emphasize the importance of significant diaspora presence in Canadian and North American gateways in order to create and foment a "holy discomfort" among North American Jesus-followers so that they seek ways to engage the diaspora with the good news and "wake up" to Acts 17:24–28 phenomenon of diaspora migration in our midst and the kingdom mission implications of that reality.

CITY	COUNTRY	CENSUS YEAR	METROPOLITAN POPULATION	FOREIGN BORN	% FOREIGN BORN
Dubai	United Arab Emirates	2005	1,272,000	1,056,000	83.02
Toronto	Canada	2001	4,647,960	2,091,100	44.99
Muscat	Oman	2000	661,000	294,881	44.61
Hong Kong	China	2005	7,039,169	2,998,686	42.60
Vancouver	Canada	2001	1,967,475	767,715	39.02
Jeddah	Saudi Arabia	1998	3,171,000	1,186,600	37.42
Miami	USA	2005	5,334,685	1,949,629	36.55
Tel Aviv-Yafo	Israel	2002	2,075,500	747,400	36.01
San Jose	USA	2005	1,726,057	614,304	35.59
Los Angeles	USA	2005	12,703,423	4,407,353	34.69
Singapore	Singapore	2000	4,017,733	1,350,632	33.62

---

15 Price and Benton-Short, "Immigrants and World Cities."

Auckland	New Zealand	2001	1,103,466	354,126	32.09
Perth	Australia	2001	1,336,239	422,547	31.62
Riyadh	Saudi Arabia	2000	4,730,330	1,477,601	31.24
Sydney	Australia	2001	3,961,451	1,235,908	31.20
Jerusalem	Israel	2002	678,300	208,700	30.77
Mecca	Saudi Arabia	1998	1,326,000	397,800	30.00
San Francisco	USA	2005	4,071,751	1,201,209	29.50
Melbourne	Australia	2001	3,367,169	960,145	28.51
Amsterdam	Netherlands	2005	742,951	211,260	28.44
Medina	Saudi Arabia	1998	885,000	247,252	27.93
New York	USA	2005	18,351,099	5,117,290	27.89
Frankfurt	Germany	2000	650,705	181,184	27.84
Tbilisi	Georgia	1999	1,339,105	370,932	27.70
London	United Kingdom	2001	7,172,091	1,940,390	27.05

Bibliography

Barrett, Matthew. "Is the Trinity Optional for Mission?" *The Gospel Coalition.* August 18, 2022. https://www.thegospelcoalition.org/article/is-trinity-optional-mission/.

Carr, Chris. "Paul's Letter to the Romans as Missiological Theocentric Document and Playbook." PhD diss., Midwestern Baptist Theological Seminary, 2021.

Carroll R., M. Daniel, and Vincent E. Bacote, eds. *Global Migration and Christian Faith: Implications Identity and Mission.* Eugene, OR: Wipf & Stock, 2021.

Global Gates Canada. "Canadian Gateway Cities: Calgary, Edmonton, Montreal, Ottawa, Toronto, and Vancouver." https://globalgates.ca/gateway-cities/.

Guenther, Bruce. "The Origin of the Bible School Movement in Western Canada: Towards an Ethnic Interpretation." In *Historical Papers 1993: Canadian Society of Church,* 135–74. History Annual Conference, Carlton University. June 8–9, 1993.

Ibbitson, John. "The Politics of 2036, When Canada Is as Brown as It Is White." *The Globe and Mail.* January 27, 2017. https://www.theglobeandmail.com/news/politics/the-politics-of-2036-when-canada-is-as-brown-as-it-is-white/article33814437/.

Price, Marie, and Lisa Benton-Short. "Immigrants and World Cities: From the Hyper-Diverse to the Bypassed." *GeoJournal* 68, no. 2 (June 2007): 103–107. https://www.researchgate.net/publication/226194863_Immigrants_and_world_cities_From_the_hyper-diverse_to_the_bypassed.

Robitaille, Edana. "How Many Immigrants Will Canada Welcome over the Coming Years? Understanding the Immigration Levels Plan 2022–2024." *CIC News*. May 19, 2022. https://www.cicnews.com/2022/05/how-many-immigrants-will-canada-welcome-over-the-coming-years-0525506.html#gs.9ci1v0.

Ryan, Ashleigh. "How Multicultural Is Toronto? Let Us Count the Ways...," *Toronto Global*. March 22, 2019. https://torontoglobal.ca/TG-Blog/March-2019/How-multicultural-is-Toronto-Let-us-count-the-way.

United Nations, Department of Economic and Social Affairs, Population Division. "World Urbanization Prospects: The 2018 Revision." New York: United Nations, 2019. https://doi.org/10.18356/b9e995fe-en.

Chapter 2
Diasporas and Multiculturalism
Social Imaginaries, Liminality, and Cultural Identity

Steven Ybarrola

In 1898 my Basque grandfather, Juan Martín Ibarrola, left his tiny, isolated village in the Pyrenees mountains on the border of Spain and France, and made his way to the United States.[1] He eventually settled in northern Montana where, along with a few of his nephews, he owned and operated a sheep ranch—an economic niche for many Basque immigrants at the time. We don't know for certain why he emigrated from his village (probably due to the Basque inheritance system which would have left the family farm to his eldest sister), but the trip from the Basque Country to Montana, via New York and California, would have been long and arduous, so there must have been a high incentive for him to make the journey.

In his later years, after moving to where his grown children had settled in California, my grandfather enjoyed spending his days interacting with other Basques who had created their own enclave in downtown Stockton, with several Basque hotels, boarding houses, and restaurants.[2] By the mid-1980s, when I conducted my Master's research on this community in Stockton, there was not much left of the Basque diaspora; subsequent generations intermarried with other groups, and largely "melted" into the American mainstream. One woman I interviewed[3] was, like me, a third generation Basque American, and, also like me, had married a non-Basque. She told me how she would often take her children for rides in the country so they could watch men tend sheep. Even though these men were now primarily Peruvian rather than Basque, she wanted her children to stay connected to their shepherding roots.

---

1 In this chapter, I refer to the Basque case frequently because I have conducted research among the Basque diaspora in California (Ybarrola, "Intermarriage, Assimilation, and Ethnicity Maintenance") as well as among internal and now Latin American diaspora communities in the Southern Basque Country of Spain (Ybarrola, "Competition and Ethnic Conflict," manuscript under review). Thus it is the case I know best.
2 Echeverria, *Home Away from Home*.
3 See Ybarrola, "Intermarriage, Assimilation, and Ethnicity Maintenance." In other cities in the American West there are still Basque cultural centers and annual Basque festivals. Most of those attending the festivals, however, are experiencing what the sociologist Herbert Gans referred to as "symbolic ethnicity."

My grandmother's migration history is also diaspora-related. We know that her family emigrated from Estonia (in a region south of the capital, Tallinn) where they had served as serfs on land owned by Germans. They left in order to join the Estonian migration moving to Crimea, likely drawn by the opportunity to acquire their own land following the Crimean War. Then, after a generation or two, the branch of the family that included my grandmother made their way to southern Canada/northern United States where they became part of the Estonian diaspora there. My grandmother eventually met my grandfather at the sheep ranch in Montana, and the rest, as they say, is history (at least my history).

What is important about my family story, at least for the purposes of this chapter, is not the details, but rather the pattern. With the exception of Native Americans and those descended from people living in what is now the southern United States before the land was annexed from Mexico, almost all of us living in the US have a story like this to tell. And it is not just a story of immigration, but of communities—diasporas—that settled in particular parts of the country for specific reasons. What these diasporas created was a multicultural society, par excellence.[4] Today, this migration pattern is increasingly found in many parts of the world, creating a much more diverse and complex multicultural milieu. In this chapter I will examine how the migration of populations and the development of diaspora communities increases the cultural diversity of their host societies, and the different responses of "natives" to this increased diversity. I will close by discussing some of the missional implications of this increasing multiculturalism.

Diasporas, Multiculturalism, and Social Imaginaries

Humans have always been a migrating species, but what we are experiencing today is unprecedented. As of 2020, it was estimated that 281 million people were living outside their countries of origin.[5] Migrations change over time, thereby changing the cultural diversity, as well as attitudes towards that diversity in receiving countries. For example, some scholars of immigration in the United States identify two main historical periods of non-Anglo migration from Europe—the "Old Immigration" of people primarily from northern and western Europe (roughly 1820–1880), and the "New Immigration" of those

---

4 As the chapter from Harvey in this volume demonstrates, the concept of "multiculturalism" is often quite different in the United States than in other parts of the world, especially the UK and other parts of Europe. Having said that, there are many people in the US who would share the "fears" of multiculturalism and its supposed failure, exhibited elsewhere.

5 IOM UN Migration, "World Migration Report 2022." Note that COVID-19 slowed the number of international immigrants significantly.

coming from southern and eastern Europe (roughly 1880–1920).[6] Of course, there were people from other parts of the world who were also arriving in the United States during these periods. But what is interesting is that even with the influx of people from Europe representing the New Immigration, there was a fear that they were too different culturally (e.g., they spoke different languages, most were Catholic) and racially (most were not considered "White" initially[7]) from the American "norm," and were coming in such large numbers that they would not be able to assimilate. As my family history indicates, my grandfather was one of these "new immigrants" who arrived knowing little, if any, English and looking to connect with his fellow Basques in diaspora. This fear of the new immigrants eventually led to very restrictive immigration laws in the 1920s which essentially staunched the flow of migrants from these parts of Europe (as well as much of Asia); these laws remained in place for the next forty years.

The restrictive immigration laws may have been based on genuine concerns for social stability, but the reaction to the demographic (i.e., cultural, "racial") change was based on a social imaginary[8] that argued that there was a distinct American culture, and that immigrants were to leave behind their previous culture and identity and become "American." Social imaginaries are the "lenses" we use to view (i.e., interpret) social reality. They represent "a way of thinking about, speaking about, and organizing relations among and within human groups."[9] In the case of the United States, it can (somewhat simplistically) be argued that there are two dominant social imaginaries that affect the way immigration in general is interpreted, as well as how different diaspora communities are viewed. The assimilationist social imaginary mentioned above is that of the "Melting Pot." In 1782 the French immigrant and writer Michel Guillaume Jean de Crèvecœur (a.k.a. J. Hector St. John de Crèvecœur) summed up this imaginary very nicely when he wrote,

> What, then, is the American, this new man? He is either an [sic] European or the descendant of an [sic] European; hence that strange mixture of blood, which you will find in no other country. I could point out to you a family whose grandfather was an Englishman, whose wife was Dutch, whose son married

---

6 See, for example, Scupin, 280–81.
7 See, for example, Guglielmo and Salerno, *Are Italians White?*
8 Taylor, "Modern Social Imaginaries," 91–124.
9 MacEachem, "Concept of Race," 36. In a similar way, the Canadian philosopher Charles Taylor writes of "social imaginaries" (2002), as previously cited.

a French woman, and whose present four sons have now four wives of different nations. He is an American, who, leaving behind him all his ancient prejudices and manners, receives new ones from the new mode of life he has embraced, the new government he obeys, and the new rank he holds. He becomes an American by being received into the broad lap of our great Alma Mater. Here individuals of all nations are melted into a new race of men, whose labors and posterity will one day cause great changes in the world.[10]

The second dominant social imaginary in the United States is that of cultural pluralism (or, more commonly, multiculturalism). This imaginary maintains that American society, from its very beginning, has been culturally diverse, and this continues to be its defining characteristic. Rather than seeing immigrant adaptation as a steady progression towards full assimilation, multiculturalists argue that immigrants tend to integrate on the civic level, but may maintain various aspects of their indigenous cultures (for example language, religious beliefs and practices, patterns of social interaction, primary friendships within the diaspora). Those holding to a multiculturalist social imaginary tend not to see immigration as a threat to social stability, but, on the contrary, as adding to the great cultural mosaic that constitutes the US. As a reflection of this social imaginary, a high school principal in Iowa wrote, "As an American, you don't have to divorce yourself from your cultural history. What's so good about America is we try to respect the rights and privileges of people different from us and teach our children to respect people's cultural integrity."[11]

The important point here is that all societies have multiple and often competing social imaginaries that are used to classify and give meaning to the immigrant or foreign "other." Elsewhere I have written about the different social imaginaries found in the Basque Country that are used to classify immigrants (and others) as either enemies/allies, or strangers/friends.[12] The first pairing is primarily political in nature—you are either with our nationalist agenda or you are against us—whereas the second has more to do with sociocultural integration and ethnic identity—you may not be "one of us" ethnically, but you can be considered a friend through integrating into our society and culture. These social imaginaries are constructed using

---

10 de Crèvecœur, *Letters from an American Farmer*, 69. See also https://avalon.law.yale.edu/18th_century/letter_03.asp.
11 *The Des Moines Register*, Sunday November 17, 1996.
12 Ybarrola, "Identity Matters," 112. See also Sarup, *Identity, Culture and the Postmodern*, 9–10.

assumptions about social reality and the social "good." As immigrants enter into host societies, they will be perceived and treated differently by various segments of the society—some with hostility, and even violence (just look at the increase in violence against Asians in the US since the outbreak of COVID-19), and others with caring concern and hospitality.

As the multicultural milieu changes with shifting migrations, so often do the boundaries of inclusion and exclusion that are assumed by the social imaginaries. When people from other parts of Spain began migrating to the Basque Country in large numbers in the 1950s and 1960s to work in the burgeoning industries, they were viewed by many Basques as unwelcomed "invaders." This migration coincided with the culturally repressive policies of the Franco regime, which outlawed the use of the Basque language among other things, so these immigrants were also seen as promulgators of Spanish culture, whereby Basque culture was displaced and largely went underground. Needless to say, there was, and still is, a fair amount of animosity between the indigenous population and the Spanish immigrants.[13]

Today, however, there is a new wave of immigrants arriving in the Basque Country, but these are now coming primarily from Latin America, Eastern Europe, and, to a lesser extent, parts of Africa. This has led to a boundary shift, at least among certain segments of the population. A friend of mine, who came to the Basque Country when she was a young girl with her parents who had migrated from the Spanish region of Extremadura, expressed to me her dismay with her father's negative attitude towards these new immigrants. From his perspective, he is now a "native" to the region compared to these new arrivals, and he wasn't too happy to have them "invading" his territory. My friend tried to get her father to see that he was treating these new immigrants the same way that he was treated by the Basques when he arrived—that is, exclusionary and discriminatory. However, from his perspective the social boundaries had now changed, and he's an "insider" in contrast to these "outsiders."[14]

---

13 See Ybarrola, "Competition and Ethnic Conflict," for a more thorough discussion of intergroup relations in the Basque Country. There is disagreement among many in the Basque Country as to what extent the descendants of those who immigrated have integrated into the local society and culture. Again, the attitude towards the subsequent generations is determined, to a large extent, by the social imaginary employed in interpreting the social context.
14 Brown, "Ethnicity and Ethnocentrism," 181.

Today boundaries are shifting quite a bit, particularly in the European context, due to what the anthropologist Ralph Grillo calls "an excess of alterity" (i.e., otherness, or difference).[15] For example, throughout most of its history the Netherlands has been known as one of the more liberal and tolerant countries on the continent, developing a consociational form of government that allowed for the peaceful coexistence of Protestants and Catholics. However, in recent years, with the influx of immigrants from different parts of the world, many of whom are Muslims, this form of peaceful coexistence has been called into question. This reconsideration is particularly true in the aftermath of the murder of the filmmaker Theo van Gogh by a Dutch-Moroccan Muslim because the latter was offended by a film van Gogh had made, *Submission*, which was critical of the treatment of women in Islam. In another example, the murders in Norway at the hands of a right-wing Norwegian was evidently triggered by the fear of a Muslim takeover of Europe due to the recent increase of Muslim immigrants not only in Norway but throughout the continent.[16] Grillo himself discusses the social imaginary of the "immigrant as threat" found in contemporary British society, and the "backlash against difference" this fear has produced. Again, this perceived "threat" is seen as mainly coming from the growing Muslim population, whose religious beliefs and sociocultural practices are seen as being based on "values at odds with those of 'Western' secular society [thereby] threatening social cohesion."[17] So great is this "excess of alterity" that the former British Prime Minister, David Cameron, stated that multiculturalism in Britain was "an outright failure and partly to blame for fostering Islamist extremism."[18]

In Spain, the sociologist Carlota Solé has written of the increased racism, triggered primarily by an immigration that is marked by "its non-White character."[19] Reflecting on this changing multicultural milieu in the Spanish context, Solé states:

> Thus, in the mind's eye of the Spanish society, the image of the "other" appeared: an image of economic immigrants from poorer countries, perceived as a "problem" and a social image which is very different from the historic "others" for the Spanish, the gypsies. Ethnic prejudice arises as this "different"

---

15 Grillo, "Excess of Alterity?" 980.
16 Bevelander and Otterbeck, "Young People's Attitudes," 404–25.
17 Grillo, "Excess of Alterity?" 980.
18 NBC, "Multiculturalism Has Failed."
19 Solé, "Labour Market and Racial Discrimination," 122.

subject is perceived as a potential threat to established interests and identities, the defense of which leads to the development of mechanisms for group identification; whilst the other, the different one, is marked out and attributed natural and social characteristics that are generally negative.[20]

A study in the Basque Country indicated a deterioration in attitudes towards the Latin American and Eastern European immigrants, which happened to coincide with an economic downturn. One finding of the study was that an increasing number of those in the Basque Country believe the immigrants pose a threat and that their society is now less secure. The Director of Immigration of the Basque Government stated that these fears are based on two unsubstantiated beliefs: (1) that the number of immigrants is greater than it actually is, and (2) that there is a direct correlation between the immigrants and the increase in crime or the abuse of social services. He concludes, in a somewhat understated manner, that these stereotypes are "generating a social imaginary that can make living together difficult."[21]

What the prior example illustrates is that immigrants and diaspora communities enter and interact within the "webs of significance" (i.e., social imaginaries) already established in the host societies, but also have a modifying effect on those imaginaries. The latter is especially true when the social and cultural differences between the immigrants and the host society are perceived to be greater than they had been with previous migrations and diasporas. If the alterity comes to be seen as "excessive," it can lead to policies that may challenge the continued existence of the diaspora communities themselves. In the United States this practice is illustrated in what happened to many German communities in the wake of the two World Wars during the twentieth century, as well as current attitudes and policies being developed to curb the influx of Latino immigrants and arrest and deport those who are there without documentation. In many cases, these policies and practices have led to the decline and demise of Mexican and other Latin American diasporas, particularly in rural communities (e.g., Postville, Iowa[22]). Local perceptions and power can have a profound impact on diaspora communities. As Miriam Adeney observed, "Multiculturalism is not a level playing field."[23]

---

20 Solé, 122.
21 *Noticias de Gipuzkoa*, June 17, 2009, 13.
22 Bloom, *Postville: A Clash*; Grey, Devlin, and Goldsmith, *Postville, U.S.A.*
23 Adeney, "Colorful Initiatives," 13.

Diasporas, Liminality, and Cultural Identity

The attitudes and imaginaries of the host societies obviously have a great influence on the adaptation of immigrants and diaspora communities. Indeed, critics of the assimilationist imaginary in the United States have argued that from its inception assimilation was only for certain groups of people (normally those considered "White") while others, viewed through America's racialist lens, were not given the option to assimilate.[24] However, the adaptation of immigrants is also affected by internal processes that affect how they view themselves within the host society. Here I will speak of two such processes—liminality and cultural identity.[25]

Liminality has to do with the sense of "in-betweenness" people often experience when they migrate to a new country or community. Being in this liminal state can certainly be disorienting and psychologically stressful as a person can find themselves neither/nor—neither accepted within the host society, nor fully identifying with the immigrant community. I recall a friend of mine in the Basque Country, who arrived as a two-year-old with his parents from Andalucía, reflecting this liminal state. In the Basque Country he was viewed as the stranger, whereas when he visited his family's village in Andalucía, he was considered the Basque. He was always the "outsider," the anomaly. As Eriksen puts it:

> If one is simultaneously a member of two groups which are partly defined by mutual contrasting, difficult situations are inevitable.... [T]his is not necessarily because the "cultures" are incompatible, but because the ethnic ideologies hold that they are.... In a social environment where one is expected to have a well-defined ethnic identity, it may be psychologically and socially difficult to "bet on two horses."[26]

But being in this liminal state can also have its benefits; it can allow a person to be both/and—both a part of the host society and a member of the diaspora community. Being in this state allows a person to develop intercultural competencies which can prove to be quite beneficial in building up social capital through the development of social networks in both the host society and the diaspora community. In this way a person in this liminal state can act as a bridge between the two communities, thereby helping both. Reflecting on this phenomenon, the global sociologist Nederveen Pieterse states, "More fruitful is to view multiculturalism as intercultural interplay

---

24 Takaki, *Different Mirror*.
25 Adeney, "Colorful Initiatives," 5–23
26 Eriksen, *Ethnicity and Nationalism*, 75.

and mingling, a terrain of crisscrossing cultural flows, in the process of generating new combinations and options; this applies in relation to political interests, lifestyle choices, and economic opportunities."[27]

The person who develops the competencies to "crisscross cultural flows" in this way will have far more opportunities available to him or her than the person who remains safely within their social boundaries. Those who have experienced liminality are often more capable of crossing these boundaries and intermingling in multiple sociocultural contexts than those in the host society who have not had this experience thrust upon them.[28]

Closely related to liminality is cultural identity. Cultural hybridity and change are certainly the hallmarks of our age. No longer can we think of people migrating from one part of the world to another, cutting ties with the home community, and assimilating into the culture of the host society. Today we live in a globalized world which permits migrants and diaspora communities to stay in as close of contact with "home" as they want. Reflecting on this change in my own family history, my grandfather came to the United States in 1898 on a ship from France, and never returned to his natal village or the Basque Country. I don't know to what extent he maintained contact with home, but to the degree that he did it would have been through the very slow process of surface mail (they don't call it "snail mail" for no reason). I, on the other hand, have traveled to the Basque Country many times, even living there for 15 months when I conducted my dissertation research, and I have maintained an active research interest there since 1984. I have been to my grandfather's village on several occasions to visit family (still not all that easy to get to, but much easier than it would have been in my grandfather's day). And I can stay in immediate contact with family there through email, phone, and even face-to-face via Zoom, Skype, or other apps.

As my family example illustrates, the technological developments associated with globalization (e.g., technology, communications, ease and relative affordability of travel) means that today's diaspora communities are much more "transnational" than in the past, creating contexts in which identity has become multi-local. Stephen Vertovec states: "However termed, the multi-local life-world presents a wider, even more complex set of conditions that affect the construction, negotiation, and reproduction of social identities. These identities play out and position individuals in the course of their everyday lives within and across each of their places of attachment or perceived belonging."[29]

---

27 Nederveen Pieterse, *Globalization and Culture*, 38.
28 Adeney, "Colorful Initiatives," 5–23.
29 Vertovec, "Transnationalism and Identity," 578.

Diaspora communities have always been reinvigorated by the influx of new members from the home country, but today's communities can maintain virtual as well as physical contact with "home," and can even eat the same foods as home through the importation of goods often purchased at stores that cater to the diaspora clientele. When I was conducting research among Latino/as in a small Iowa town, I was surprised to smell the spices from Latin America in a chain grocery store popular in the Midwest. Clearly the management of this store knew they had to adapt to the local diaspora community in order to compete with the newly opened Latin American grocery stores in the town.

An important issue when it comes to diaspora identity is what happens with the 1.5 and 2nd generations?[30] The pattern for the descendants of many "White" diasporas in the United States was to assimilate into the mainstream (as with the Basques in Stockton). Indeed, for many of the immigrants, this is what they wanted their children to do—learn English, get a good education, and become productive members of the larger society. The parents were willing (or forced) to take low paying jobs that required long hours and hard work, looking to a better future for their children. In other cases, the 1.5 and 2nd generation, being in the liminal, or anomalous, state, rejected the culture and identity of their parents, much to the latter's chagrin. However, by the 3rd generation there was often a desire to learn about the culture and identity of the grandparents who had migrated to the country. So common was this pattern in the United States that some social scientists studying immigration in the first half of the twentieth century referred to it as "third-generation return" ("what the son wishes to forget, the grandson wishes to remember").[31] Bender and Kagiwada summarize the thesis in this way: "Grandchildren of the immigrant classes, already secure in their Americanness, took pride in the past and formed historical societies to record their ethnic history."[32]

However, this pattern of assimilation was not true for all immigrant groups, not even all "White" groups. In 1963, sociologists Nathan Glazer and Daniel Patrick Moynihan published an important work that challenged the assimilationist assumptions of the melting pot. Their book, *Beyond the Melting Pot*, was a study of diaspora communities in New York City. What they found was that in this urban context, different groups were not "melting" into the American mainstream, but rather were maintaining much of their

---

30 The 1.5 generation refers to those who migrated as children with their parents, whereas 2nd generation refers to the children of immigrants who were born in the host country.
31 Hansen, "Problem of the Third," 9.
32 Bender and Kagiwada, "Hansens's Law," 360–70.

cultural identity within neighborhood enclaves. These diaspora communities remain to this day in many of the larger urban centers. For example, when my family and I moved to Providence, Rhode Island, in 1985 for me to attend graduate school, we first moved into an Italian neighborhood where you could hear people speaking Italian with their neighbors, and where stores and restaurants catering to this diaspora could be found. After a year we moved closer to the university, and into a Portuguese neighborhood. When my wife and I would go to the local bakery, owned by our landlord, to get fresh-baked bread and rolls, we would almost always be the only ones there speaking English. Again, stores and restaurants in the neighborhood catered to this clientele.[33] These types of diaspora enclaves are found in many countries throughout the world.

What the above indicates is that the cultural identity of the 1.5 and subsequent generations is varied and complex. They often take on more of a hybrid identity (both/and) which, as I stated above, can be used as a way to bridge the cultural gap between their diaspora community and the larger host society.

By Way of Conclusion: Diasporas, Multiculturalism, and Mission

In this volume, Dr. Tira will address many of the missional implications of the different chapters, so I will conclude by just touching on a few that I believe are pertinent to what I've presented here. First, today there are diaspora communities from the Global South and East that are practicing what has been called "reverse mission" (or "echo mission"). As these migrants enter Western societies, they need to be aware of the social imaginaries that will impact, to a great degree, their missional endeavor.

Just as Western missionaries were viewed through the imaginary lenses of those they were trying to reach in the non-Western world, so too are these new missionaries to the West so viewed and affected. In some cases, these efforts have been quite successful. However, in other cases it looks as though the existing social imaginaries (particularly the imaginary of "race" in the US) of the host society have had a negative impact on the missionary effort. This seems to be a problem among the Nigerian Pentecostals in the Atlanta, Georgia area who, in spite of their stated goal of reaching the American population with the gospel, have, thus far, succeeded primarily in reaching fellow Nigerians in the diaspora.[34] In addition to the social imaginaries in the host society (or perhaps feeding into them), part of the problem here

---

33 Kazin, *Walker in the City*.
34 Udotong, *Transnational Migration*.

might be the transnational nature of the missional diaspora. In maintaining such close connections with the church and leadership back in Nigeria, the churches in the US may not be as effective at translating the message, worship style, and even theology to their new context.[35] As a result, the churches and services may be seen as very foreign (an excess of alterity) to the indigenous population.

A second missional implication, related to the first, has to do with the 1.5 and 2nd generation members of the missional diasporas. If the first generation is less successful at reaching the host society than they had hoped (and prayed), perhaps the succeeding generations will be more successful, if they see their liminal state positively as a bridge between the diaspora and host society, and if they maintain the missional vision of their ancestors. Both of these are big "ifs," because, as I've discussed, liminality can also be psychologically and socially stressful. One response to this stress can be the rejection of the immigrant identity and culture in an attempt to assimilate (or at least integrate) into the host society and culture (as happened with some previous migrations discussed above). Also, since the reason these diaspora communities migrated in the first place is because they viewed the host society as needing to be evangelized, their children and grandchildren might be affected by the secularizing influences of the host society, thereby abandoning the missional vision of their ancestors. An encouraging sign comes from a recent review by Kate Bowler of Duke Divinity School. In reviewing the book *Religion and Spirituality in Korean America*, she states, "Second-generation Korean American Christians are forging new connections between their generational, ethnic, and religious identities. In short, they find new ways to be all three: Koreans, Americans, Christians."[36]

A final missional implication (at least from me) has to do with the fact that liminality can also make people more open to the gospel. As individuals migrate, they are "uprooted" from their home society and culture, and are "replanted" in a new socio-cultural context. As a result, they can often feel disoriented, alone, frustrated, and even terrified. It is in these situations that Christians can demonstrate to them, in deed as well as in word, the love of Jesus. We can reach out to them with what Brian Howell has called "radical hospitality."[37] The need for this is especially true with the growing Muslim

---

35 In addition to the communications technologies of the internet and cell phones, there is now a direct flight from Atlanta to Lagos, which makes the transport of people and materials much easier.
36 Bowler, "Generation K."
37 Howell "Rethinking Contextualization," 79–85.

migrant population. As I discussed above, the response to this migration by states in Europe has been to question the boundaries of tolerance as well as multicultural policies. But we, as Christians, are not states, though at times we respond as though we were. I've had conversations with Christians in the United States about the Muslim population, and on many occasions, they have responded from a nationalist rather than Christian perspective. The nationalist perspective, informed by the "immigrant as threat" imaginary, is "They are invading and taking over our country. They need to be stopped." In some of these conversations I've pointed out that it is the gates of hell that will not withstand the furtherance of the church, not the other way around; as Christians we are not to have a "fortress mentality" where we are the ones trying to keep the gate shut. The Christian perspective should be "God is bringing these people, from countries where missionaries are not allowed to go, to our doorsteps. How can we reach them with the love of God?" If we, as Christians, take this opportunity and calling seriously, it can have a profound impact on the revitalization of the church worldwide.[38]

Bibliography

Adeney, Miriam. "Colorful Initiatives: North American Diasporas in Mission." *Missiology* 39, no. 1 (2011): 5–23.

Alvite, J. P. "Racismo e Inmicración." *Racismo, Antiracismo e Inmigración*, edited by J. P. Alvite, 8–65. Donostia: Tercera Prensa-Hirugarren Prensa, 1995.

Bender, Eugene, and George Kagiwada. "Hansen's Law of 'Third-Generation Return' and the Study of American Religio-Ethnic Groups." *Phylon* 29, no. 4 (1968): 360–70.

Bevelander, Pieter, and Jonas Otterbeck. "Young People's Attitudes towards Muslims in Sweden." *Ethnic and Racial Studies* 33, no. 3 (2010): 404–25.

Bloom, Stephen G. *Postville: A Clash of Cultures in Heartland America*. Chicago: Harcourt, Inc., 2000.

Bowler, Kate. "Generation K: Korean American Evangelicals." *Books and Culture*, *Christianity Today*, May/June, 2009. Retrieved May 18, 2023, online: http://www.booksandculture.com/articles/2009/mayjun/generationk.html.

Brown, Donald E. "Ethnicity and Ethnocentrism: Are They Natural?" In *Race and Ethnicity: The United States and the World*, 2nd ed. Edited by Raymond Scupin, 178–204. Boston: Pearson, 2012. PDF Ebook published December 2020: https://www.researchgate.net/publication/347937513_Race_and_Ethnicity-_The_United_States_and_the_World_2nd_edition_edited_by_Raymond_Scupin_2012.

---

38 Ybarrola "Diasporas and Revitalization."

de Crèvecœur, Jean, and Michel Guillaume. *Letters from an American Farmer and Sketches of Eighteenth-Century America*. New York: Penguin Classics, 1981.

Echeverria, Jeromina. *Home Away from Home: A History of Basque Boardinghouses*. Reno: University of Nevada Press, 1999.

Eriksen, Thomas Hyland. *Ethnicity and Nationalism: Anthropological Perspectives*. 3rd ed. New York: Pluto Press, 2010.

Gans, Herbert. "Symbolic Ethnicity: The Future of Ethnic Groups and Cultures in America." *Ethnic and Racial Studies* 2, no. 1 (1979): 1–20.

Glazer, Nathan, and Daniel Moynihan. *Beyond the Melting Pot*. Cambridge, MA: The MIT Press, 1963.

Grey, Mark A., Michelle Devlin, and Aaron Goldsmith. *Postville, U.S.A.: Surviving Diversity in Small-Town America*. Boston: Gemma Media, 2009.

Grillo, Ralph. "An Excess of Alterity? Debating Difference in a Multicultural Society." *Ethnic and Racial Studies* 30, no. 6 (2007): 979–98.

Guglielmo, Jennifer, and Salvatore Salerno, eds. *Are Italians White?: How Race Is Made in America*. New York: Routledge, 2003.

Hansen, Marcus. "The Problem of the Third Generation Immigrant." *Commentary* 14, no. 5 (1952): 492–500.

Howell, Brian. "Multiculturalism, Immigration and the North American Church: Rethinking Contextualization." *Missiology* 39, no. 1 (2011): 79–85.

IOM UN Migration. "World Migration Report 2022." https://worldmigrationreport.iom.int/wmr-2022-interactive/.

Kazin, Alfred. *A Walker in the City*. New York: Harcourt Brace Jovanovich, 1969.

MacEachem, Scott. "The Concept of Race in Contemporary Anthropology." In *Race and Ethnicity: The United States and the World*. 2nd ed. Edited by Raymond Scupin, 34–57. Boston: Pearson, 2012.

NBC. "Multiculturalism Has Failed." Published February 5, 2011. https://www.nbcnews.com/id/wbna41444364.

Nederveen Pieterse, Jan. *Globalization and Culture: Global Mélange*. New York: Rowan & Littlefield, 2009.

Sarup, Madan. *Identity, Culture and the Postmodern World*. Athens: University of Georgia Press, 1996.

Scupin, Raymond (ed.), et al. *Race and Ethnicity: The United States and the World*, 2nd edition. Ebook PDF, December 2020. https://www.researchgate.net/publication/347937513_Race_and_Ethnicity-_The_United_States_and_the_World_2nd_edition_edited_by_Raymond_Scupin_2012.

Solé, Carlota. "The Labour Market and Racial Discrimination in Spain." *Journal of Ethnic and Migration Studies* 29, no. 1 (2003): 121–40.

Takaki, Ronald. *A Different Mirror: A History of Multicultural America*, rev. ed. Boston: Back Bay Books, 2008.

Taylor, Charles. "Modern Social Imaginaries." *Public Culture* 14, no. 1 (2002): 91–124.

Taylor, Charles. *Modern Social Imaginaries*. Durham, NC: Duke University Press, 2004.

Udotong, William. "Transnational Migration and the Reverse Mission of Nigerian-led Pentecostal Churches in the USA: A Case Study of Selected Churches in Metro Atlanta." PhD diss., Asbury Theological Seminary, 2010.

UN DESA, Population Division. "International Migration 2020 Highlights." https://www.un.org/development/desa/pd/sites/www.un.org.development.desa.pd/files/undesa_pd_2020_international_migration_highlights.pdf.

Vertovec, Steven. "Transnationalism and Identity." *Journal of Ethnic and Migration Studies* 27, no. 4 (2001): 573–82.

Ybarrola, Steven. "Competition and Ethnic Conflict: The Dynamics of Native/Migrant Relations in the Basque Country of Spain." PhD diss., Brown University, 1995.

Ybarrola, Steven. "Diasporas and Revitalization." *Interpretive Trends in Christian Revitalization for the Early Twenty-First Century*. Edited by J. Steven O'Malley, 117–32. Lexington, KY: Emeth Press, 2011.

Ybarrola, Steven. "Enemies and Allies, Strangers and Friends: Immigration and Identity in the Peninsular Basque Country." Unpublished manuscript, Center for Basque Studies. University of Nevada, Reno.

Ybarrola, Steven. "Identity Matters: Christianity and Ethnic Identity in the Peninsular Basque Country." In *Power and Identity in the Global Church: Six Contemporary Cases*. Edited by Brian Howell and Edwin Zehner, 107–30. Littleton, CO: William Carey Library, 2009.

Ybarrola, Steven. "Intermarriage, Assimilation, and Ethnicity Maintenance: Basque American Case Study." Master's thesis, Brown University, 1987.

Chapter 3
La Mamá as Missionary to the Next Generation
A Case Study of a US Latina Immigrant Mother and Her Influence on the Religious Identity Formation of Her Gen Z Daughter

Rebekah Clapp

"*Ten ánimo. Yo soy. No tengan miedo.*" Mateo 14:27

Global Migration

For a mother to leave her home country along with her husband and children, uproot her family, abandon her career, and establish a new life in a new nation takes courage. For Sandra Diaz that courage was found in her Christian faith. The above Scripture reference from Matthew 14:27 came to Sandra after praying about whether leaving Colombia to move to Panama and then later to the United States was the right decision. She prayed that God would reveal to her whether or not they should migrate, and she heard the response, "*Yo voy contigo*" ("I will go with you"). So, Sandra, her husband, and their three young children left Colombia for Panama, and eventually immigrated to the United States, where they planted a Hispanic/Latino church and raised their family among fellow Latino migrants, with their Christian faith at the center.

Global migration has brought about the formation of diaspora communities as immigrants establish themselves in host societies that are different from their countries of origin. The theory of diaspora argues that globalization influences migration and the ways in which migrant communities interact with and maintain connection to their host society and culture. Diaspora communities serve as an expansion of immigrants' societies of origin, cultivating and fostering a strong ethnic identity. Diaspora theory, therefore, has important connections to ethnicity theory. Ethnicity is a collective identity which arises from shared language and culture, which is produced and passed on to the next generation, while undergoing change. Identification with an ethnicity results in inclusion in a community because of shared physical, linguistic, cultural, or religious practices; these characteristics also bring about exclusion of this community by others in the host society. The migrant community's identification with an ethnic group or culture is constantly changing as they live and interact within a diaspora community, connected to both their country of origin and their host society. They are constructing and reconstructing their cultural identities through shared beliefs and practices forged across diverse societies, communities, and generations. The changing nature of their culture often produces hybrid ethnic identities, as we can see in the US Latino population.

In the United States, the majority of the immigrants received are from Latin America, especially Mexico and Central America. More immigrants cross the southern border of the United States than any other in the world. At times, Latin American immigrants form themselves into diaspora communities. Because of a long history of migration, shared language, and similar cultural backgrounds, Latin American immigrants have become a pan-ethnic group, expanding beyond their nation-based diaspora communities to form a shared Latino community.

The Latino Community

The Latino community is a multi-cultural and multi-ethnic diaspora, made up of individuals from many Latin American countries and ethnic groups. As the number of Latinos have grown in US society across generations, the community has diversified. Because of an "eternal first generation," the Latino community maintains features of the diaspora, yet US-born Latinos, as well as those who migrated as children and were raised within the United States, interact with society differently while maintaining some degree of their Latino identity and membership within said community.

The Latino community's ethnic identity has emerged in the United States as a cultural community based on heritage, association, and relationship to the broader society. This Latino cultural and ethnic identity is marked by *mestizaje* and *Latinidad,* which becomes evident when the community gathers in their shared spaces, in contradistinction to the majority culture. The majority culture identifies Latinos by their language use, their cultural ancestry, and their racial phenotype. For the Latino population, the shared experience of immigrating to and living within the United States is what brings together the diverse nations, races, and cultures of Latinos living there. This experience is common among new immigrant groups and certainly impacts Latino cultural identity; however, a shared history of Spanish colonialism, a shared language, and marginalization as a racialized people group in the US also bring Latinos together despite distinctions in their cultures of origin.

The succeeding generations of Latinos in the United States also influence the construction of their community's cultural identity. Later generations have a number of distinctions from their parents' experiences, as they were raised in the United States, either having been born here (second generation) or arriving here as young children (1.5 generation).

These children have been raised in the majority culture, attending school, and often living in neighborhoods populated by majority culture children. Even when both of their parents are Latinos, their experience is increasingly marked by *mestizaje* as they grow up interacting in two cultures and two languages. For this reason, they often have difficulty finding their place within the Latino cultural identity of their parents. This distinction of cultural identity within the Latino diaspora between the immigrant and US-raised generations is interesting; while both have elements of hybridity and the first generation has an influence on the succeeding ones, they each relate to the diaspora and the majority society in different ways. Diaspora and ethnicity theory recognize the significance of shared identity for the Latino migrant community and its changing nature across generations. These two pieces are foundational to understanding development of religious identity of Latinos born and/or raised within the context of the US Latino diaspora community.

To understand the influence of the first-generation immigrant Latina mother on the religious identity development of the succeeding generations of the US Latino diaspora, we need grounding in the anthropology of mothering. Mothering has become a key area of research within the discipline of anthropology due to its relevance to understanding culture and its impact on the same. There is an important link between mothering and culture as mothers are the primary channel through which culture is communicated. Arriving at a definition of mothering proves difficult, as the topic speaks to both biological and social processes; however, this chapter will focus on the sociological role of mothering, rather than biological, as it is in the social engagement of mothers with their children, within their cultural contexts, that we see their influential role in their children's religious identity take shape.

Latina Motherhood

The role of mothering encompasses a wide array of practices and perspectives. While the distinct behaviors and approaches vary significantly across cultures, there is also a great deal of commonality to be found. Essential to the mothering role is the relationship or bond between the mother and child. When it is one of strength, engagement, and emotional commitment, it creates an inextricable tie between the identities of the mother and child.[1]

---

1 Kitzinger, *Women as Mothers*; Walks and McPherson, *Anthropology of Mothering*; Martin, "Motherhood and Power."

The diverse ways in which the mother-child relationship is lived out involve practices of caring for the development of children. The social practices and responsibilities are of vital importance because through them mothers shape and develop their children's identities.[2] The identity development of the next generation is essential to the role of mothering. A mother's role, then, is of social significance because it influences the development of the next generation's identity, both through relationship and responsibilities; this relationship also influences the mother's own identity.

There is diversity across cultures in the ways in which the relationships and responsibilities of mothering are lived out. Just as a mother influences her children and forms their cultural understanding, so culture influences mothering. Cultural values which imbue a mother's role and influence her mothering are passed along from one generation to the next because on some level, mothers recognize that they work, serving both society and their children. Mothers are active participants in the acculturation of their children, applying their cultural values to form their children's identity, personally and spiritually, with the goal of developing them into a certain kind of adult, depending on their society. While different cultures have different goals and practices in their parenting, all seek to influence their children's development in some way.

These kinds of cultural differences are particularly notable in immigrant communities. When mothers immigrate or when women immigrate and then become mothers in diaspora, they bring with them the cultural forms of mothering from their home culture, but they are also influenced by the parenting styles of their host country. Whenever parents from the South and East immigrate to the West they "abandon traditional ways" and adapt to the parenting styles of the West. Immigrant mothers are "transnational," as they bridge two or more cultures of mothering, sometimes with children in multiple cultures and countries as well, impacting both the women themselves and their children. This situation can negatively influence the mother-child relationship due to all they must endure: "separation from their children, alienation and loneliness, anti-immigrant laws, xenophobia, lack of educational opportunities, and cultural and language denigration."[3] Despite all of these challenges, immigrant mothers justify their decisions to migrate because of the better life it offers their children. For immigrant mothers to offer their children this better life, they must mother in a new, transnational way as they choose to apply different aspects of the cultural and social influences of their host and home cultures in raising their children.

---

2 Walks and McPherson, *Anthropology of Mothering*; Oliveira, *Motherhood across Borders*.
3 Smith Silva, *Latina/Chicana Mothering*, 4.

Within the Latino diaspora in the United States, Latina immigrant mothers raise their children, shaping their identities, with the influences of both their Latin American culture and that of the United States. Latina mothers who migrate demonstrate strength and resiliency, in the face of oppression, hostility, and discrimination. The strength of the mother-child bond is exemplified in the self-sacrifice of a Latina mother making the migration journey for her children. This migration experience can have a transformative impact on the very way Latina immigrants mother. They may continue to emphasize their Latin American cultural and religious heritage and their value of strong family connections, while also seeing their role extending to political and social activism for the benefit of their children and community. The Latina immigrant mother seeks to impart her cultural heritage to her children while living in a new context and experiencing its challenges, also while working for a better society for her children's future.

Members of this US-raised generation of Latinos are raised by immigrant mothers who are engaged in the religious life of diaspora Latino churches, ministries, and communities and who practice and model their religion in the home. Yet, just as the US-raised generation's ethnic and cultural identities differ from those of their parents, it follows that their religious identities do as well. This chapter utilizes a case study to begin to examine how this difference impacts the religious identities of US-raised Latinos and the role that the diaspora religious experience, mediated through faithful mothers, has in influencing the religious identity of its next generation. The case study will examine the impact of immigration, multiculturalism, identity formation, and the role of mothering and religious identity development in the lives and experiences of Sandra Diaz, the Colombian immigrant mother referenced at the beginning of this chapter, and the youngest of her three adult children, Evangelina, who was raised in the United States in order to give insight into the relationship between the role of mothering and the development of religious identity within the broader US Latino population.

A Mother's Journey

Sandra Diaz (not her real name) is a member of the transnational Latino diaspora. After spending over twenty years living in the United States, ministering among the Latino community, and raising her children here, she and her husband have recently returned to Colombia. Her three adult children reside in the United States, studying and working. It was the shared faith of Sandra and her husband and their conviction that God had called them that brought their family to the United States initially. Though, it wasn't easy, they believed they were making the right decision.

Tides of Opportunity

Sandra shares that one of the most difficult and frustrating things about moving to the United States was the language. She had to depend on others to communicate with people. Even though she was the mother, even though she was a professional, having had a successful career as a lawyer in her home country, she had to have her children's help at times to be understood by their teachers. She recognizes that her eldest daughter, who was eight years old when they moved to the US, had an especially significant emotional burden to bear, along with her parents, because she was so heavily depended upon. There were also financial pressures as the family figured out how to sustain themselves and their church in a different culture and system on a small income. In spite of these difficulties, or perhaps due to them, the Diaz family had a strong bond of unity. Sandra remarked that God had called the whole family, to come to the United States as a family, and minister among Latinos here. The five of them were very integrated, especially because they didn't have other family close by. So, the surrounding Latino community was very influential for them.

For Sandra, identifying with the Latino community was meaningful because of shared roots. Apart from her immediate household, this broader Latino population provided her with a connection to her cultural roots. Sandra remarks that even though she is Black, being able to speak in Spanish and share many customs, experiences, and values strengthened her identification with the Latino community. Her participation in the Latino community was largely through her family's community of faith—the church which her husband pastored. Their church was made up of fellow immigrants with similar needs, similar experiences, similar hardships, and shared cultural roots. However, for Sandra, their shared faith was most important. She believes that her religious identity must take precedence over her cultural identity, because sometimes faith and culture clash. Sandra states that it is important to know how to respond with your faith in the midst of these tensions.

These cultural and religious tensions were not the only difficulties in Sandra's life. Though she was confident in their family's decision to move to the US, it had a significant impact on her career and her personal identity. In Colombia she had a professional career. She was a mother, a wife, and a woman of faith. She was also a successful, educated, lawyer and she worked outside of the home while hired help cared for her children. When she moved to the United States, she set her career aside. She believed that just as God had called her family to move to the United States, he had called her to focus on being a mother for this period. So that role became her primary identity and mission as she raised her children in the US Latino diaspora community.

La Mamá as Missionary to the Next Generation

As a Christian mother with what she perceived to be a missional calling from God to focus on raising her children in a new country, Sandra believed she had a personal responsibility to educate her children spiritually. Her own spiritual development had been different from what she sought to provide for her children. She grew up in a Catholic home in Colombia, and while her family had her participate in her first communion, her mother did not have them regularly attend church or engage in religious practices. When she was a young adult, before heading to university, her mother had a religious conversion and started attending a Protestant church. Sandra attended with her mother, and while there, Sandra had a spiritual experience which brought her to tears and brought her back to church each week. A few years later, her mother had a heart problem which was miraculously healed, and this strengthened Sandra's faith. So, while Sandra's mother did not raise her in a highly devoted religious environment, Sandra's mother's faith had a significant influence on Sandra during her young adult years. She believed that as a Christian mother, teaching her young children about God was her responsibility. Additionally, her religious belief and practice was meaningful and influential in the way she mothered her children, especially living in diaspora.

"*Una no sabe cómo ser mama ...*" Sandra stated, "No one knows how to be a mom. I had three children. Three different children ... it was only God who knows each of them. I would ask God for wisdom. Only he knows the heart."[4] Even though she experienced God speaking to her when she was frustrated and had asked for wisdom, being a mother still wasn't easy. She remarked that she had a practice of recognizing the presence of God, especially when she was particularly frustrated. She learned to put her faith into practice. For her, this meant seeking God's word and applying it to the situations in her life and the lives of her children. For example, she may have been frustrated with her children at times, but she would read in Scripture that children were a blessing, and so she would believe those words and apply it to her life. Her children were a blessing and therefore she and they were blessed. She would pray, asking God for a word for her child, for a specific adverse situation. She would then have words come to mind or would read Scripture verses, which she believed came from God as a specific answer to her situation. So, she said she would believe that word and "launch it" to her children, praying it over them and seeking to apply it to their lives. Sandra believes that whatever happens to a person, God is using it in that person's favor. "Whenever you live through something, God will use it for you or another person."[5] As an Afro-Latina, an immigrant, and a mother, Sandra

---

4 Sandra Diaz, interview with the author.
5 Sandra Diaz, interview with the author.

had her share of difficulties, but she found strength in her religious identity and sought to teach her faith to her children.

Generation Z

Her youngest daughter, Evangelina, is a part of the 1.5 generation; though not born in the United States, she left Colombia as an infant, and her first memories are of leaving Panama when she was only three years old to move to the United States, where she grew up. She and her two elder siblings were all children when they arrived in the US. They were raised by their Colombian parents among a Latino diaspora church community, while living and attending school in a very white and affluent neighborhood in western Ohio.

Evangelina shares at length about her experience growing up as a Black Latina in this context. "But living in [this community] ... it was very White, there were like four Black people ... the family and the church were my community. My cousins and grandparents were very far away ... and the rest of life was in English, but in these moments, [in] the private family and the church, the atmosphere [was] Latina and in Spanish."[6] Evangelina identifies as Afro-Latina. While her family is made up of Colombian immigrants and she grew up participating in the life and culture of the US Latino community, her family is also Black. The experience of being Black in America also had a significant impact on Evangelina's upbringing and cultural identity development.

She remembers feelings of being different, both within the broader White community with whom she attended school and even within the Latino community. She remarks that her mother used to try to help her feel better about being of African descent, doing her hair in particular ways to help her feel beautiful and proud of who she was. Within the church community she was more comfortable in her skin and could more easily be herself, surrounded by others with shared experiences of immigration, marginalization, racism, and shared language and culture. But she also recognized that there was a distinction in her experience as a Black Latina and her experience of racism, even within the Latino community.

While discussing her Afro-Latina identity, Evangelina remarked: "White Latinos don't understand the struggle of the double or triple minority that it is to be Black and Latino."[7] In her experience, she could relate more easily with Latinos with browner skin or with people who had been exposed to

---

6 Evangelina Diaz, interview with the author.
7 Evangelina Diaz, interview with the author.

Black culture. In addition to the struggle of being raised in an immigrant family and a Latino family, Evangelina recognized that her skin color and hair type added another layer to the discrimination she experienced through micro-aggressions: questions about her hair or skin-color or assumptions about her cultural background or Spanish-language ability.

Even within the Latino community she sometimes felt there were efforts to erase the Afro-Latino identity. She spoke of *mestizaje* as a way of explaining how the Latino community sought to unify themselves through shared struggle, but she pushed back because as a dark-skinned Latina, as an Afro-Latino she faces additional struggles. For example, she pointed to a phrase she heard growing up within the US Latino culture, *Mejorando la raza*. "Bettering the race," which refers to the idea that members of the Latino community can improve their race by marrying a white or a lighter person. Finally, Evangelina criticized the portrayals of Latinos in media, which do not tend to feature Black Latinos, which she felt was not representative of the reality that Black Latinos make up a meaningful part of the Latino community. Identifying as both Black and Latina while growing up in a very White, suburban area of the United States, Evangelina faced discrimination and tension in relationship to both the broader culture and within the Latina community. However, she had a solid foundation for her self-understanding in her family relationships and her community of faith, remarking, "I always had community in my home and in the church."

For Evangelina, her cultural identity and her religious identity are intertwined. She shared:

> Being Afro-Latina growing up in the church, my dad was a pastor, he used to preach to us in Spanish, and the sermon was in Spanish, he used to read the Bible to us in Spanish ... all those comforting verses, I'm ... more receptive to it being Spanish, it's ... comforting to me. I found out that when I went to Anglo churches ... they were a lot more formal with their church services ... punctual, a lot more rigid. It was harder for me to make a connection. Also, being ... the only Black person in that space, the undertone of it, kind of made it feel like, the structure of it, like you don't belong here. But ... Latinos and ... people of color have a tendency to be more warm [sic] or we just interact differently a little bit ... I feel ... more understood there... . In my experience, I don't have to feel worried about being looked down upon or not accepted.[8]

---

8 Evangelina Diaz, interview with the author.

It was at home and at her church where Evangelina had the opportunity to engage and grow in her Latina identity; however, both of these places were also heavily influenced by her parents' religious faith, with which she also identifies. The religious practices in the Diaz home while growing up revolved around the church and their family life, the same places where they had a shared cultural community and identity. Because the father of the Diaz family was a pastor, there were expectations about church attendance and involvement, which created extra pressure in Evangelina's life. She remembered feeling as if she had to live up to a standard of perfection or an image that church people had of her because of who she was as a pastor's daughter. Yet, this community was also a comfortable place for her where she could be herself. Even at home she felt some of this same pressure through sibling relationships. It was also at home where religious faith was put into practice. Evangelina talks about how her mother modeled a life of prayer and demonstrated a trust that God would respond to their prayers and sustain their family through hard times. This practice of prayer and trust in God continues as an important part of Evangelina's religious life today.

Evangelina's religious belief and practices today differ somewhat from that of her childhood. She no longer attends worship every single week, though she still finds community in church. After moving to California, a professor of Evangelina's, who is from Trinidad and also a Black woman, invited Evangelina to her church. Although the church is not made up of Latinos and does not worship in Spanish, Evangelina was reminded of her church community growing up. Gathering with other Christians who were Black and immigrants made her feel like she could relate to them, even though they were from a different culture. Another change in Evangelina's religious belief has to do with some of her social beliefs, in areas such as abortion or LGBTQ rights. Growing up, she was taught at home and in church from a more conservative perspective; however, she believes that her change in perspective is related to her Christian identity and her understanding of who Jesus is. She says that her faith is more liberal now, "but as you grow up you just try to follow how Jesus set the example ... not condemning anybody for the choices they make, be loving, helping your neighbor."[9] During her adolescence there was a period of time when she did not call herself a Christian and was entertaining a more nihilistic worldview. During childhood, she thought that she had to be perfect, but after experiencing some hardships and receiving treatment for emotional health as well, she learned that she doesn't have to be so religious, as religiosity isn't as important as

---

9 Evangelina Diaz, interview with the author.

maintaining her faith and hope. Today she calls herself a child of God and identifies as a Christian, even though some aspects of her religious belief and practice have changed.

Sandra and Evangelina have a close mother-daughter relationship, which they have maintained throughout Evangelina's childhood, adolescence, and into young adulthood. Theirs is the kind of relationship which Kitzinger remarks creates a particularly strong bond between the mother's and child's identities, strengthening the passing on of cultural knowledge.[10] While there have been periods of tension, as is common in these relationships, Evangelina has always felt that her mother was there for her, and she recognizes that her mother's faith was an integral part of her upbringing and her development into the person she is today. "My mother's faith is a part of my faith today ... because she started the foundation."[11] She speaks about the way that her mother's vibrant personality, generosity, encouragement of others, treatment of others, and willingness to help other people taught her how to live out her own faith. Whenever there is a problem, whenever she is worried, she still calls her mom to confide in her and receive encouragement. During these interactions, her mother will often pray for her in Spanish, and Evangelina feels as if her mother's faith is a shield of protection for her. She remarks how grateful she is to her mother for constantly reminding her of who she was, a beloved daughter, for helping her to identify with her culture and with her faith, and for making her more connected to her identity and to God. Sandra also recognizes the ways that being an immigrant, living in another country, and mothering three children in another culture have shaped her own beliefs. It has been for her, a journey by faith, not by sight. Sandra remarks how she has become more flexible and tolerant. Her mind is more open to many situations, and she recognizes the difference in her own faith: "I am the same in Christ, but not so much in the rituals."[12]

All three of the Diaz children have grown into young adulthood and each in different ways remain connected to their family, their cultural roots, and their Christian identity. Sandra's two elder children have both studied theology at the graduate level and are involved in the church, and Evangelina has also remained connected to her Christian faith. Sandra speaks to her understanding of the mission of motherhood that she felt God gave to her as her personal focus and calling when they moved to the United States: "The mission isn't so your children follow your same pathway. God has

---

10 Kitzinger, *Women as Mothers*.
11 Evangelina Diaz, interview with the author.
12 Sandra Diaz, interview with the author.

another territory for them. Be there so they grow. But after [they grow], I am behind them so they can see their own horizon. Because I have a different horizon. Their equipping no longer belongs to me, if they fly or if they fall, because it is no longer the same flight." So, her faith sustains her now, as she places her children's lives and their own religious identity in God's hands.

The Latina Diaspora

This case study of Sandra and Evangelina is only one story which shares the experiences of one mother and one daughter who are a small part of the large, diverse US Latina diaspora. It is a story of culture, faith, and identity, a story about two women who overcame hardship and endured the difficulties of immigrant life in the US through reliance upon their Christian faith and within their familial and cultural community. Each woman relies upon a meaningful prayer life, connection to a faith community that understands her experience and culture, unity with her family, and most importantly, faith in God to sustain her throughout the difficulties of life's circumstances. When Sandra moved their family from Colombia, she took this risk because she felt that God had called them to go. Recently, Evangelina made the journey from Ohio to California, to start a new life in a new state as a young person. Though it was a financial risk, Evangelina attributes the courage she had to make this move, to the faith that was formed in her as a child. She had faith that God would sustain her, and she believes he has. There may be differences between the women's approaches to their individual religious beliefs and practices, but each has influenced the other. As a mother, Sandra formed for Evangelina and her siblings a foundation upon which they could build their own faith as they became young adults.

Within diaspora missiology, further study of the influence of the first generation of the diaspora on the religious faith of the next generations is warranted. It is clear through current scholarship in the anthropology of mothering that a mother's influence in areas of identity and culture is significant; religious belief and practices are important parts of this development as well. Additional ethnographic work among immigrant mothers and their adult children will provide further insight into the way that the mission of the church can be furthered in and through the diaspora, between mothers and their children. This research will also provide missiological implications for evangelization beyond the diaspora as this next generation engages the broader host culture, of which they are also a part, with the faith that formed them in the diaspora community of their childhood.

Bibliography

Castles, Stephen, Hein de Haas, and Mark J. Miller. *The Age of Migration: International Population Movements in the Modern World*. 5th ed. New York: Guilford Press, 2014.

Clapp, Rebekah. Interview with a Latina immigrant adult child (name is withheld to protect the privacy of the interviewee). PhD Candidate, Asbury Theological Seminary. Dayton, OH. August 17, 2022.

Clapp, Rebekah. Interview with a Latina immigrant mother (name is withheld to protect the privacy of the interviewee). PhD Candidate, Asbury Theological Seminary. Interview conducted via Zoom. Dayton, OH. June 21, 2022.

Clapp, Rebekah. Interview with Latina immigrant mother and her adult child (names are withheld to protect the privacy of the interviewees). PhD Candidate, Asbury Theological Seminary. Dayton, OH. August 23, 2022.

Crespo, Orlando. *Being Latino in Christ: Finding Wholeness in Your Ethnic Identity*. Downers Grove, IL: InterVarsity Press, 2003.

De La Torre, Miguel A., and Gaston Espinosa. *Rethinking Latino(a) Religion & Identity*. Cleveland, OH: Pilgrim Press, 2006.

Kitzinger, Sheila. *Women as Mothers*. Oxford: Fontana, 1978.

Levitt, Peggy. *The Transnational Villagers*. Berkeley: University of California Press, 2001.

Martin, Joann. "Motherhood and Power: The Production of a Women's Culture of Politics in a Mexican Community." *American Ethnologist* 17, no. 3 (1990): 470–90.

Martinez, Juan Francisco. *Walk with the People: Latino Ministry in the United States*. Nashville, TN: Abingdon Press, 2008.

Mize, Ronald L., and Grace Delgado. *Latino Immigrants in the United States*. Cambridge: Polity, 2012.

Oliveira, Gabrielle. *Motherhood across Borders: Immigrants and Their Children in Mexico and New York*. New York: New York University Press, 2018.

Ragone, Helena, and France Winddance Twine, eds. *Ideologies and Technologies of Motherhood: Race, Class, Sexuality, Nationalism*. New York: Routledge, 2000.

Rodriguez, Daniel. *A Future for the Latino Church: Models for Multilingual, Multigenerational Hispanic Congregations*. Downers Grove, IL: InterVarsity Press, 2011.

Small, Meredith F. *Our Babies, Ourselves: How Biology and Culture Shape the Way We Parent*. New York: Anchor Books, 1998.

Smith Silva, Dorsia, ed. *Latina/Chicana Mothering*. Bradford, ON: Demeter, 2011.

Walks, Michelle, and Naomi McPherson, eds. *An Anthropology of Mothering*. Bradford, ON: Demeter, 2011.

Chapter 4
Pluralism, Multiculturalism, and Diaspora Mission
Discovering the Relevance of Apostolic Mission Today

Thomas Alan Harvey

As the archaeologist in Xinjiang China brushed the final layer of sand off the four-thousand-year-old corpse, he was surprised to find himself face to face with a beautiful European woman. The discovery of the ancient Tarim diaspora was a reminder that humans have been on the move for millennia and grappling with the issues that arise with our restless wandering. Indeed, the crucible of Judaism and Christianity was diaspora. Out of the bowels of the Babylonian captivity arose the Hebrew Canon and in bustling cities from Jerusalem, to Antioch, to Rome, Paul preached the gospel and penned his letters to the churches.

Shortly, we will also reflect on mission in that ancient diaspora, but first we will consider the postmodern cultural and pluralistic milieu where mission amongst the diaspora takes place today. We begin with the ways modern peoples seek to understand and manage urban diversity. In this regard we will examine modern pluralism and multiculturalism in their descriptive and ideological senses. In particular we will consider the ways that pluralism and multiculturalism seek to provide a sense of unity, the common good, continuity, vocation, and identity.

This framework is not accidental, but provides a lens by which we will relate modern pluralism and multiculturalism to the practical wisdom of the early church's missionary activity in their own pluralistic and multicultural milieu of late antiquity. The gospel gathered, displaced, and dispersed people into the "one, holy, catholic, and apostolic" ecclesia. These marks of the church describe the unity, common good, divine vocation, and rich sense of identity which was the fruit of diaspora mission. In turn, the marks of the church serve as an appropriate lens to examine not only the social implications of Christian mission of the early church as a holistic and practical communal engagement that transformed their world, but also as a framework for understanding effective mission today.[1]

---
1 Pelikan, *Excellent Empire*.

Pluralism, Multiculturalism, and Diaspora

Though common terms, the meaning of pluralism and multiculturalism are by no means fixed. They shift depending on who is using them and why. In general, they refer social, religious, political, and cultural diversity in modern urban society. Their use in all spheres of life reflects increasing awareness of the reality and effects of cultural diversity and the desire of modern societies to effectively engage their changing demographics. Though the terms are used globally, their origin and definition have arisen primarily out of the UK and North America—a fact which should be kept in mind when noting how and by whom these terms are understood and employed.

As simple descriptions of human diversity in modernity, pluralism, and multiculturalism often appear synonymous. When used categorically, however, distinctions become apparent. Whereas pluralism tends to classify individuals according to their religious, political, social, economic, or civil affiliation and beliefs, multiculturalism classifies groups according to fixed characteristics, identities, or cultural/ethnic boundaries. Moreover, pluralism tends to classify individual identity in light of an assumed greater and more foundational national identity. Thus, individual members of society may have various religious, political, or ethnic ties, yet in their national identity they are viewed as one. Multiculturalism, however, classifies and describes according to difference and seeks to bring to light the significance of cultural, ethnic, religious, and moral diversity in modern society. Group identity is foundational and therefore precedes individual or national identity. Thus, political or even religious affiliation are viewed as subsidiary to one's more foundational racial, ethnic, gender, or sexual identity. In this regard, religion tends to be viewed as a matter of volition and thus secondary to one's cultural or biological nature.

The Roots of Pluralism

The roots of modern pluralism lie in the gradual rise of large European nations in the seventeenth century. Whether this was due to abhorrence of the so-called "religious wars" or the pangs of nascent state nationalism remains sharply contested. In either case, as larger states enfolded contending religious constituencies, recognition and growing tolerance of religious pluralism became the order of the age. National identity increasingly absorbed religious identity within national churches, national history, and the standardization of national languages.

As power was consolidated in growing European nations, advances in navigation and military technology fueled their imperial expansion around the globe. Those they conquered they conscripted. And those they conscripted they trained to exploit resources, extend markets, staunch rebellion, and fend off imperial rivals. This led to an ever-increasing flow of foreign laborers and economic migrants into Europe.

By the twentieth century, Western nations were inundated with ever-welling tides of immigrants who brought with them a dizzying variety of faiths, values, histories, and loyalties. This diversity strained older understandings of national and ethnic identity. As these new immigrants became citizens, only rarely were they referred to as "French," "English," "German," "Spanish," or "Italian." Instead, new ethnic monikers or derogatory racial epitaphs were used to label the confusing influx of tribes, races, and ethnicities now inhabiting Western societies.

Securing the ardor and loyalty of their new foreign-born citizens would hardly be gained by tales of imperial glory, national conquest, and stolen riches. Thus, outmoded national sagas were supplanted by new revisionist histories to critique and cleanse an uncouth imperial legacy and promote a common good that could unite the conqueror and the conquered in a common national unity and identity.

"Pluralism" as Political Ideology

The ideological foundations of political pluralism appear in any perusal of Western citizenship rituals. Regardless of one's ethnic, historical, economic, cultural, or religious backgrounds, what one shares with other citizens is a commitment to democratic values and civil rights. Thus, government and justice should be blind to difference that could ignite sectarian violence as groups vie for power, resources, and political influence.

Such violence is stemmed by what pluralism refers to as "liberal democratic equilibrium." Democratic equilibrium is the fruit of political systems that provide room for dialogue, negotiation, and reasonable compromise. What makes these possible are a minimal commitment to democratic values and fundamental human rights (the right to vote, right of assembly, free speech, religious freedom, regular open elections, and protection of minority rights). Pluralism holds that this minimal concord works because it appeals to reasonable self-interest and avenues for citizens to access relative goods in democratic market societies.

The produce of this approach is what Michael Sandel has called a "procedural republic," namely, a liberal, diverse, and democratic society where there is no mechanism to accommodate any one notion of the good.[2]

---

2 Sandel, *Democracy's Discontent*, 276.

Rather than a view of the common good, what democratic values and human rights provide are procedural liberties that underwrite individual choice and self-realization. In this way, the role of liberal secular government is to remain neutral in regard to what constitutes the "good life" or communal fruition, and simply ensures that individuals are able to pursue unencumbered their own vision of the good life.

Multiculturalism as Ideology

Multiculturalism and the politics of identity have their roots in the civil rights movement of the latter half of the twentieth century. Emphasis upon universal human rights and equal access did little to redress the damage of social, political, and economic exclusion based on race, gender, culture, or sexual orientation. Only attention to cultural, ethnic, gender, racial, or sexual difference would allow society to identify, understand, and thus effectively redress injustices that were based on discrimination and prejudice fueled by difference.[3]

Attention to difference has brought identity politics to the fore in Western societies. Here political association does not orbit around beliefs, programs or even party affiliation, but rather around constituencies of those marginalized and oppressed because of inherited biological characteristics or inherited cultural traits. Thus, rather than defining nationalism in terms of the values and rights citizens hold in common, multiculturalism defines society as diverse and held together through attention to dignity, diversity, and mutual tolerance.

Multiculturalism is but one aspect of a larger critique of historical European imperial, patriarchal, and racist domination of the globe. Thus, multiculturalism is a demand that dignity, representation, just restitution, and redistribution be spread equally across cultures. Because the privilege, power, and wealth of White Western culture have been the seedbed of domination and its associated injustice, only when power, wealth, and influence are fairly redistributed in favor of historically marginalized groups will social justice be realized.

This shift in emphasis from individuals to groups can be seen in academic circles. Prominent Western universities now sport cultural study centers that focus on racial, gender, sexual, and cultural studies. Their growing influence in academic circles has nurtured the post-modern turn in contemporary thought that questions the notion of "objective truth." Instead, it is argued that all knowledge is to some degree interested, partial, and arises out of

---

3 Taylor, "Politics of Recognition," 3–73.

cultural presuppositions. Thus, situatedness and cultural perspective is crucial to knowledge. Moreover, this approach opens the door to marginal perspectives that have been systematically excluded due to social and economic marginalization.

In terms of a common good, multiculturalism turns to the collective goals and goods of specific marginalized constituencies. Recognizing the collective good of a discernible group provides insight into adequate remedies. A classic example of this has been the insistence in Canada of the *Quebecois* that the city of Quebec uphold the collective goals of its French-speaking citizens. In this instance the recognition of the collective goals necessary to nurture and extend the historic French culture of the city required that collective goals and the goods associated with it be given special protection that favored minority French-speaking citizens over the majority of English speakers.[4]

Pluralism and Multiculturalism in Tension

Though concern for fairness, justice, and equal respect are important for both pluralism and multiculturalism, they differ sharply regarding how these are to be achieved. For Pluralism justice must be blind and without bias in regard to race, religion, or culture. For multiculturalism justice ignored is justice denied, and the failure to take into consideration awareness of race, gender, and culture leave pluralism blind to injustice and just redress. Indeed, multiculturalism argues that pluralism remains blind to its own cultural bias. Appeals to liberal, universal values and human rights fail to recognize how those values arose out of dominant Western cultures and preserve an unequal status quo. As Charles Taylor has noted, "the worrying thought is that this bias might not just be a contingent weakness of all hitherto proposed theories (of universal human rights), that the very idea of such a liberalism may be a kind of pragmatic contradiction, a particularism masquerading as the universal."[5] Accordingly, pluralism's claim to rest the equilibrium and peace of civil society upon a shared commitment to universal democratic values and universal human rights in fact conceals the cultural imperialism that has historically subsumed difference in the crucible of dominant White, Western, European culture.

In spite of being fashionable in some academic and political circles, multiculturalism and "identity politics" have also come under increasingly sharp criticism. Emphasizing difference, critics claim, has encouraged the

---

4 Taylor, 55.
5 Taylor, 44.

isolation, exclusion, dangerous divisions, and extremism bedeviling modern society. In light of increasing ethnic tensions and race riots in both London and Paris, UK Prime Minister David Cameron argued: "Under the doctrine of state multiculturalism, we have encouraged different cultures to live separate lives, apart from each other and the mainstream. We have failed to provide a vision of society to which they feel they want to belong. We have even tolerated these segregated communities behaving in ways that run counter to our values."[6]

Defenders of multiculturalism argue that analysis has shown that the violence stemmed from a complex seedbed of unemployment, family breakdown, racism, discrimination, gang culture, and the glorification of violence. Thus, they argue that it is unfair to lay these tensions at the feet of multiculturalism. Instead, they assert that only attention to cultural differences will enable society to understand and thus alleviate the tensions that gave way to rioting.

This debate between ideological rivals, however, reveals their dearth of moral resources to arrive at a common good. Pluralism's appeals to self-interest, self-realization, and democratic values may be good at producing amorphous, self-directed, high-achieving individuals. Nonetheless, to establish the common good requires that self-interested individuals begin to consider what is good for all. Doing so, however, requires more than tolerance, democratic values, and procedural rights. What's needed is wise discrimination between communally wise and foolish ends and to promote behaviors and pursuits that enrich the common good and actively discourage those that destroy it. Nonetheless, pluralism's obsession with the self-referential individual bent in on themselves provides little that could inform communal well-being. Reduced to procedural means, liberalism lacks the richer resources that come from tradition and reason nurtured in a community that shares goals, values, and virtues by which to forge a common good.

Certainly, multiculturalism defends the role of communities that affirm a diversity of goods, but given the multiplicity of cultures, the only social virtues multiculturalism can offer across cultures are a "politically correct" but substantially empty tolerance and diversity. Indeed, if the only stable virtues on offer in modern society are tolerance and diversity, the only achievable goal is at best a nervous truce between diverse diaspora groups that inhabit modern mega-cities.

The upshot is an ever-increasing sense of anomie in the public square. Standards and values fray given the inability of pluralism or multiculturalism

---

6 Euractiv, "Multiculturalism Has Failed."

to provide any coherent vision of the common good. The result is not only social turmoil, but a society stripped of the moral language and practical wisdom necessary to identify the problem, diagnose its effects, and arrive at suitable responses to address the ailment. As some commentators have noted, the common denominator of the banking crisis of 2008, the riots in London in 2011, and the Occupy Wall Street movement are the inconsistency and incoherency of the grievances. Without some shared sense of what is good, determining what precisely is wrong, why it is wrong, and how it might be remedied is not conceivable. The subsequent confusion reigns not only in the streets but in the marketplace, legislative halls, and universities as business leaders, bureaucrats, and academics are left stammering and increasingly unable to offer coherent responses to the disarray of modern urban society.

Pluralism, Multiculturalism, and Mission: Grappling with Diaspora

We have looked at two modern ideological approaches that have sought to cope with diversity. Though the ideologies of pluralism and multiculturalism abide side by side in modern society, they do so uneasily for they begin at contested starting points and lack any coherent vision that might forge a greater harmony. Both struggle due to a lack of moral resources needed to fashion a coherent social and communal vision necessary to nurture social unity and the common good.

In what follows, we will compare that deficit with the Roman Empire in late antiquity and social transformation wrought by the early church through its mission to the Jewish and Gentile diaspora. We will note the ways in which the early church's embodiment of a spiritual, political, and social unity, its understanding and engagement to secure the common good, as well as a social and communal vision flowed out of its sense of mission to preach the gospel and to reveal the kingdom of God.

Jaroslav Pelikan has sought to explain how the early church emerged from small insignificant gatherings to a movement that triumphed over pagan Rome in light of the four "notes," or marks of the early Nicene Creed: the "one, holy, catholic, and apostolic church."[7] We will extend that analysis to show that the "social triumph of the early church" was in large measure the result of effective Christian mission whose evangelical and social engagement made decisive inroads in the pluralistic and multicultural urban milieu of late antiquity. Later on, we will examine what relevance these four "notes" might have for effective diaspora mission today.

---

7 Pelikan, *Excellent Empire*, 15.

The Early Church's Diaspora Mission Was One

Religiously, the Roman Empire was relatively tolerant. Various sects from across the empire could worship their preferred deity so long as that worship fit into its assigned place beneath the Roman Pantheon and the ultimate lordship and worship of Caesar. Even diaspora Jewish communities that abhorred the defiling idolatry of the pagans were allowed by imperial edict to defer from emperor worship so long as their worship of the "one true God" remained within the confines of the synagogue and the Jewish ghetto.

Paul, however, ventured beyond the Jewish quarter in his zeal to claim Gentile converts and establish Gentile congregations. The new ecclesia included former sorcerers who burned their scrolls and others who abandoned the Temple of Artemis, the city's guardian deity. This level of conversion threatened not only the purse of idol makers, but the public order. At issue was more than the exclusive monotheism of the gospel—various stoics and Platonists held to a rudimentary monotheism. No, the disruptive power of Christian worship and mission was its claim that Christ was Lord. In placing the crucified Messiah as the supreme deity who brought rebellious principalities and powers to heel, the Apostle Paul preached a gospel that debased local deities and inverted the Roman order whose coercive dominion was reflected in the hierarchy of pagan worship. In this way the crucified Christ's triumph from below deconstructed, exposed, and seriously qualified secular authority.

Christian worship, God's sovereignty, Christ's suffering, and diaspora mission were thus of one cloth. From baptism to the Lord's Supper, converts to faith in Christ were now united in a transformed order. It wasn't that Scythian, barbarian, slave, or free shed their cultural vestments when they joined the church, rather as Scythian, Roman, Jew, or barbarian, they turned their back on the spiritual and physical captivity of the pomp, hedonism, domination, and spiritual enslavement of pagan or emperor worship. Thus, conversion represented a personal and cultural transformation. Many were now one in Christ as they sought to honor, magnify, worship, and emulate individually and corporately their crucified Lord. They still represented many tribes, but that diversity found its greater unity in the life, mission, and witness of the church.

The Early Church's Diaspora Mission Was Holy

For Christians cannot be distinguished from the rest of the human race by country or language or customs ... They live in their own countries, but only as aliens ... They busy themselves on earth, but their citizenship is in heaven. They obey the established laws, but in their own lives they go far beyond what the laws require. They love all men, and by all men are persecuted. They are unknown, and still they are condemned; they are put to death, and yet they are brought to life... . They are defamed, and are vindicated. They are reviled, and yet they bless; when they are affronted, they still pay due respect. When they do good, they are punished as evildoers; undergoing punishment, they rejoice because they are brought to life.[8]

Roman values and virtues in the late antiquity took into account the vast hierarchy of being that inhabited empire. Every person was due the degree of honor their status possessed. Masters were due greater honor than slaves, fathers greater honor than sons, husbands greater honor than wives and so on down the chain of being. Status was usually gained at birth and maintained in an intricate and at times dangerous social network that required skillful navigation to sort when and where deference and patronage applied. An individual's social and civic rank was a matter of communal perception and social encounters demanded display and bearing; countenance and comport exhibited one's station in life as personal honor and pursuit of glory were woven into the political, social, and economic fabric of society.

On the route from birth to death, life's compass was guided by the virtues appropriate to one's station in society. Rulers were to embody the civic virtues of magnificence, munificence, high-mindedness, personal ambition, and equipoise in dominion. Soldiers inculcated courage, loyalty, and dedication, and slaves were noted for deference, obedience, docility, and assiduity. Each in their place contributed to the stability and extension of Roman dominion.

The Galatian epistle's spiritual virtues reflect a very different order. Meekness, temperance, gentleness, goodness, etc. would to the imperial eye be only fitting for plebeians or slaves, not patricians or masters. Yet Paul's inversion reflects the lordship of the crucified Christ. As such they are the Spirit's antidote to hatred, wrath, strife, sedition, heresy, murders, drunkenness, and revelry eating away the foundations of the empire.

---

8 Baillie, McNeill, and Van Dusen, "So-Called Epistle to Diognetus," 187–88.

Although a firm moral line was drawn between the way of Christ and the way of the pagan, it did not exclude but rather offered a compelling alternative. This transformative openness created a society that complicated the traditional niche of culture, class, cosmos, or empire. Here shared experience of transformed conduct and character changed formerly fixed relationships. Thus in Paul's letter to Philemon, a slave returns to the service of his master but now paradoxically as a brother in Christ who is a valued companion of Paul. Indeed, the pagan Celsus complains of this inordinate Christian "love of sinners" who welcome "whosoever is unwise, whosoever is a child, and in a word, whosoever is a wretch" and assures that "the kingdom of God will receive him."[9] For Celsus, such a collection of dubious characters would only be a holy society in a theatre of the absurd.

Indirectly, Celsus's revulsion brings out the disturbance the moral and social inversion wrought by the witness of Christ's death and resurrection had brought into being. This witness of the church was not a radical withdrawal from the public square, but a transformative missional engagement with it that was beginning to get under the skin. Certainly, God's redemption was a call to conversion and purity of life but the inversion of the cross was a radical social engagement.

This Christian emphasis upon purity and the cross was not a withdrawal but a provocative entry into the public sphere. As Bruce Winter has noted, to do "good works" to those beyond the church was a command whose effect was two-fold: "This would not only benefit others and the city generally, but it would also silence the 'ignorance of uninformed people.' They concluded that the Christians were 'evildoers' and not 'doers of good.' The doing of good in the public domain was declared to be 'the will of God' and it was also aimed at correcting misconceptions about Christianity."[10]

Rather than simply good works to avoid persecution, Peter, echoing Jeremiah 35, reminded his readers (1 Pet 1:1; 2:11) they were the "elect sojourners of the dispersion" and "resident aliens" seeking the welfare of the city even as they sought to avoid the defiling snare of pagan decadence. Augustine summed up this diaspora relationship well in *The City of God*. Augustine refers to the true ecclesia as a city within a city that reflects the true peace and prosperity in Christ. This city, hidden in the folds of the eschaton, is disclosed discreetly in the communion of believers on their pilgrimage to the heavenly city. Thus, the Christian pursuit of the common good blesses the earthly city and the church; in order that through "this mortal condition

---

9   Origen, *Contra Celsum*.
10 Winter, "Pilgrims and Citizens," 31.

shared by both cities, a harmony may be preserved between them in things that are relevant to this condition."[11]

The Early Church's Diaspora Mission Was Catholic

Within the vast sea of the Roman Empire, small fellowships of Christian believers appeared from Palestine to Asia Minor and eventually in Rome. An odd mix of messianic Jews and Gentile converts, their identity, continuity, and cohesion were threatened both from within and without. Within, "Judaizers" demanded Jewish ritual and kosher Jewish distinction that threatened to divide these fragile fellowships along ethnic lines. Meanwhile the lure of pagan intemperance questioned communal norms and encouraged pagan syncretism that threatened to untie the narrative cord that bound prophets, apostles, and redemption in Christ.

Paul, however, embraced "all who invoke the name of our Lord Jesus Christ in every place" (1 Cor 1:2). Thus, each distinct fellowship was but one member of the universal body of Christ. The political term that captured this union was *ecclesia*. In ancient Greece, the term referred to civic gatherings where free male citizens made public decisions. The writers of the New Testament give the word a new elasticity. Thus, *ecclesia* refers to the local congregation as when Paul refers to the "ecclesia of the Thessalonians," or a province of churches as in the "ecclesia of Asia," or ethnicity in the "ecclesia of the Gentiles," or finally to the universal church as in the "ecclesia of God," or the "ecclesia of the Lord." In the ecclesia disparate believers, ethnicities, cultures, and peoples entered a common household as brothers and sisters "in the Lord." This intimacy was afforded to Paul's emissaries who were to be received as fellow workers and family members of the household of faith.

In this way, each local congregation was tied into a wider universal mission. Gentiles give funds to Paul in Asia Minor to relieve Jewish brethren in Palestine. No wonder the letter to the Ephesians can speak of the wall of hostility between Jew and Gentile crumbling. Indeed, other walls and separations that had defined society crumble as masters and slaves, parents and children, husbands and wives, and members of the church and the churches are reconciled in Christ.

In his letter to the Colossians, Paul extends this unity in Christ to encompass all of creation as all things are brought under the authority and dominion of Christ. Paul sees himself as part of the greater work of Christ reconciling all things to himself through his people. Thus, the particular

---
11 Augustine of Hippo, *Concerning the City*, 877.

fellowship and their universal mission become definitive of what it means to be part of the unfolding story of God's peace that brings human beings back into proper fellowship with each other and with the living God. Here believers discover their identity in the mission of God through the preaching of the word, and in their regular fellowship and embrace of each other both locally and universally.

The Early Church's Diaspora Mission Was Apostolic

> To whom does the Faith belong? Whose are the Scriptures? By whom, through whom, when, and to whom it has been handed down the discipline by which we are Christians? The answer is plain: Christ sent his apostles, who founded churches in each city, from which the others have borrowed the tradition of the Faith and the seed of doctrine and daily borrow in order to become churches; so that they also are Apostolic in that they are the offspring of the Apostolic churches. All are that one Church which the Apostles founded, so long as peace and intercommunion are observed. Therefore, the testimony to the truth is this: We communicate with the apostolic Churches.[12]

In this "Demurrer against the Heretics," Tertullian ties the "rule of faith" to the church and its mission. This rule is the authoritative, sacred deposit handed down to the church from the apostles. This "rule" referred to the Scriptures and appears to be an early, rudimentary creed that sums up the basic narrative of God, Christ, the Spirit, salvation, and the church. Unlike the pagan texts and nostrums, the Scripture is of divine origin and is thus sufficient to order the life and discipline of the church.

Tertullian's logic was simple: "any group of things must be classified according to its origin" and the origin of the true church was the "primitive church of the apostles." Thus, the mission of the church derives from this apostolic trunk that flows through true branches of the church spreading over the known world. Thus, the later creed that would affirm that church is apostolic as doctrine is of one cloth with it being social and missional in the same breath.[13]

Given the growing size and diversity of the church, the "rule of faith" served to tie its identity and mission back to the primitive church and allowed it to retain its coherence, unity, and truth. It was the plumb line in new culture that allowed diversity and unity to dwell together.

---

12 Tertullian, "Demurrer against the Heretics," 290.
13 Pelikan, *Excellent Empire*, 25.

At first glance, this might appear extremely culturally conservative and reduce mission to the displacement of difference. In fact, apostolic sanction allowed for dynamic mission engagement that assured continuity even as it creatively allowed the embrace of diversity. This creative paradox can be seen in the result of the Jerusalem Council of Acts. Its decision to include Gentiles on the basis of the spiritual circumcision of faith and not circumcision of the flesh would allow mission to gather the nations to the Messiah without their having to become Jewish.

Thus, the rule of faith led to discernment in mission by providing an identifiable set of truths whose implications went beyond doctrine. This discernment can be seen in subsequent councils that would address a host of ecclesial, social, ethical, and political matters. They grappled with matters as diverse as whether Christians could serve in the military or whether priests who had denied the faith under the compulsion of torture could be forgiven. These had missiological implications as the body of authoritative teaching brought a continuity in identity and vocation to ever new situations and cultures. Thus, apostolicity brought with it a sense of clarity to cacophony and meaning amongst the growing anomie.

Pluralism, Multiculturalism, Diaspora, and Mission

> Urban society in the early Roman Empire was scarcely less complicated than our own.... It's complexity—its untidiness—may well have been felt with special acuteness by people who were marginal or transient, either physically or socially or both, as so many of the identifiable members of the Pauline churches seem to have been. In any case, Paul and the founders and leaders of those groups engaged aggressively in the business of creating a new social reality.[14]

As we have seen, this new social reality was not extrinsic to mission but integral. The one, holy, catholic, and apostolic ecclesia in mission provided a compelling and transformative alternative to Roman decadence and division. Indeed, the multicultural and pluralistic urban centers of the empire were a catalyst to the gospel that penetrated all classes, cultures, and ethnicities. In light of this fact, and given the multicultural and pluralist urban centers of today, what might mission viewed through the lens of the one, holy, catholic, and apostolic ecclesia offer?

---

14 Meeks, *First Urban Christians*, 105.

The church as one in identity and mission kept the church from simply taking the place set for it within Roman religious pluralism. Instead, it inverted the Roman social and religious hierarchies and categories thus qualifying Roman rule by the rule of faith. In our own day, pluralism and multiculturalism perceive Christianity as simply one religious sect in an urban marketplace of diverse faiths. For pluralism, this should lead Christianity to shed its exclusive and universal claims so as to promote the secular public square and national unity which should transcend private religious sentiment. Pluralism might allow Christians the right to religious belief as long as it doesn't impinge on public debate or public policy. Instead, pluralism would suggest that faith and mission belong to the private realm of "spiritual needs" and "eternal yearnings," or what William James referred to as the "experiences of individual men in their solitude."[15]

Nonetheless, it is precisely here that effective mission should escape the private walled community pluralism offers. Where this has been discovered is with the churches of the Global South. Here holistic evangelical mission has been crucial to its relevance and power. Since the 1974 Lausanne Congress, Global South church leaders, missionaries, and scholars have reminded their Western Evangelical brethren that a gospel that involves only the private conversion of individuals and personal emotional experience of God is not in accordance with the mission of the early church. Indeed, the radical embrace of the principles and practical wisdom of Christ and the power of transformative suffering to combat injustice has informed powerful engagements with society from St. Francis to Tolstoy, Gandhi, Martin Luther King, and Nelson Mandela. This point is not to claim that their views were orthodox or evangelical, but they are a reminder of the practical relevance of the teaching of Christ to diagnose and confront injustice and transform society.

Multiculturalism, on the other hand, would hem the church and mission within the cultural bounds of the ecclesia's own community. They point to the poisonous tie between imperialism and global missions that forced conversions, denigrated and displaced cultures, and whose sense of superiority blinded them to their own failings. Given that legacy and the need for harmony between cultures, that emphasis on conversion should give way to dialogue, and disparagement of other religions to appreciation of the truths of other faiths.

Certainly, Christian missions should begin with repentance for insensitivity and failure to treat others with dignity. Indeed, where Christian mission fell into league with imperial power that embraced dominion,

---

15 James, *Varieties of Religious Experience*, 31.

coercion, and manipulation it embodied more often the lordship of Caesar rather than the crucified Christ. Nonetheless, precisely here it was a distortion of an earlier evangelism that reached beyond its cultural boundaries so as to reveal Christ as the power of the powerless.

In today's multicultural and pluralistic milieu the church has the opportunity to shed its imperial garments for the vestments of the crucified Lord. Nonetheless, like the early church, mission should recognize that it is Christ's inversion of power that leads to the church's critique of idolatry, superstition, polytheism, the glorification of violence, and the defiling enslavement to cults of hedonism, fertility, and depersonalized sexual license. At each point, multiculturalism would seek to silence the church, but it is precisely at each of these points that personal and social transformation merge in mission.

In terms of the common good, mission in a multicultural and pluralistic milieu has opportunity to rediscover the early church's insistence upon the unity of truth revealed in Christ. We have discussed how both modern pluralism and multiculturalism are unable to avail themselves of the spiritual and moral resources of a coherent rational tradition. Moreover, the members of many diaspora churches come from non-Western cultures where sacred and secular, spirit and matter, faith and knowledge are not rigidly separated. Thus, they represent a rich resource for mission engagement spiritually, socially, economically, and politically. As with the early church, diaspora churches can give witness to a common good that is at once holistic and extending across the church in its manifold cultural diversity. Nonetheless, this witness will require a willingness to challenge regnant secular reason that would consign faith and revelation to the realm of the private and inconsequential.

Perhaps the greatest challenge will be to rediscover the catholic nature of mission. Certainly, the particularity of the church is represented in the cultural diversity of diaspora churches. Nonetheless, their universality is suspect given the legion of sects, ethnic fellowships, and denominations. In most churches, the language of worship and communal fellowship is usually mono-cultural. Too often diaspora churches only reach out to their own. As a result, diaspora churches tend to reflect the divisions of multicultural, postmodern, urban existence.

On the positive side, recognition of the catholic nature of mission is a reminder that the gospel links the local congregation to the global church. Diaspora churches are increasingly doing evangelism in lands that in the nineteenth and early twentieth centuries were sending out waves of missionaries, but where the church now is in serious decline. Christians who emigrate from the Global South remind increasingly secular Western leaders, scholars, and diplomats that Christianity is neither a dying religion nor is the church an obsolete and irrelevant institution but rather a dynamic faith that empowers a globally relevant ecclesia.

This vitality of the global churches inspires courage in their Western brethren and is a reminder that mission begins with the marginal and the displaced who know what it means to speak truth to secular power. In diaspora movements and mission, we are reminded that Jesus moved from Galilee to confront the religious leaders in Jerusalem, and Paul ventured from Jerusalem to Rome to preach the gospel and establish the church. In diaspora the church reflects its mission roots as the church from the margins now engages great urban centers of the world with the gospel.

Ties to persecuted believers around the globe allow diaspora churches to support and nurture the gospel in the lands from which they've sojourned. As expatriate citizens of other nations, they give voice to the suffering of their people, work to provide education, economic assistance, and shelter, and serve as a voice for those imprisoned or silenced in their homelands. In this way, they bear public witness to the lordship of Christ and his universal rule in a hostile world.

Finally, in contrast to the growing sense of anomie beguiling pluralism and multiculturalism, diaspora churches and diaspora mission can offer the sense of identity, meaning, and vocation in Christ that accounts for yet transcends culture or tribe. The early church discovered that identity, continuity, and discernment flowed from the apostolic deposit of the rule of faith. In word, sacrament, shared ministry, and mission, the church through diverse congregations can do the same in urban centers today. Nonetheless, the ecclesia's apostolic identity remain frayed and forgotten in modernity as divisions that have haunted the church now multiply exponentially in our post-modern age.

Yet, there are powerful centripetal forces at work in the churches which have much to do with diaspora churches and mission. Paradoxically, it is often pressure placed upon churches by secular governments that encourage ecumenical identity, common cause, and mission engagement. In Singapore, churches have joined together to present a united front to the government in regards to protection of church property, ethical concerns regarding life sciences, and preserving the right to witness to Christ with persons of other religions or no religion at all.[16] Large gatherings of evangelicals such as at

---

16 Harvey, "Engagement Reconsidered."

Cape Town 2010 or more Mainline Protestant church conferences such as Edinburgh 2010 have brought together diverse church and mission leaders from around the globe in common cause and mission. Global conference leaders and delegates were a catalyst towards greater unity. Indeed, their voices held sway as can be seen in the subsequent statements of both conventions which questioned the false dichotomy between evangelism and social action that has dominated Western missions over the past century.

As Christians join in mission with others beyond the walls of their own cultures and denominational frameworks, they are able to reveal a solidarity seriously lacking in modern urban society. In so doing they have the opportunity to rediscover the continuity and identity of the ecclesia's apostolic roots.

The One, Holy, Catholic, and Apostolic Church and Mission

In an age of rapidly expanding migration, urban centers sprawl outward filled with enclaves of people from around the globe. It is not uncommon to walk along and hear several languages in a single block or sense tension between rival ethnic communities living amongst each other. With so much difference in cultures, beliefs, economic classes, and moral persuasions where do people turn to find common ground so as to promote peace, nurture unity, receive justice, uphold morality, and flourish personally and communally?

Pluralism and multiculturalism have sought to either transcend this diversity or simply to embrace it. We are to take our cues from the mission of the early church. However, rather than a problem to be solved we would recognize this grand diversity as part and parcel of the plans and purposes of God. The early church did not seek to transcend human diversity, nor simply affirm it. Rather, as Christ's disciples they were "to go and make disciples of all nations baptizing them in the name of the Father and of the Son and of the Holy Spirit" (Matt 28:19). That commission does not deny diversity, but affirms it; for it is only in diversity that the ecclesia reveals the one, holy, catholic, and apostolic church.

Bibliography

Augustine of Hippo. "Concerning the City of God against the Pagans." Chap. 17 in *City of God*. Translation by Henry Bettenson. London: Penguin Books, 1972.

Baillie, John, John McNeill, and Henry Van Dusen, eds. "The So-Called Epistle to Diognetus." In *The Library of Christian Classics, Early Christian Fathers*, 176–93. Philadelphia: Westminster Press, 1953. PDF available at https://ccel.org/ccel/r/richardson/fathers/cache/fathers.pdf.

Euractive. "After Merkel, Cameron Too Says Multiculturalism Has Failed." Updated December 22, 2011. https://www.euractiv.com/section/uk-europe/news/after-merkel-cameron-too-says-multiculturalism-has-failed/.

Harvey, Thomas. "Engagement Reconsidered: The Fall and Rise of a National Church Council in Singapore." *Trinity Theological Journal* 14. Singapore: Trinity Theological College, 2004.

Ho, Engseng. *The Graves of Tarim: Genealogy and Mobility across the Indian Ocean*. Berkeley: University of California Press, 2006.

James, William. *The Varieties of Religious Experience*. London: Longmans, Green, 1915.

Meeks, Wayne. *The First Urban Christians: The Social World of the Apostle Paul*. New Haven, CT: Yale University Press, 2003.

Origin. *Contra Celsum*. The Gnostic Library Society. N.d. http://www.gnosis.org/library/orig_cc2.htm.

Pelikan, Jaroslav. *The Excellent Empire: The Fall of Rome and the Triumph of the Church*. The Rauschenbusch Lectures, n.s., 1. San Francisco: Harper & Row, 1987.

Sandel, Michael. *Democracy's Discontent*. Cambridge, MA: Harvard University Press, 1996.

Taylor, Charles. *Multiculturalism: Examining the Politics of Recognition*. Edited by Amy Guttmann. Princeton, NJ: Princeton University Press, 1994.

Tertullian. "The Demurrer against the Heretics." In *Faith of the Early Fathers*. Vol. 1. Collegeville, MN: Liturgical Press, 1970.

Winter, Bruce. "Pilgrims and Citizens: The Paradox of the First Christians According to 1 Peter." In *Pilgrims and Citizens: Christian Social Engagement in East Asia Today*, 25–36. Edited by Michael Nai-Chiu Poon. Adelaide: ATF Press, 2006.

Chapter 5
Religious Pluralism in the Twenty-First Century Global Diaspora
A Case of Canadian Pluralistic Communities and the Evangelical Response

Sadiri Joy Tira

Migration or diaspora, the movement of people from one region to another, has at least four major off-shoots. These are: urbanization, multi-culturalism, "hybridity," and, in places where cultural diversity is embraced, religious pluralism. This observation is true in my own country, Canada, and of our diverse nation. In this chapter, I will focus on religious pluralism vis-à-vis migration and multi-culturalism, and will suggest to you that diverse diaspora communities, and the religious pluralism that they bring, has made Canada a fertile mission field, necessitating a thoughtful and pragmatic response from the Canadian church, particularly from the evangelical Canadians.

Religious pluralism is not a new phenomenon. Like human migration, it is an age-old reality of human experience. As such it should not be feared, but embraced as an opportunity to engage in society, inviting people "from everywhere" to a relationship with Jesus Christ. This chapter is delimited to the Canadian context where I have lived for the past forty years. Moreover, this chapter is divided into four parts: (1) "diversity is Canada's strength:" official multiculturalism—a description of the Canadian government's multicultural policies; (2) immigration and historico-religious landscape—a brief description of the historico-religious landscape among immigrant and migrant communities; (3) the Lord Jesus Christ in the pluralistic, diaspora communities in Canada—the response or reaction of the Canadian evangelical church; and (4) conclusion. Also included is a section entitled "Questions for Reflections and Further Research."

"Diversity Is Canada's Strength:" Official Multiculturalism

"Diversity is Canada's strength" is the mantra of current prime minister, Justin Trudeau's media machine. From school social studies lessons to doughnut commercials on television, the motto is celebrated from the Pacific to the Atlantic. Though the current government has thrust "diversity" center stage, this motto is a deeply Canadian value. Canadian children are taught that Canadian commitment to diversity goes back to when indigenous nations networked across the North American continent, which is evidenced by the initial trade partnerships between the host First Nations and the migrant French and English settlers. Perhaps there is truth in all of this, but the type of cultural diversity Canada is known for in the twenty-first century is the one that started with a new immigration act legislated by the Canadian government in 1967, Canada's centennial year.

In 1967, Canada became the first country in the world to assign "points" to people based on criteria including language fluency in English or French, levels of education, and work experience. The introduction of a new discrimination-free, points-based system for immigration into Canada ended preference for white immigrants from the British Isles, Western Europe, Australia, New Zealand, and the United States. This new immigration policy welcomed qualified people from all over the world to become "New Canadians." Prior to this change, migrants from outside protestant Western Europe, were discriminated against, and were seen only as solutions to labor shortages.

Shortly after, in 1971, Canada became the first country in the world to formalize multiculturalism as an official policy in the Canadian Multiculturalism Policy. In this policy, the government committed to "support and encourage the various cultures and ethnic groups that give structure and vitality to our society. They will be encouraged to share their cultural expression and values with other Canadians and so contribute to a richer life for us all."[1]

The implementation of official multiculturalism developed as immigrants arrived. The 1988 Canadian Multiculturalism Act committed to "promote the full and equitable participation of individuals and communities of all origins in the continuing evolution and shaping of all aspects of Canadian society."[2] The government now formally "recognizes the diversity of Canadians as regards to race, national or ethnic origin, color, and religion as a fundamental characteristic of Canadian society and is committed to a policy of multiculturalism designed to preserve and enhance the multicultural heritage of Canadians while working to achieve the equality of all Canadians in the economic, social, cultural, and political life of Canada."[3]

Laurence Brosseau and Michael Dewing of the Legal and Social Affairs

---

1 Canada House of Commons, October 8, 1971.
2 "Canadian Multiculturalism Act," 1988.
3 "Canadian Multiculturalism Act," 1988.

Division, and Parliamentary Information and Research Service of Canada's Library of Parliament define *multiculturalism* for Canada:

> As a sociological fact, multiculturalism refers to the presence of people from diverse racial and ethnic backgrounds. Ideologically, multiculturalism consists of a relatively coherent set of ideas and ideals pertaining to the celebration of Canada's cultural diversity. At the policy level, multiculturalism refers to the management of diversity through formal initiatives in the federal, provincial, territorial and municipal domains.[4]

By formalizing multiculturalism, Canada has paved the way for diversity of race, ethnicity, and unavoidable pluralism of ideology.

Immigration and Historico-Religious Landscape

The most recent Canadian census figures came close to 21.9 percent of Canadians reporting as being or having been an immigrant or permanent resident. The census report compared statistics from 1971 and 2016. In 1971, 5 percent of the population originated in Asia, 50 percent from Europe, and 30 percent from the British Isles. In contrast, in 2016, 48 percent of the population originated in Asia, with 21 percent from Europe, and 7 percent from the British Isles. It is important to note the top source countries for immigration to Canada in 2016. These are the Philippines (15.6%), India (12.1%), and China (10.6%). New predictions from Statistics Canada estimate immigrants could represent up to 30 percent of all Canadians by 2036.[5]

The four offshoots of migration and diaspora are evident in Canadian cities, in particular the Greater Toronto Area, Montreal, Vancouver, Calgary, and Edmonton, as they grow and are greatly enhanced by the New Canadians. In my own province of Alberta, demographics are rapidly shifting. According to the Canadian Broadcasting Corporation, "Alberta has surpassed British Columbia as a destination for recent immigrants.... . Over the past two years, Alberta lost more than 30,000 residents to interprovincial migration. During that same time, it gained more than 75,000 people from international migration."[6]

The major tenet of the Canadian Multiculturalism Act in 1988 is "equality in diversity"; it encourages Canadians to social integration and assimilation, but without force or pressure from the government. Therefore, all Canadians, old and new, who came from East or West, Global South

---

4 Canada Library of Parliament, "Background Paper."
5 Canada Statistics, "150 Years of Immigration."
6 Grenier, "Alberta Demographics."

or Global North, arriving in Canadian territory at different times, are equal before the law. Canada's commitment to pluralism was visibly demonstrated in 2006 when the Centre for Pluralism was established in Ottawa, the nation's capital. Consequently, Canada, is now hailed, by some as, "the most successful pluralist society" in the world.[7]

These statistics are not mere numbers but representations of the changing face of Canadian demographics and religious alignment.

The Lord Jesus Christ in the Pluralistic Diaspora Communities in Canada

In 2005, Jack Jedwab of the Association for Canadian Studies wrote that 2017 would bring considerable change to the profile of the Canadian mosaic: "Once considered a predominantly Christian country, Canada is in for a dramatic shift in the religious composition of its population when it reaches its 150th birthday. Statistics Canada forecasts major changes to the religious landscape of the country by 2017. Based on 2001–2017 projections issued by Statistics Canada," Jedwab writes, "non-Christian groups will be concentrated in Canada's largest cities."[8]

In the greater Toronto area, approximately one out of six residents will be either Muslim or Hindu and the two groups combined will pass the one million mark. In the nation's capital, much like in Montreal, the Muslim population will be greater than all other religious groups combined as it will near the one hundred thousand mark. Calgary will see growth in all non-Christian groups while in Vancouver, the Sikh population will remain the largest non-Christian group.

These changes in demographics are reflected in Canada's institutions. Notably, in 2010, Calgary, Alberta became the first larger North American city to elect a Muslim mayor, Naheed Nenshi. Born in Toronto, Ontario, and educated at University of Calgary and Harvard University, Nenshi is a second-generation Canadian—the son of immigrants from Tanzania. In 2017 he was re-elected to a third term.

The Pew Research Center reported on "Canada's Changing Religious Landscape" based on findings from the 2011 census:

> In the 1970s and 1980s, Canada's foreign-born population was smaller, largely European and overwhelmingly Christian. In recent years, however, rising numbers of immigrants—nearly

---

7 *Globe and Mail*, "Aga Khan's World View."
8 Jedwab, "Canada's Demo-Religious Revolution."

half of Canada's immigrant population—have come from Asia, Africa, and the Middle East. In the US, by comparison, three-in-ten of all foreign-born residents have come from these three regions.

Adding perspective, it observes that New Canadians are generally more religiously observant.... Immigrants do not appear to have contributed to Canada's decline in self-reported attendance at religious services. On the contrary, religious attendance is higher among immigrants than among the general public, and it has been fairly stable: 43 percent of immigrants report in 2011 that they attend religious services at least once a month, the same share as in 1998. By contrast, 22 percent of native-born Canadians in 2011 say they attend religious services at least once a month, down from 31 percent in 1998.[9]

In 2011, of the 32 million people surveyed, 22,102,745 identified as Christian (including major denominations—Catholic, Christian Orthodox, Anglican, Baptist, Pentecostal, Lutheran, Presbyterian, and "Other Christian"); 1,053,945 as Muslim; 497,965 as Hindu; 454,965 as Sikh; 366,830 as Buddhist; 329,495 as Jewish; 64,935 as practitioners of "Traditional (Aboriginal) Spirituality; and 130,835 as practitioners of "Other religions."[10]

The question on religion was not included in the 2016 Census of Population and the National Household Survey. This question has only been asked every 10 years, since 1871. Religious pluralism is an ancient reality. Before the Hebrews entered the Promised Land, God warned in Exodus 20:2–5 (NIV):

> I am the LORD your God, who brought you out of the land of Egypt, out of the house of slavery. You shall have no other gods before me. You shall not make for yourself an idol, or any likeness of what is in heaven above or on the earth beneath or in the water under the earth. You shall not worship them or serve them; for I, the LORD your God, am a jealous God, visiting the iniquity of the fathers on the children, on the third and the fourth generations of those who hate me, but showing lovingkindness to thousands, to those who love me and keep my commandments.

---

9 Pew Research Center, "Canada's Changing Religious Landscape."
10 Canada Statistics, "Two-thirds of the Population."

Biblical history shows that the Hebrews were not faithful to their Redeemer-God following their deliverance from the land of slavery. They transgressed his commandment many times. Centuries later, the Psalmist declared: "I will praise You with my whole heart, before the gods I will sing praises to You; ... all the Kings of the earth shall praise You, O LORD, when they hear the words of Your mouth, yes they will sing the ways of the LORD for great is the glory of the LORD" (Ps 138:1, 4–5).

These scriptures reveal the syncretistic worship among the Hebrews and the existence of pluralistic milieus in their geographical context. Indeed, many times, the nation Israel was chastised and severely punished by God for their unfaithfulness to him. Their punishment was banishment from their country and scattering of their nation. God used the Assyrians, the Babylonians, and the Romans to force them to live as exiles. Amidst these challenges, brokenness, dislocations, harsh judgment, and pluralistic environments, the Psalmist declared his worship of the living God. No other religious forces can change his allegiance to the living God. But for the psalmist, it was not enough to personally worship God; he expressed his missional responsibilities to proclaim "the words of the living God" so that the kings and their kingdoms will also sing the "ways of the Lord." This desire is the eschatological hope of the Psalmist; a hope that has been fulfilled in Christ!

We read in John 14:6, the Lord Jesus Christ's claim: "I am the way the truth and the life. No one comes to the Father except through me." His claim clearly galvanized the demarcation line between Christianity and other religions.

In 2004, missiologist Ralph Winter wrote: "[Diaspora missiology] may well be the most important undigested reality in missions thinking today. We simply have not caught up with the fact that most of the world's people can no longer be defined geographically."[11]

William Lacy Swing, director general of the International Organization for Migration, had similar words on September 19, 2016:

> We live in a world on the move—there have never been so many people in movement. Then, unprecedented human mobility: one billion of our seven billion world are migrants; one in every seven of us is a migrant. Were the 244 million international migrants to constitute themselves as a country, they would have a population slightly smaller than Indonesia's and slightly larger than Brazil's. They would have a gross domestic product roughly that of a small to medium size European country and far exceed all foreign aid.[12]

---

11 Winter, "Endorsement," 2004.
12 Swing, "Migration Is Not a Problem."

The primary driving forces of migration are "demography; disasters; the digital revolution; distance-shrinking technology; north-south disparities; and environmental degradation."[13] At a simplistic level, migration can be viewed as a result of both involuntary factors (including regional instability and conflicts, etc.) and voluntary causes (e.g., educational and career advancement, long-term tourism, job deployments, family reunification,). However, in actuality, these are directly related to the primary forces and global processes previously listed.

From a biblical perspective, Acts 17:26–28 provides us with a redemptive context for migration:

> And he has made from one blood every nation of men to dwell on all the face of the earth, and has determined their pre-appointed times and the boundaries of their dwellings, so that they should seek the Lord, in the hope that they might grope for him and find him, though he is not far from each one of us; "for in him we live and move and have our being," as also some of your own poets have said, "For we are also his offspring."

Luis Pantoja, Jr., a Filipino diaspora theologian, writes:

> The fact is that God created nations (Gen 25:23; Ps 86:9–10) and languages/cultures (Gen 11:1, 6–7, 9), and determined the place (space) and the timing (time) of our habitation. The passage in Acts 17:26–29 implies that he not only "uses" the "diasporas"; but designs, conducts, and employs such "diasporas" for his own glory, the edification of his people, and the salvation of the lost. Every dispersed person and people group has a place and a role to play in God's redemptive history.[14]

On December 22, 2017, *The Globe and Mail*, a leading national newspaper, published the article "Immigrants Providing a Boost to Declining Church Attendance in Canada" written by Xiao Xu in Vancouver:

> The Washington-based Pew Research Center found the percentage of Canadians who identify as Catholics dropped to 39 percent from 47 percent between 1971 and 2011, while the share that identified as Protestant fell even more sharply, to 27 percent from 41 percent.
>
> According to statistics collected and analyzed by Reginald Bibby, a sociologist at the University of Lethbridge

---

13 Swing.
14 Lausanne Diasporas Leadership Team, "'Diasporas' and God's Mission," 12.

and a prominent researcher of spirituality, about half of the immigrants who came to Canada between 2005 and 2010 were either Catholic or Protestant. Churches with large Asian congregations in particular are growing.[15]

The article further explores and reports of New Canadian conversions to Christianity. Rev. Rich Kao of Five Stone Church outside of Vancouver is quoted: "Canadians are inoculated; they think they know about Christianity … whereas you have people from Asia who have no exposure, and it's so fresh and so new."[16] Migrant people are coming to Christ in diaspora churches. The growing influence of the new immigrants brings hope for the Canadian church revitalization.

I am convinced that human migration serves the missional purpose of God. Christian Canadians, while enjoying freedom of diversity and the benefits that accompany official multiculturalism, must remember the challenge to declare the truth, the gospel of Jesus Christ in Canada's "walled" pluralistic society that embraces all religious beliefs including Islam, Hinduism, Sikhism, Judaism, and even Voodoo.

Conclusion

Religious pluralism is pervasive. What is happening in Canada is also true in other countries and other regions of the globe. The global church of Jesus Christ must embrace this reality and take up this missional role in our borderlessness. In this context we take seriously the declaration of the psalmist: "declare his glory among the nations" (Ps 96:3).

Several years ago, while living in Toronto, I was a frequent diner in my neighborhood Vietnamese restaurant. Inside the restaurant I noticed a golden Buddha statue, a red dragon, a green banner with a mosque and moon crescent, and the Virgin Mary statue displayed on a prominent shelf. One day, I asked the owner if he was Buddhist. He said, "Yes, but since opening this restaurant a lot of my customers are South American Roman Catholics, Pakistani Muslims, Thai and Chinese Buddhists. So I please everyone, but I remain Buddhist!" The owner of this restaurant opened my eyes to the pluralistic Canadian context.

Here are four realities from his simple statement:

1. He remains Buddhist, but he welcomes his diverse customers.
2. He offers his customers a space of identity in a multicultural mega city. His restaurant is a place to belong.

---

15 Xu, "Immigrants Providing a Boost."
16 Xu.

3. He uses the religious motifs and symbols for his customers to engage with other worldviews, beliefs, and culture.
4. He attempts to engage in religious dialogue with his customers.

Across from this restaurant were three historic church buildings: Baptist, United, and Anglican. These buildings were half-empty on Sunday mornings. My observation of these local congregations was that they were not missional in their local context. They were operated more like community monuments because they were not active in welcoming members of their changing community—the migrants. Their doors were locked throughout the week—the buildings unused, unlike the Vietnamese restaurant. The leaders were available to their parishes, but did not engage in the community beyond the church buildings. Perhaps they were not interculturally competent and had not discipled their congregations to engage with their diaspora neighbors.

The church of Jesus Christ in Canada and around the globe must be made up of disciples who live like their Master—trained in intercultural competence to engage people with different faiths and worldviews. Our buildings must be open for interfaith dialogue; they must be a space where people come to learn more about Christianity. Our people must embrace God-appointed diversity.

In London, during his 2015 address at Canada House, Prime Minister Justin Trudeau declared: "our diversity isn't a challenge to overcome or a difficulty to tolerate. Rather, it's a tremendous source of strength."[17] For the church, local diversity and the plurality it brings is also a tremendous opportunity to reflect the heart of Jesus, and to be his face, hands, and feet, inviting people into relationship with him in what has always been a pluralistic world.

Questions for Reflection and Further Research

Pluralism is not an enemy of the church, but a door to be opened for authentic dialogue. It is a pathway for Christians to engage non-Christian adherents. However, followers of Jesus Christ must also know how to share their faith (evangelism) and how to defend their faith (apologetics). It seems that many Christians have departed from church dogma; their moorings have loosened because they were not taught the doctrines (e.g., Apostles' Creed, Nicene Creed) of the church. We can confidently engage in a pluralist society, if we know what and why we believe our faith.

---

17 Trudeau, "Diversity Is Canada's Strength."

1. How can the academy help local congregations understand their pluralistic context?
2. How can the academy best prepare students to engage increasingly interfaith communities? Are the curricula helping develop missional leaders among the diasporas?
3. How can church leaders effectively disciple their parishioners to become effective witnesses to the diasporas?

Bibliography

Canada. Citizenship and Immigration Canada. "Canadian Multiculturalism: An Inclusive Citizenship." Last modified October 19, 2012. https://web.archive.org/web/20140312210113/http://www.cic.gc.ca/english/multiculturalism/citizenship.asp.

Canada House of Commons. Debates, 28th Parliament, 3rd Session, Volume 8, October 8, 1971. 8545-8548, Appendix, 8580-8585. https://pier21.ca/research/immigration-history/canadian-multiculturalism-policy-1971.

Canada Library of Parliament. Legal and Social Affairs Division and Parliamentary Information and Research Service. "Background Paper on Canadian Multiculturalism." Prepared by Laurence Brosseau and Michael Dewing. September 15, 2009, revised January 3, 2018. https://bdp.parl.ca/content/lop/ResearchPublications/2009-20-e.pdf.

Canada Statistics. "150 Years of Immigration in Canada." Modified May 17, 2018. https://www150.statcan.gc.ca/n1/pub/11-630-x/11-630-x2016006-eng.htm.

Canada Statistics. "Two-Thirds of the Population Declare Christian as Their Religion." Modified February 19, 2016. https://www150.statcan.gc.ca/n1/pub/91-003-x/2014001/section03/33-eng.htm.

"Canadian Multiculturalism Act." Canadian Multiculturalism Act (justice.gc.ca).

Globe and Mail. "The Aga Khan's World View." *The Globe and Mail.* Published May 28, 2010. Updated May 1, 2018. https://www.theglobeandmail.com/news/world/the-aga-khans-world-view/article4321039/.

Grenier, Eric. "Alberta Demographics." *Canadian Broadcasting Corporation,* October 25, 2017. http://www.cbc.ca/news/politics/census-2016-immigration-1.4368970.

Jedwab, Jack. "Canada's Demo-Religious Revolution: 2017 will bring considerable change to the profile of the Mosaic." Association for Canadian Studies. March 30, 2005. http://www.muslimpopulation.com/pdf/Canada_demography2017.pdf.

Lausanne Diasporas Leadership Team. "'Diasporas' and God's Mission." In *Scattered to Gather: Embracing the Global Trend of Diaspora*, 11–28. Manila: LifeChange Publishing and Lausanne Committee for World Evangelization, 2010.

Lo, Elsie, Mark Chapman, and Robert Cousins. "Listening to the Diaspora Church." *Faith Today*, May/June 2017. http://digital.faithtoday.ca/faithtoday/20170506?pg=45#pg45.

Peritz, Ingrid. "Haitian Diaspora Spreading the Gospel of Voodoo." *The Globe and Mail* (Montreal). Published September 27, 2010, updated May 1, 2018. https://www.theglobeandmail.com/news/national/haitian-diaspora-spreading-the-gospel-of-voodoo/article4327066/.

Pew Research Center. "Canada's Changing Religious Landscape." *Pew Research Center: Religion & Public Life*, June 27, 2013. http://www.pewforum.org/2013/06/27/canadas-changing-religious-landscape/.

Swing, William Lacy. "IOM Director General's Speech at the UN Summit on Refugees and Migrants." https://weblog.iom.int/iom-director-general-william-lacy-swings-speech-un-summit-refugees-and-migrants%C2%A0and-signing-iom-un.

Swing, William Lacy. "Migration Is Not a Problem to Be Solved; It's a Reality to Be Managed." United Nations Regional Information Centre for Western Europe, www.unric.org/en/latest-un-buzz/29774-migration-is-not-a-problem-to-be-solved-its-a-reality-to-be-managed.

Trudeau, Justin. "Diversity Is Canada's Strength." Canada House address by the Right Honorable Justin Trudeau, Prime Minister of Canada. London, UK. November 26, 2015. https://pm.gc.ca/eng/news/2015/11/26/diversity-canadas-strength.

Winter, Ralph. "Endorsement." In *Scattered: The Filipino Global Presence*. Manila: LifeChange, 2004.

Winter, Ralph, and Bruce Koch. "Finishing the Task: The Unreached Peoples Challenge." *Perspectives on the World Christian Movement: A Reader*. Kindle. 4th ed. Ralph Winter and Steve Hawthorne, eds. Pasadena, CA: William Carey Library, 2014.

Xu, Xiao. "Immigrants Providing a Boost to Declining Church Attendance in Canada." *The Globe and Mail* (Vancouver). Published December 22, 2017. https://www.theglobeandmail.com/news/british-columbia/immigrants-providing-a-boost-to-declining-church-attendance-in-canada/article37423409/.

Chapter 6
Ethnic and Cultural Hybridity
Jewish-Gentile Intermarriage in North America

Tuvya Zaretsky

Jewish-Gentile Intermarriage in North America

The Jewish people have lived the diaspora experience for more than twenty-five hundred years. They have existed as cross-cultural observers and outsiders possessing an internal worldview of *us* and *them*. It is simple and straightforward. World Jewry identifies as an ethnically singular nation distinct from all other nations. In Hebrew it is expressed as *Am Yisrael*, the nation Israel, and *Kol Ha-goyim*, all the (other) nations. This simple ethnocentric classification, as one nation versus all the others, presents an interesting "petri dish" for an anthropological, missiological study of a diaspora people. Viewed from the perspective of a current phenomenon of Jewish intermarriage presents a fascinating study of hybridity. We will show some of the implications of this trend and opportunities for discipleship of the next generation of Jewish-Gentile couples and their families.

Since the 1990s, Jewish demographic reports have shown an increasing global trend toward intermarriage. This chapter is focused on the American dramatic shift toward Jewish-Gentile intermarriage that first made headlines in 1990. We will note how the broader Jewish community has reacted to the phenomenon. To better understand that reaction, we will consider some of the implications in the issues and challenges faced by the couples and examine the biblical perspective of Jewish intermarriage. The current American Jewish-Gentile intermarriage trend offers a laboratory in which we may study the impacts of hybridity and some of the missiological implications for Jewish evangelism.

The Changing Demographic

Over the past thirty years, intermarriage has been a dominant pattern of life in the American Jewish diaspora. The 1990 National Jewish Population Survey (NJPS) made public the seismic sociological shift among American Jewry.[1] The American Jewish intermarriage rate rose slowly from 6 percent

---
1 Kosmin et al., "Highlights of the 1990 CJF."

in the 1960s to 12 percent in the 1970s. By 1990, the NJPS reported the Jewish-Gentile intermarriage rate was 52 percent, having doubled in each preceding decade. This report marked the first time American Jewish sociological reports found Jewish-Gentile exogamy exceeding endogamous Jewish marriage.

In 1997, then Harvard law professor, Alan Dershowitz, in *The Vanishing American Jew: In Search of Jewish Identity for the New Century*, warned the trend would lead to the total assimilation of American Jewry, apart from the Orthodox community.[2] In the same year, American diplomat, educator, and legal expert, Elliott Abrams, warned of the threat to Jewish survival in *Faith or Fear: How Can Jews Survive in Christian America*. Before the 2000 decadal report, Jewish Theological Seminary historian, Jack Wertheimer, warned American Jewish exogamy had become "self destructively ... accommodated."[3] The fact of Jewish intermarriage was a feature of diaspora life in America and signaled the increased hybridity of the next generations.

In 1990, Jewish sociologists and religious leaders responded with anguish and aggression. Jewish institutions increased funding and programs designed to promote Jewish reattachment to Judaism and conversion of Gentile spouses. At the same time, American sociological studies showed the trend continuing to move toward the 63 percent Jewish disaffiliation from Jewish institutions. American Jews were turning their backs on traditional Judaism, disconnecting from synagogue life, and trending toward assimilation.

The 2001 NJPS showed that none of the reattachment efforts were having the desired impact. The intermarriage trend was not abating. The decadal rate of Jewish intermarriage showed no decrease at all, but rather a slight increase to 54 percent. At that point the American Jewish Federation stopped providing decadal studies.

In 2013, the Pew Research Center's "A Portrait of Jewish Americans" found that fully 44 percent of all American Jews were married to non-Jewish spouses.[4] The Jewish rate of exogamy continued to rise to 58 percent by the end of that year. Further, if you were to remove the small community of Orthodox or Haredi religious Jews from the American Jewish population sample, the intermarriage rate was actually a whopping 73 percent.[5]

---

2 Dershowitz, *Vanishing American Jew*.
3 Wertheimer, "Surrendering to Intermarriage."
4 Lugo, Cooperman, and Smith, "The 2013 Pew Research Center Survey of U.S. Jews."
5 Lugo, Cooperman, and Smith.

America isn't the only place where Jewish intermarriage has increased.[6] It has been a global phenomenon continuing into the twenty-first century. This is not the first time in history that Jews have married out, yet over the millennia God promised the eternal existence of the descendants of Abraham, Isaac, and Jacob. When he addressed implications of Jewish intermarriage, his greater concern was the potential harm to the faith of the people and their relationship with him; so we will briefly look at those considerations as they are presented in biblical history.

Intermarriage in the Bible[7]

After the Hebrews' survived their first four-hundred-year diaspora in Egypt, God cautioned them to remain separate from the Canaanite nations they encountered on entry into the Promised Land. While at Sinai, the Lord was visibly present amid the nation in a pillar of fire by night and a pillar of cloud by day. His presence was among them from above the tent of meeting. They received instruction in the *Torah* and were promised blessings if they would look to God continually with trust and obedience.

It was there that God warned the Israelites against marrying the Canaanite people in the land they were to inherit. The issue was not about racial hostility against the Canaanites. However, it was a protective warning against the risk of spiritual corruption of the Hebrews. The Lord cautioned that mingling with religious perversions of the Canaanites would turn the Hebrews from him.[8]

The Lord God was jealous for the hearts of the Israelites, but their intimacy with him was not consistent. Therefore, he warned them against exposing their families, and the generations of children yet to come, to spiritual influences that would lead them away from Adonai. This principle could be applied today by partners in Jewish-Gentile marriages who believe in Messiah Jesus. Ignoring or diminishing the importance of their own sanctification in the Messiah can impose a cost to their spiritual well-being or to their loved ones.

Today, many Christians are aware of Paul's teaching in 2 Corinthians 6:14 against being "unequally yoked." Still, too many believers forgo purity to pursue passion under the influence of contemporary cultural views of sexuality. The "unequally yoked" warning is drawn from Deuteronomy 22:10, "You shall not plow with an ox and a donkey together." The point

---

6 DellaPergola, "Jewish Out-Marriage," 13–39.
7 Zaretsky, "Intermarriage in the Bible," 121–26.
8 Exod 34:10–17; Deut 7:1–4.

was to show the foolishness or harm in such a dissimilar pairing in the plow yoke or in attempts to build a spiritual home and life. Jewish people will be preserved as a unique nation, sanctified by God's covenant faithfulness. Individual Israelites can miss the blessing of knowing God by failing to honor and trust him through the choices they make.

Even knowing this, King Solomon, the son of David, took some seven hundred wives, many from foreign nations.[9] Scripture is powerfully direct in charging that Solomon allowed his heart to be "turned away" from the God of his father and his people. He was "not loyal to the LORD his God, as was the heart of his father, David."[10] Solomon's bad example caused the Jewish nation to pay a terrible price in the centuries that followed. He disregarded God's instruction, allowing the idols of his foreign wives into the land and environs of the holy temple. They polluted the hearts and faith of the Israelites. They brought spiritual confusion and chaos in and among the Jewish people, turning many from the Lord and subsequently leading to the split from one another as the northern and southern kingdoms divided.

The spiritual harm of that era eventually led to dispersion of Jewish exiles from the northern kingdom of Samaria at the hands of Assyria in 722 BC, followed by the deportation of Jews in the southern kingdom of Judah to Babylon in 586 BC. Upon return from the exile, both Ezra and Nehemiah describe their dismay at the compromised faith and assimilation of their nation's priests who brought foreign wives back with them from captivity.[11] The issue was and is God's jealousy for the hearts of the remnant, those who are his people. The identity of the Lord's chosen ones, from whatever nation, depends on their abiding trust in him. This truth must be one of the contemporary issues in considering how the growing community of Jewish-Gentile couples and their children will establish hybrid identities that are spiritually healthy. Here, we can consider missiological implications and opportunities.

Intermarriage Implications and Opportunities

Jewish Responses

The 2013 Pew Research of American Jewry found that, over the past three decades, 83 percent of the children from Jewish-Gentile marriages have also married a non-Jewish spouse. A generation of Jewish-Gentile children from these intermarriages are now adults presenting a new hybrid Jewish identity.

---

9   1 Kgs 11:1–5.
10 1 Kgs 11:2–5.
11 Ezra 9:1–10:44; Neh 13:23–27.

They are the American Jewish Millennials. They have proceeded through higher education and moved into the professional workplace. Jewish leaders, like Rabbi Aaron Lerner, executive director of Hillel at UCLA, observed a totally new self-identity among American Jewish college students. To the wider Jewish community, these children from Jewish intermarriages do not look like past Jewish generations. Lerner cautioned, "If we don't give these men and women a right to be part of our Jewish community, we risk losing them forever."[12]

Opinions from institutional American Jewish leaders have trended toward the viewpoint that Jewish hybridity from intermarriage is bad for the Jews. Emma Green wrote in the *Atlantic*, "what's at stake is actually the future of Jewish identity and pluralism."[13] However, in our "missiological laboratory," we should see implications and opportunities from the natural openness that comes with cross-cultural experiences and the creation of new, hybrid identities among Jewish-Gentile couples and the growing population of their Millennial and Gen Z children.

A Hybridity Picture of Jewish-Gentile Identity

The *2013 Pew Research Center Survey of US Jews* highlighted the impact of intermarriage and secularization on the children of Jewish-Gentile marriages—mostly Millennials (the generation born from 1981–1996). It should be no surprise that more than half of the Jewish Millennials are from Jewish-Gentile couples.

The Pew study found only 19 percent of Jewish Baby Boomers self-identify as "Jewish without any religion," or "nones." By contrast, 32 percent of Jewish Millennials self-identify as Jews of no religion—that's a 41 percent increase! Further, 62 percent of all Pew respondents said that being Jewish is more about "culture and ancestry—not about religion."[14] The hybrid Jewish identities, particularly in America, reflect a disconnect from religious identity. Where traditional Judaism maintained a high "hedge" to prevent Jewish curiosity about Christian faith, the non-religious trend implies a greater openness to other expressions of spirituality—a fact that has significant implications for younger American Jewry.

---

12 Lerner, "On College Campuses."
13 Green, "We're Headed Toward."
14 Lugo, Cooperman, and Smith, "2013 Pew Research Center Survey of U.S. Jews."

Over the past ten years, Barna Group has interviewed 27,140 Millennials in 206 studies. They commonly find Millennials making a distinction between *spirituality* and *self-identity according to religion*. This was one characteristic found in the Barna Group study of American Jewish Millennials in 2017, and is reported in the Barna article, "The Evolving Spiritual Identity of Jewish Millennials."[15] Now, religion doesn't necessarily mean affiliation with any religious organization. Barna highlighted that Jewish youth seek identity that is spiritual, but not necessarily religious in an institutional sense of a connection.

The Barna Group 2017 Study on American Jewish Millennials

Perhaps the most exciting barometer of the opportunity for ministry to Jewish-Gentile couples is revealed by Barna in October 2017.[16] A few significant observations of that study point toward opportunities for ministry:

- Jewish Millennials are open-minded to spiritual conversations and do not find them scary.
- Millennial Jews see a difference in *affiliating* as opposed to *believing*. They are asking, "What will work for me?" and "Where is my community?"[17]
- Jewish Millennial relationships are often experienced through one-dimensional contact such as social media and digital devices. Millennials tend to crave meaning and connection as one result of such social isolation.
- Jewish Millennials are discovering value in Jewish wisdom literature in the Bible. Examples include:
  - Ecclesiastes says a lot about ambition: "Young person, think about what it means to live a long and meaningful life."
  - Lamentations sees ways to express deep sorrow in the horrific events and relational tragedies presented in life.
  - Song of Songs has a lot to teach about sexuality.
  - Proverbs, the original Twitter feed, has good advice to offer about wise living.

Here are some specific findings for our consideration: the Barna Group report found that while 38 percent of American Jewish Millennials say they

---

15 Barna Group, "Evolving Spiritual Identity."
16 Barna Group.
17 Sales, "Jews for Jesus."

are not religious, 82 percent said they were "somewhat" or "very interested" in *spirituality*. What kind of spirituality? Surprisingly, 73 percent were interested in learning about the spirituality of other faiths besides Judaism, including Christianity. That's a significant change in American Jewish culture.

One of the biggest surprises in Barna's work was the new perspective of Jesus among Jewish Millennials. Even the *Jerusalem Post* took notice reporting, "The survey found that 21 percent of Jewish Millennials believe Jesus was 'God in human form who lived among people in the first century.'"[18] Here is evidence of hybridity's impact. Since demographics indicate more than half of Jewish Millennials have one non-Jewish parent, it can safely be assumed that the spiritual influence of Gentile Christian parents is exposing more of their children to Jesus's teaching. Jews for Jesus was interested enough to commission (but did not influence) the 2017, Barna Group study.[19]

American Jewish leaders have been doing their own analysis of the Barna Group findings and are adjusting to the evidence about the changes in how American Jewish Millennials think about Jewish identity. Ari Kelman, Jewish Studies professor at Stanford University, responding to the Barna report said, "These don't look like Jews I recognize ... maybe these are Jews we've never seen before."[20]

The *Jerusalem Post,* noted that while 21 percent of Jewish Millennials believe that Jesus was God, 42 percent of respondents celebrate Christmas.[21] Barna also found that a Jewish Millennial majority said that, in their view, they could "hold other faiths and still be Jewish."[22] That is a distinction of Jewishness as an ethnicity which is not defined by a culturally religious affiliation. Put another way, 34 percent of Jewish Millennials said, "belief in Jesus as the Messiah was compatible with being Jewish." This statistic reflects the growing awareness and acceptance of Messianic Jews in American and Israeli Jewish cultures.[23]

Sara Weissman, editor of the web-zine *New Voices*, was one of the younger Jewish editors to opine regarding the significance of the Barna Group study.[24] She expressed incredulity but also familiarity with American Jewish Millennial culture. Weissman described how she knows the Barna

---

18 JTA, "One-Fifth of Jewish Millennials."
19 Perlman, "Barna Releases New Study."
20 Sales, "Jews for Jesus."
21 Sales.
22 Sales.
23 Sales.
24 Weissman, "Did Jews for Jesus."

assessment is true, because she *knows* the Jewish Millennials the study described. Nevertheless, she found the survey description disquieting: "The young adults describe themselves as religious, and practice Jewish ritual, but are unaffiliated. They value tradition and family, but don't plan on marrying only Jews. They are proud to be Jewish, but don't feel that contradicts with practicing other religions."[25]

Weissman offered a surprisingly eclectic ethnographic description from her experience of American Jewish Millennial life. She knows the people who could be "dating a Buddhist," or "laying *tefillin* daily even though he couldn't find a synagogue," or the young lady who goes "clubbing on Friday nights but insisting on turning off her phone and the computer" to observe Shabbat. Weissman noted, they say that being *Jewish* is "very important" to them. In fact, 80 percent would self-identify as "religious Jews." She conceded, "the point is, our Judaism looks different ... as millennials stray from traditional Jewish institutions and movements."[26]

These Jewish Millennials are the next growing wave of Jewish-Gentile couples. The Barna data indicates their hybrid identities, grown in the American Jewish diaspora, are leading them to be more spiritually open to new ways of defining Jewishness, spirituality, and loving God. That means new and exciting opportunities are present for gospel conversations among Jewish-Gentile couples and their children.

Challenges and Opportunities

While American Jewish leaders lament that assimilation, secularization, and intermarriage are dangerous to Jewish survival, the Christian community has been unresponsive to this spiritual opportunity. As noted here, there are Gentile partners in almost half of all American Jewish marriages today. Often those non-Jewish partners are familiar with the Bible, desire to know more about Jewish holidays, customs, and traditions, and may maintain faith in the Lord Jesus Christ.

Studies by sociologists and psychologists report interfaith couples experience greater threat to marital stability and satisfaction than do same faith couples.[27] These studies also indicate that 75 percent of mixed-faith couples experience marital dissatisfaction or divorce. Christians have a message of hope for such a situation—the potential for finding a mutually satisfying spiritual harmony.

---

25 Weissman.
26 Weissman.
27 Vaughn, Call, and Heaton, "Religious Influence on Marriage."

Finding Spiritual Harmony

It is important to state at the outset that we have a perspective about the way to spiritual harmony. That perspective is based on the biblical belief that the one Creator God accomplished reconciliation with himself through his messianic Redeemer, Jesus. When marital partners find vertical relationship with the same God and through the same faith, they may find horizontal intimacy and shared spirituality with one another.[28] In the Scriptures, God promised he would answer anyone who earnestly opens their heart to him and invites him to be known. If anyone is open to the words of Jesus, it is important that they know his offer, "Ask and it will be given to you; seek and you will find; knock and the door will be opened to you."[29]

In the ministry to Jewish-Gentile couples, we believe that if each partner would seek God in the way he wants to be known, he will lead them to himself through the person of Messiah Jesus. Such confidence is founded on biblical statements by Jesus and the apostles. See for examples John 14:6; Acts 4:12; and 1 John 5:11, 12.

Issues and Challenges

There seem to be at least three contemporary issues that drive the conversation around Jewish-Gentile intermarriage. Those are Jewish survival, enculturation of children, and finding spiritual harmony.

Survival is an imperative core value for world Jewry. That impulse was intensified by the extermination of one third of the people during the Holocaust. Contemporary rabbis in America are especially concerned about the massive disaffiliation from Judaism and Jewish institutions. In their perspective, intermarriage is a direct threat to the survival of the Jewish religion. The natural conclusion, for them, means the end of the Jewish people since Jewish identity is established by religious attachments and religious culture. Such an outlook discounts the immutability of Jewish ethnicity. No similar outlook generally exists among Christians. Christians who marry a non-Christian are viewed as making a choice that could put their own spiritual well-being in jeopardy. However, such an intermarriage isn't viewed as a threat to gospel truth.

Enculturation of children in a Jewish-Gentile marriage is a second pressing issue. Couples need to be intentional about their choices in enculturating the next generations. Marianne Husby Callahan at USC identified four strategies

---

28 Wan, "Paradigm of 'Relational Realism'."
29 Matt 7:7 NIV.

of enculturating children: (1) *delegation* to one partner; (2) *cooperation* where both partners share in the enculturation of their children in one or both faith traditions; (3) *abdication* where they intentionally choose not to offer religious training so the children "may decide for themselves"; and (4) *avoidance* where the failure to adequately discuss the process of enculturation usually results in tension, mistrust, frustration, and anger. The choices come down to one faith, two faiths or none at all.[30]

A third issue is finding spiritual harmony. American Jewish Millennials are rejecting religion, while showing an interest in tradition and a hunger for spirituality. This, I believe, is an opportunity with missiological implications related to identity hybridization occurring in the subsequent generation of Jewish-Gentile couples.

An Approach

A 2004 ethnographic study of cross-cultural challenges as reported by Jewish-Gentile couples identified five key challenges.[31] Underlying all of them was the inability to find a satisfying spiritual harmony. I suggest an approach that utilizes tools of missiological cultural anthropology. We serve Jewish-Gentile couples by helping them seek greater understanding of the cross-cultural challenges in their experience. While spiritual rebirth or renewal is the desired goal, this ministry does not start with a conversionary agenda. We absolutely believe that salvation in Christ can lead to satisfaction and stability in marriage through spiritual harmony. See the methodology presented by Donald K. Smith in *Creating Understanding: A Handbook for Christian Communication across Cultural Landscapes*.[32]

Missiological cultural anthropology seeks to understand how partners use words, concepts, and presuppositions that inform their world view. We serve them as cross-cultural translators, helping build bridges between their two identities, cultures, and world views. At the same time, we must be mindful of our own intervening culture during this process. Some practices have been developed and presented as a training manual for Christians desiring to engage in Jewish-Gentile couples ministry.[33]

The 2017 Barna study described religious outlook and identity of American Jewish Millennials. It began the description of them as, "free-thinking and flexible in their spiritual and religious identity, yet they

---

30 Callahan, "Interfaith Family Process."
31 Zaretsky, *Challenges of Jewish-Gentile Couples*, 93–97.
32 Smith, *Creating Understanding*.
33 Zaretsky, "Intermarriage in the Bible," 121–26.

gravitate toward formal customs and ancient expressions of faith."[34] Along with Gen Z, this population makes up the majority of American Jewry today. They reflect a hybrid identity coming out of the Jewish-Gentile marriage phenomenon dating back thirty years to 1990. A key issue for them is where can they find community? A beginning point, and a surprise to most, comes with informing them that they are the majority of American Jewry today. A booklet is available that introduces couples to a discussion around their cross-cultural differences as a Jewish-Gentile couple. It is intended as a guide toward finding spiritual harmony. Couples are encouraged to read chapters together, then complete a self-assessment at the end of each chapter. The results are shared with one another as a stimulus toward safe conversations for building understanding.[35]

The Barna Group found that a third of American Jewish Millennials would say they are not religious. Yet more than two-thirds of them are interested in spirituality. These are people in a unique diaspora community that is part of a larger Jewish diaspora. They have turned away from religious conventions, while respecting traditions that convey history, story, and meaning.[36] Jewish-Gentile intermarriages are forming new hybrid identities for their families and children. That is a significant population to engage for gospel ministry. Their expressions of hybrid identity may appear unconventional to traditional perspectives. However, Jewish-Gentile couples are a perfect example of a unique population, Jews and Gentiles, "us and them," in the human tidal wave that is coming for spiritual harmony in the Lord Jesus.

Bibliography

Barna Group. "The Evolving Spiritual Identity of Jewish Millennials." *Barna. Com*, 10 October 2017. https://www.barna.com/research/beliefs-behaviors-shaping-jewish-millennials/.

Callahan, Marianne Husby. "Interfaith Family Process and the Negotiation of Identity and Difference." Dissertation, University of Southern California, 2001.

DellaPergola, Sergio. "Jewish Out-Marriage: A Global Perspective." In *Jewish Intermarriage around the World*, 13–39. London: Routledge, 2009.

DellaPergola, Sergio. "World Jewish Population 2020." In *The American Jewish. Yearbook 2020*. Edited by Arnold Dashefsky and Ira M. Sheskin, 273–370. Cham, Switzerland: Springer, 2022. https://www.jewishdatabank.org/content/upload/bjdb/2020_World_Jewish_Population_(AJYB_DellaPergola)_FinalDB.pdf. 2022.

---

34 Barna Group, "Evolving Spiritual Identity."
35 Zaretsky, "Finding Spiritual Harmony."
36 Zaretsky, "They're Spiritual, but Not Religious."

Dershowitz, Alan M. *The Vanishing American Jew: In Search of Jewish Identity for the Next Century.* New York: Little, Brown, 1997.

Green, Emma. "We're Headed Toward One of the Greatest Divisions in the History of the Jewish People." *The Atlantic*, July 16, 2017. https://www.theatlantic.com/politics/archive/2017/07/intermarriage-conservative-judaism/533637/.

Heilman, Uriel. "Pew Survey of U.S. Jews: Soaring Intermarriage, Assimilation Rates." *Jewish Telegraphic Agency*, October 1, 2013. http://www.jta.org/2013/10/01/news-opinion/united-states/pew-survey-u-s-jewish-intermarriage-rate-rises-to-58-percent.

JTA. "Study: One-Fifth of Jewish Millennials Believe Jesus Is the Son of God." *Jerusalem Post*, November 1, 2017. https://www.jpost.com/diaspora/study-one-fifth-of-jewish-millennials-believe-jesus-is-the-son-of-god-512015.

Kosmin, Barry, Sidney Goldstein, Joseph Waksberg, Nava Lerer, Ariella Keysar, and Jeffrey Scheckner. "Highlights of the CJF 1990 National Jewish Population Survey." New York: Council of Jewish Federations, 1991.

Lerner, Aaron. "On College Campuses, the Intermarriage Debate Is Already Over." *The Jewish Forward Online*, September 14, 2017. https://forward.com/community/382685/on-college-campuses-the-intermarriage-debate-is-already-over/.

Lugo, Luis, Alan Cooperman, and Gregory A. Smith, principal investigators. "The 2013 Pew Research Center Survey of U.S. Jews: A Portrait of Jewish Americans." Jewish Federation of North America. http://www.jewishdatabank.org/Studies/details.cfm?StudyID=715.

Perlman, Susan. "Barna Releases New Study on Jewish Millennials: The Results Offer Some Surprises." *Jews for Jesus*, October 30, 2017. https://jewsforjesus.org/press/barna-releases-new-study-on-american-jewish-millennials-the-results-offer-some-surprises.

Sales, Ben. "Jews for Jesus Commissioned a Study on Jewish Millennials. Here's What It Found." *Jewish Telegraphic Agency*, October 31, 2017. https://www.jta.org/2017/10/31/news-opinion/unitedstates/jews-for-jesus-commissioned-a-study-on-jewish-millennials-heres-what-it-found.

Sharon, Jeremy. "At Least 85,000 Jewish Intermarried Couples in Israel." *Jerusalem Post*, November 17, 2021. https://www.jpost.com/israel-news/at-least-85000-jewish-intermarried-couples-in-israel-685251.

Smith, Donald K. *Creating Understanding: A Handbook for Christian Communication Across Cultural Landscapes.* Grand Rapids, MI: Zondervan, 1992.

Spokoiny, Andrés. "The Jews in the Pew: What the 2021 Pew Report Tells Us about Modern Identity." *EJewishPhilanthropy*, June 4, 2021. https://ejewishphilanthropy.com/the-jews-in-the-pew-what-the-2021-pew-report-tells-us-about-modern-identity/.

Vaughn, R., A. Call, and Tim B. Heaton. "Religious Influence on Marriage Stability." *Journal for the Scientific Study of Religion* 30, no. 3 (1997): 382–92.

Wan, Enoch. "The Paradigm of 'Relational Realism'." *Evangelical Missiological Society* 19, no. 2 (2006): 1–4. https://www.enochwan.com/english/articles/pdf/Relational Realism-EMS-OB-Spring2006.pdf.

Weissman, Sara. "Did Jews for Jesus Get Jewish Millennials Right?" *New Voices*, November 6, 2017. http://newvoices.org/2017/11/06/did-jews-for-jesus-just-get-something-right-about-jewish-millennials/.

Wertheimer, Jack. "Surrendering to Intermarriage." *Commentary Magazine*, March 2021. https://www.commentary.org/articles/jack-wertheimer/surrendering-to-intermarriage/.

Zaretsky, Tuvya. "Finding Spiritual Harmony in Your Interfaith Relationship." *Inherit* (blog) *Jews for Jesus*, June 13, 2019. https://jewsforjesus.org/publications/inherit/finding-spiritual-harmony-in-your-interfaith-relationship.

Zaretsky, Tuvya. "They're Spiritual, but Not Religious," Billy Graham Center for Evangelism's www.Gospel-Life.net (blog), September 20, 2017. Accessed archived page on August 21, 2023, https://web.archive.org/web/20171005092742/http://www.gospel-life.net/theyre-spiritual-but-not-religious/.

Zaretsky, Tuvya. "Intermarriage in the Bible." In *He Said ... Then She Said: Helping Jewish-Gentile Couples Find Spiritual Harmony*, 121–26. San Francisco: Jews for Jesus, 2016.

Zaretsky, Tuvya. "The Challenges of Jewish-Gentile Couples: A Pre-Evangelistic Ethnographic Study." DMiss diss., Western Seminary, Portland, Oregon, 2004.

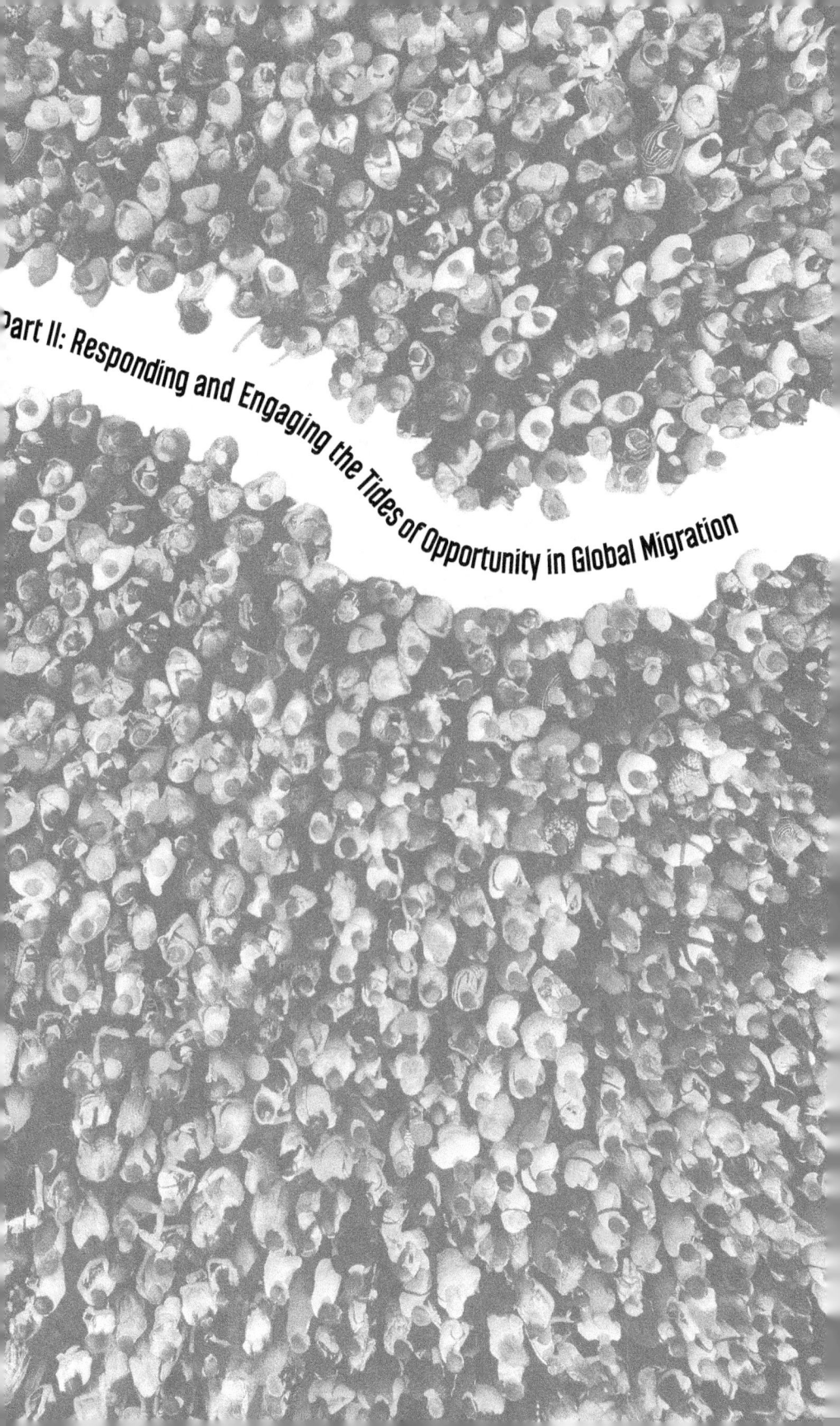

Part II: Responding and Engaging the Tides of Opportunity in Global Migration

Chapter 7
Models of Diaspora Communities for Missiological Application

Jason Richard Tan

Diaspora communities behave differently even when composed of people of the same ethnic identity. Filipino diasporic communities in the US or Canada present peculiar traits compared to Filipino Overseas Workers (OFWs) in Hong Kong or Saudi Arabia. This chapter explores and proposes five different models of diaspora communities based on characteristics observed and identified by social scientists (including Robin Cohen, William Safran, Alex Weingrod, and Jonathan Clifford). Each model offers a unique perspective on understanding diasporic communities' behavior concerning their homeland, aspirations, and ambivalence toward their host country as they wrestle with social forces and expectations. These models offer theological and missiological applications that may help missiologists and ministry practitioners recognize distinctive attributes and respond appropriately.

Introduction

Diaspora study is a relatively new discipline in missiology. Although it has been around for almost twenty years, the field is still developing.[1] Resources on the subject have exploded over the last decade due to an increased awareness of the influence of globalization on labor, economy, migration, global politics, and, more importantly, on the global church.

Despite the voluminous materials, the church has yet to understand this elusive subject. This lack of understanding is due to the volatile nature of diaspora, which involves human behavior, migration, travel, transnationality, national and ethnic sentiments, and political discourses. More importantly, the current definition, concept, and use of the word *diaspora* in theological and missiological applications has become too erratic.

This chapter will propose five models of diaspora communities based on various concepts espoused by social theoreticians. It will then consider the missiological and theological ramifications for the mission of the church.

---

1 Lausanne Congress for World Evangelization (LCWE), Thailand and Cape Town.

Diaspora Missiology

The word diaspora comes from the Greek word *diaspora*, an agricultural term for "fruitful scattering away of seeds."[2] It first occurred in the Septuagint (LXX) in verses including Isaiah 49:6; Jeremiah 13:14; 15:7; 34:17; and Daniel 12:2. The word may be translated as follows: removed, driven out, scattered, banished, exiled, dispersed, outcast, exiles, preserved, remnant [which were scattered], even horrified.[3] The last translation, "horrified," may rightfully illustrate the experiences of many refugees today, especially those forced out of their country due to war or ethnic hostilities.

Mercy Corps estimates that there are about 6.6 million Syrian refugees today. Added to this growing number are 2.7 million Afghan refugees, 2.2 million South Sudanese refugees, 1 million Rohingya refugees, and 0.9 million Somali refugees. All were dispersed due to horrific violence and political unrest.[4] Additionally there are some 4.8 million refugees from Ukraine due to the ongoing war with Russia.[5]

In a biblical sense, the word diaspora simply refers to the dispersion of the Jews outside of their homeland and all the Jewish communities outside of Palestine.[6] This definition is insufficient to describe other forms of social, labor, demographic, and conflict induced migration today.

Take for example, a community of Filipino seafarers, entertainers, and cooks on board a luxury tourist liner. Can this community of seafarers who serve for a year or so be considered a diaspora community apart from a host country or geographic space while cruising on international waters? Or can a community of American-raised Jews be considered a diaspora community within Israel? What about Filipino Muslims fighting for independence within a nation-state? Can they be considered a diaspora community?

The concept of diaspora as understood by theologians and missiologists is either too restrictive or too broad and over-simplified to account for other variables such as politics, economics, ethnicity, social dynamics, and culture. A theologian may use the word diaspora to refer to the Jewish community living in exile in Babylon. In contrast, a missiologist could simply use the term to define Filipino Christian labor migrants working in Hong Kong. William Safran points out, "Today, 'diaspora' and, more specifically, 'diaspora

---

2 Tololyan, "Rethinking Diaspora(s)," 10.
3 Im and Casiño, *Global Diasporas in Mission*, 2.
4 Mercy Corps, "World's 5 Biggest Refugee Crises."
5 Operational Data Portal, "Ukraine Refugee Situation."
6 Moo, *Letters of James*, 50.

community' seems increasingly to be used as metaphoric designations for several categories of people—expatriates, expellees, political refugees, alien residents, immigrants, and ethnic and racial minorities, *tout court.*"[7]

Over the past decade, evangelical scholars have adjusted the working definition of the term *diaspora* to accommodate other forms of social migration. One such work comes from Chandler H. Im and Tereso C. Casiño, who define the term as: "Diaspora refers broadly to the global phenomenon of the dispersion or scattering of people in various parts of the world, occurring either by a voluntary act or coercive conditions in both domestic and global contexts."[8]

This broad definition allows theologians and missiologists to apply the word diaspora to labor migrants, immigrants, as well as war refugees. But how do we distinguish between migrant communities and diaspora communities? The usual approach that theologians and missiologists take is to interpret the concept of diaspora in terms of theological, eschatological, or ecclesiological themes.

Im and Casiño define diaspora missiology as an "interdisciplinary field" of study that focuses on the "geographic and demographic" movement of people around the world as it relates to "God's redemptive plan for the nations."[9] Similarly, when asked to develop a theology of the Filipino diaspora, Luis Pantoja argues,

> For the purposes of this consultation, we borrow the term diaspora—technically used of Jews who for one reason or another lived or lives outside of Palestine. Because only the Jews received a special election and a "promised land" from God, and because being driven away from it had the notion of a curse and due punishment, and furthermore, because there is the promise and hope of an eschatological return to the land, then only with those specifications can diaspora truly apply.[10]

These tendencies to attach the concept of diaspora too ideally and closely to the biblical, Jewish, historical experience and eschatological hope only constricts our perspective as we seek to apply this concept to the church.[11] Consequently, we tend to use sweeping missiological applications based on generalization or narrow theological views.

---

7   Safran, "Diasporas in Modern Societies," 83.
8   Im and Casiño, *Global Diasporas and Mission*, 3.
9   Im and Casiño, 3.
10 Pantoja, Tira, and Wan, *Scattered*, 68.
11 Clifford "Diasporas," 305.

Diaspora Missiology

Prominent advocates of this new field of study are Sadiri Joy Tira and Enoch Wan. They proposed its development against what Wan labels as "traditional missiology" in light of the changing nature of global Christianity.[12] Although the diaspora phenomenon has been around since man discovered travel, theologians in this century have only begun to reflect on the concept of diaspora as it relates to missiology, ecclesiology, and theology.

Wan highlights three strategic principles of what he calls a "diaspora mission." It is a mission strategy that deliberately reaches out *to*, *through*, and *beyond* the migrant diasporic community. For Wan, diaspora mission intentionally engages the diaspora community for evangelistic purposes (mission *to*), trains them to evangelize and disciple their fellow migrants (mission *through*), and prepares them to reach out to those outside the diaspora community (mission *beyond*).[13]

While this approach has been helpful in articulating how a local church may engage a migrant community, it has its drawbacks: not all migrant or diasporic communities behave the same way. Each has its shared history, uniqueness, and felt needs that a responding local church might not be prepared to handle. Without discounting what Wan has proposed, perhaps models of diasporic communities that could supplement the current definition and refine our approach to the diaspora mission are necessary.

Models of Diaspora Communities

The following are various models of diaspora communities as explained by multiple social theoreticians. These models will highlight a unique element in the study of diaspora as offered by its proponents. A few caveats are in order:

1. None of the theoreticians below were trying to create a model. Instead, their main work consists of defining, expounding, and applying their concept of diaspora. Based on their ideas, I have attempted to create models to help illustrate their visions.

2. The illustrations of each model did not come from any of our theoreticians; these illustrations are my attempt at capturing their ideas. They may not entirely capture what the theoreticians are trying to say, since not all ideas can be transformed into a drawing.

Nonetheless, it is my hope that these models can open new ways of approaching this study, and perhaps lead to better models that might be developed in the future.

---

12 Wan, *Diaspora Missiology*, 5.
13 Wan, 5.

The models utilize shapes and figures to illustrate different cultures. Generally, the circle represents the "homeland," while other shapes stand for other cultures.

Homeland-Diaspora Model

The most common diaspora model is the Homeland-Diaspora Model or the Solar System Model.[14] It is also called the "Jewish typology model."[15] This model is most popular because it highlights stereotypical ideals of a Jewish diaspora in the past which most people with Judeo-Christian backgrounds are familiar with. This model affirms the biblical historical narrative and closely reflects the Jewish communities exiled during the 6th century BC.

Although William Safran was not the first to use this model for diaspora studies, his description of essential features is most helpful. According to Safran, the Jewish typology model has six essential features that distinguish it from other migrant communities.

- They are dispersed from one original homeland or "center" to at least "two peripheral places" or diaspora.
- They maintain a "memory, vision, or myth about their original homeland."
- They believe their host country cannot fully accept them.
- They see their ancestral home as a place of eventual return.
- They are committed to maintaining their culture and restoring their homeland.
- They are committed to maintaining their relationship with their homeland.[16]

Although this model is too synthetic to capture the realities of modern-day global diaspora communities, it continues to be an excellent starting reference in studying a shifting social phenomenon. The model captures in essence what a particular Jewish diaspora meant in the past; therefore, it is a crucial concept in developing theories. As Weingrod and Levy affirm, "There can be little doubt that the 'homeland-diaspora' paradigm has firmly entered into the contemporary social-science vocabulary."[17]

---

14 Weingrod and Levy, "Paradoxes of Homecoming," 692.
15 Safran, "Diasporas in Modern Societies," 83–99.
16 Clifford "Diasporas," 304–5; Tololyan "Rethinking Diaspora(s)," 12–14.
17 Weingrod and Levy, "Parodoxes of Homecoming," 691.

As illustrated below, the homeland-diaspora model maintains a center (homeland) while the dispersed (diaspora) communities serve as its periphery. There is a shared experience of memory, vision, and myth of the homeland and a desire to return to it. The solid circle around the diaspora community signifies its resistance to assimilation with the host country, illustrated as a box.

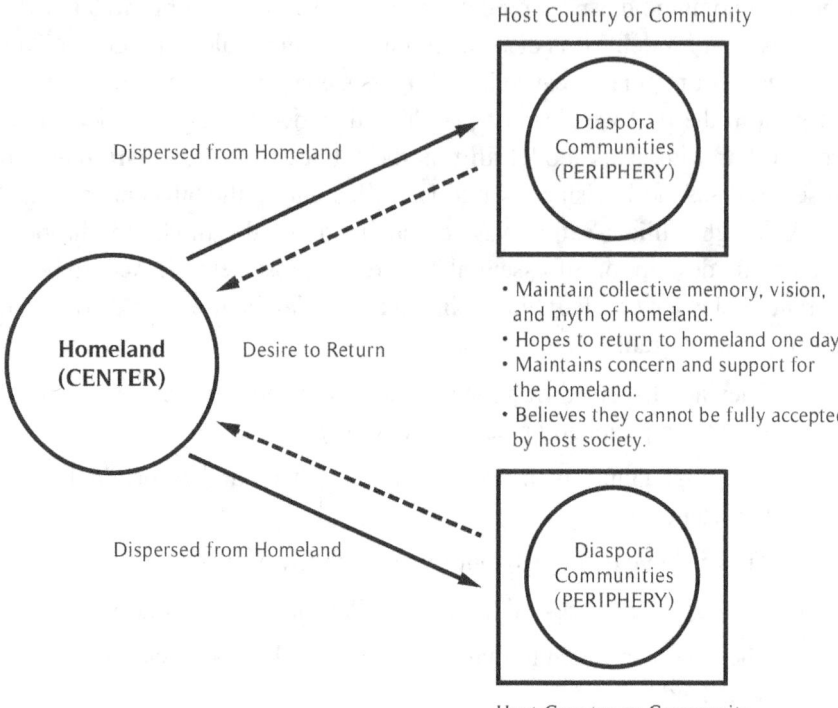

Figure 7.1: Homeland-Diaspora Model

Robin Cohen followed Safran's model of the homeland-diaspora paradigm but highlighted the element of "victimization" in an effort to make the model inclusive of refugees and other migrant groups who were coerced to live outside of their homeland. Cohen calls this model the "victim diaspora tradition." He underscores the "experience of enslavement, exile, and displacement." He juxtaposes it with the experiences of the Jewish exiles of 600s BC, who were subjugated and removed from the Promised Land and whisked away to Babylon to serve as enslaved people.[18]

Like Safran's model, Jerusalem is the center while Babylon has become the periphery and a code word for "affliction, isolation, and oppression."[19]

---

18 Cohen, *Global Diasporas: An Introduction*, 3.
19 Cohen, 3.

Cohen slightly reconstructs Safran's model and suggests the following standard features of a diaspora:

- Traumatic dispersal from original "homeland" to two or more regions
- "A collective memory and myth about the homeland"
- "Idealization of the ancestral home"
- Collective commitment to restore or return to their homeland
- Ethnic group consciousness fueled by a shared past and fate
- Animosity between the community and the host society
- Empathy and solidarity among members of the ethnic community[20]

According to Cohen, this diaspora model allows us to include the "Palestinian, Irish, African, and Armenian diaspora."[21] Perhaps the first-generation African Americans who were victims of the transatlantic slave trade may be considered under this model as a diaspora community since they were taken out of their homeland as adults with vivid "collective memory myth about the homeland, its location and its achievements."[22]

However, the same cannot be said of the second or third generation of African Americans. More importantly, African Americans have no collective memory of their homeland since their ancestors were taken from different African countries. There is a tragic tendency even among scholars to think of Africa as a country with a mono-cultural ethnic identity. Since Africa is a vast continent, the assumption that African Americans have a shared collective memory is unfounded.

This model may account for modern-day war refugees and migrants forced to flee from their homeland, but it still falls short in accounting for the Chinese, Indian, Filipino, or Pakistani labor migrants who have decided to leave the country of their own volition to seek better opportunities. Nor does it account for student migrants from South Korea, Myanmar, Nepal, India, and Iran who are training as nurses, engineers, and doctors in the Philippines.

Homeland-Center Model

In the previous model, Safran highlighted a diaspora community's collective memory and experience, while Cohen underlines their collective traumatic experience. These elements prevent a diasporic community from being assimilated into a host culture.

---

20 Cohen, 26.
21 Cohen, 3.
22 Cohen, 55.

The question, however, is whether these emotions (desire to return) get resolved the moment they return home. According to Alex Weingrod and André Levy, this is not the case. In their study of Jewish populations migrating to Israel (such as Moroccan Jews, Ethiopian Jews, Russian Jews, and Ashkenazi Jews), they discovered that most of these returnees maintained a strong attachment with their diasporic communities. In fact, the bond was so strong that one wonders which was the center and which was the periphery.[23]

This phenomenon forced Weingrod and Levy to rethink the homeland-diaspora model. They concluded that the homeland-diaspora paradigm is insufficient to account for these new feelings of ambiguity and forces one to assume that their ambivalence would be resolved when these exiled communities return home. Furthermore, a fundamental flaw in the homeland-diaspora model (Safran model) is traced back to the use of the terms "homeland" and "diaspora." They explain, "as we see it, a basic flaw in the model is that it is typically phrased in terms of a single 'homeland' and its 'diasporas,' or, as is often the case, a number of diasporas. Irrespective of the scope or intensity of these relationships, the model assumes that the perception and understanding of which place is 'homeland,' and which is 'diaspora,' is always clear and unambiguous."[24]

Weingrod and Levy discovered that feelings of ambivalence between homeland and diaspora traverse geographical boundaries, meaning migrants bring these feelings with them into their new home. Such ambiguous feelings are never resolved. Many of these returnees created their own diaspora communities within Israel because they struggled to assimilate into their new social space.

For many of these returnees, the diaspora communities outside Israel have become their new "center." Weingrod and Levy explain:

> Return to the homeland does not necessarily bring about the end of ties and identifications with one's former land, or the formation of new links with what we call symbolic and other centers. On the contrary, in each instance return to the homeland has initiated processes in which some group-members find themselves to be part of a new "diaspora" linked to old/new centers, or being to organize trans-national identities, while, at the same time they continue to live their lives in "the homeland."[25]

---

23 Weingrod and Levy, "Paradoxes of Homecoming."
24 Weingrod and Levy, 692.
25 Weingrod and Levy, 694.

If this is the case, then there is a sense of "re-centering," and "one might better conceptualize the homeland-diaspora pair as being 'fluid, historically conditioned, and even multidirectional.'"[26]

Instead of the homeland-diaspora paradigm, Weingrod and Levy suggested that this phenomenon be called the "homeland-center paradigm" in order to account for the ambivalence as well as the periphery as the "new center" which "may persist and prosper without any important, let alone a concrete, link with their cherished 'mother/father/sun.'"[27]

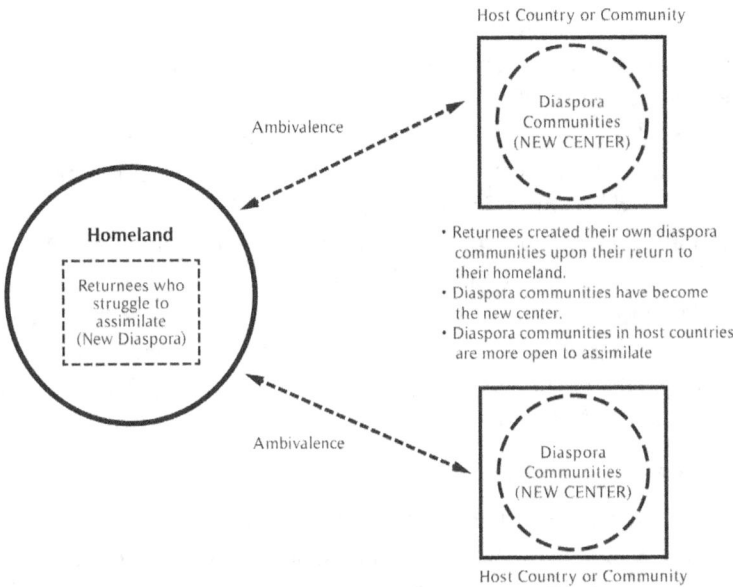

Figure 7.2: Homeland-Center Model

In figure 7.2 (homeland-center model), one would notice that in the "homeland," the new diaspora reflects the same shape as their host country. In contrast, those living in the host country, or "new center," espouse the form of their homeland. This is my attempt to show the ambivalence of migrants as they move from new center to homeland and perhaps to the new center again. The dotted lines with two arrowheads connecting the homeland with the new center or host country further illustrate that for some migrants, "home" is a relative term.

This model affirms the historical and cultural importance of the homeland without downplaying the diaspora communities that exert significant influence on the lives of its former members. In a sense, diasporic communities that exist outside of the homeland play a central role

---
26 Weingrod and Levy, 693; cf. Levy and Weingrod, *Homelands and Diasporas*, 72.
27 Weingrod and Levy, "Paradoxes of Homecoming," 693.

in sustaining certain peculiarities of returnees that, in turn, prevent total assimilation within their homeland. This phenomenon is similar to Goitein's work on Jewish Mediterranean communities of the thirteenth century.[28] According to Goitein, these Jewish communities sustained and defined their Jewishness despite having no existing homeland (or center); they served as the center of Jewish culture instead.

This state is undoubtedly the case for most career missionaries and their families who have lived for an extended period in their fields of assignment. When these missionaries retire and are called home, many feel that a significant portion of themselves died, metaphorically, but for some, it has become literal. Stories of old missionaries who have died of loneliness upon returning home to the US are not uncommon. For these missionaries, home is no longer the homeland. What once was considered a mission field has now become their new center's real home. This is why some missionaries prefer to die and be buried in their "mission field."

Missionary kids also struggled to adjust and felt socially awkward. As a result, missiologists have identified them as "third-culture kids" who struggled with social and emotional stress. In severe cases, missionary kids have attempted suicide as they struggle to cope with the new context. This is where a missionary diaspora support community is essential. Missionary families of the same mission field could form a group to help ease re-entry stress.

Displacement-Resistance Model

James Clifford suggests that a legitimate diasporic community does not need to have all six characteristics to be identified as such. Instead, he offers that we "focus on diaspora's borders, on what it defines itself against."[29] He states, "Rather than locating essential features, we might focus on diaspora's borders, on what it defines itself against ... Diasporas are caught up with and defined against (1) the norms of nation-states; and (2) indigenous, and especially autochthonous, claims by 'tribal' peoples."[30]

For Clifford, a diaspora community could consist of a displaced (but not dispersed) community that fights to define itself in contrast with a hegemonic nation-state that, on the other hand, seeks to assimilate them. These communities may share collective "histories of displacement and violent loss,"[31] but they continue to inhabit a portion of their ancestral land. Therefore, there is no homeland (or center) to return to nor nation-state to defend or support.

---

28 Clifford, "Diasporas," 305.
29 Clifford, 307.
30 Clifford, 307.
31 Clifford, 307.

Models of Diaspora Communities for Missiological Application

The people's ethnic identity, language, religion, and shared history bring them together, contributing to their resolve to resist assimilation and fight for self-determination. Thus "merging [them] into a new national community" is next to impossible. In this model, diaspora becomes, "A signifier, not simply of transnationality and movement, but of political struggles to define the local, as a distinctive community, in historical contexts of displacement."[32]

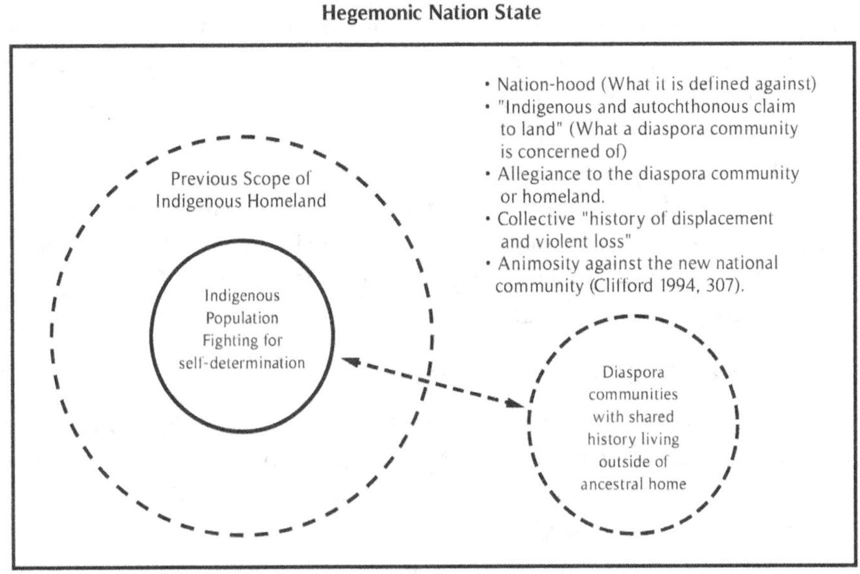

Hegemonic Nation State

- Nation-hood (What it is defined against)
- "Indigenous and autochthonous claim to land" (What a diaspora community is concerned of)
- Allegiance to the diaspora community or homeland.
- Collective "history of displacement and violent loss"
- Animosity against the new national community (Clifford 1994, 307).

Previous Scope of Indigenous Homeland

Indigenous Population Fighting for self-determination

Diaspora communities with shared history living outside of ancestral home

Figure 7.3: *Displacement-Resistance Model*

Clifford's model may shed light on the current socio-political tension between the Philippine government, and the Bangsamoro people (the ethnic Filipino-Muslim community) who claim that their land has been violently taken from them. These communities were forced to embrace armed resistance in an effort to recover parts of their ancestral home lost to colonial nation-states and to fight for self-determination.

In a sense, these communities have become diaspora communities within a nation-state. Today, multiple such armed communities are fighting for autonomy. The Moro National Liberation Front (MNLF), the Moro Islamic Liberation Front, and other armed groups share the same sentiments.

On the other hand, other ethnic-Muslim groups choose a more peaceful approach and have decided to join the nation-state. Many of these Muslim communities have set up their own Masjid and, when possible, a Mosque in non-Muslim cities in the Philippines. These religious centers allow them

---

32 Clifford, 307–8.

to participate in nation-building while maintaining their ethnic identity. There is ambivalence in these Muslim diaspora communities as they walk a tightrope between assimilation and supporting the armed struggle of their fellow Muslims. Clifford stresses, "Thus the term diaspora is a signifier, not simply of transnationality and movement, but of political struggles to define the local, as distinctive community, in historical contexts of displacement."[33]

Furthermore, it is possible for ethnic groups within a nation-state to behave as diasporic communities within their own country. The Chin ethnic group is often forced to create their own community as they live among the majority Bamar people of Myanmar. Although they belong to the same nation-state, their ethnic identity causes social discrimination among the majority Bamar people.

Similarly, ethnic Filipino groups may form their diasporic communities in Metro Manila due to ethnic differences despite living in their own country. This is well illustrated even among local churches in Metro Manila, which tend to draw people of the same ethnic group.[34]

Transnational-Linkages Diaspora Model

The next model is patterned after Jonathan Okamura's research among Filipino migrants in Hawaii. He argues that diaspora communities must retain two principal attributes, "transnational linkages" and "social constructiveness." Okamura states,

> By this proposition, I mean that diasporas should be understood as consisting of transnational linkages between an immigrant/ ethnic minority and its homeland (or cultural center) and its counterpart communities in other host societies. As for being socially constructed, diasporas should be viewed as resulting from the development and maintenance of those transnational relations by people in diaspora that link them culturally, economically, and politically with their homeland.[35]

Okamura argues that any migrant community that loses transnational connection with their former culture, even if they retain their cultural or ethnic distinctiveness, is merely an immigrant group. These communities have become socially and culturally bound within a host culture, feeding on the values and ideals of the majority. On the other hand, a true diaspora community retains its ethnic uniqueness. It maintains a "porous boundary" where cultural artifacts, values, and ideals from the homeland and other

---

33 Clifford, 330.
34 Tan, "Diaspora Within."
35 Okamura, *Imagining the Filipino American*, 14.

diaspora communities traverse national boundaries. "These relations include cultural, economic, and social linkages evident in the circulation of people, money and consumer goods, and information and ideas."[36]

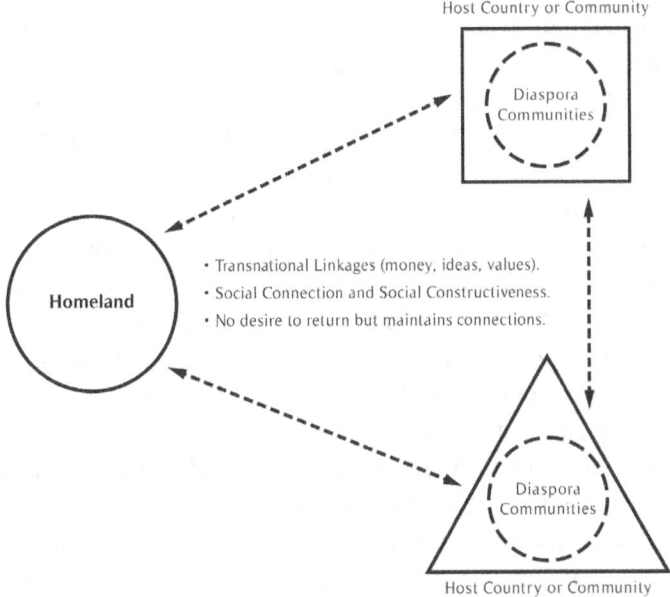

Figure 7.4: *Transnational-Linkages Diaspora Model*

Second, according to Okamura, a diaspora community would eventually lose its distinctiveness unless the people who composed it maintain and revitalize its cultural and ethnic identity. Okamura argues,

> Advances in transportation and communication technology are necessary but not sufficient conditions to explain fully the emergence, proliferation, and nature of late twentieth-century diasporas. A sufficient explanation must include the agency of diasporic peoples to create and sustain transnational linkages through their own actions, resources, and decision making. The continuously expanding scope and number of contemporary diasporas throughout the world clearly indicate their ongoing social construction and extension in space and time.[37]

Okamura stresses that these two components, transnational linkages and social constructiveness, define a diaspora community from an ethnic minority group such as Polish, German or Russian immigrants who have successfully assimilated into the mainstream US society. These immigrant communities

---

36 Okamura, 17.
37 Okamura, 23.

may retain certain peculiar features of their culture but do not have to deal with the disparity caused by racialization. Thus, there is no need to construct and redefine their ethnic boundaries. On the other hand, "diasporic peoples resist the assimilationist national strategies and ideologies of the nation-state and extend their identities and communities beyond its borders"[38] as a political reaction against discrimination.[39]

Filipino communities around the world (Israel, Italy, and Hong Kong) are usually forced to organize themselves in order to provide mutual economic and social support due to their collective experiences as "oppressed" and discriminated people. This was certainly the case for Filipino Americans who were marginalized and discriminated against in Hawaii and California. These communities formed labor organizations to bolster their civil rights. These social constructs enabled Filipinos to erect boundaries that strengthened their ethnic values and relations.[40] This behavior is similar to Chinese diaspora communities that have created social, geographical, and political boundaries within their host societies. As a result, "Chinatown" has become a landmark in many cities in the world, including Manila, New York, San Francisco, Chicago, Vancouver, and Sydney.

Furthermore, Okamura states, "The notion of return to the homeland does not necessarily involve a literal, physical, permanent return but instead a 're-turn, a repeated turning to the concept and/or the reality of the homeland' through memory, written and visual texts, visits, and charitable contributions."[41]

Based on Strobel's and Espiritu's studies of second-generation Filipino Americans, their desire to return to their homeland is in keeping with their ethnic identity and not so much as to settle.[42] This notion of "re-turn" to their ethnic identity strengthens and encourages transnational linkages.[43]

These linkages create healthy traffic of trade, goods, remittances, and ideas that traverse geographical boundaries not only between homeland and diasporic communities but also between diasporic communities abroad. These linkages create a global diasporic network among people of the same ethnic background.

While this model allows us to define the modern Filipino labor migrants in Hong Kong or Singapore as a diaspora community, it prevents us from using the same model for Filipino Canadian migrants who have no desire

---

38 Okamura, 14–15.
39 Clifford, "Diasporas," 308.
40 Crouchett, *Filipinos in California.*
41 Okamura, *Imagining the Filipino American*, 17; cf. Tololyan, "Rethinking Diaspora(s)."
42 Strobel, "Born Again Filipino," 41; Strobel, "Coming Full Circle," 62–79; and Espiritu, "Intersection of Race, Ethnicity," 258.
43 Tololyan "Rethinking Diaspora(s)," 12.

to return to their homeland. In the same way, this model would fail to accommodate the Irish, Germans, Italians, African American, and Latin-American migrants as diasporic communities because "they no longer maintain a 'myth of return' to their respective homelands."[44]

Imagined Homeland Model

For Epifano San Juan Jr., "homeland" is not merely a geographic place but a caring political state. He argues that since the Philippines was just recently recognized as a republic, all prior migration of Filipinos should not be considered a diaspora. Furthermore, since the present republic has been an oppressive entity serving foreign capitalist nations (further strengthening neo-colonial purposes), Filipinos, in reality, have no nation to return to. Dispersed Filipinos are:

> A fusion of exile and migration: the scattering of a people, not yet a fully matured nation, to the ends of the earth, across the planet throughout the 60s and 70s, continuing up to the present. We are now a quasi-wandering people, pilgrims or prospectors staking our lives and futures all over the world—in the Middle East, Africa, Europe, North and South America, in Australia and all of Asia, in every nook and cranny of this seemingly godforsaken earth. A whole people dispersed, displaced, dislocated.[45]

San Juan is not alone in his contention. Basch, Schiller, and Blanc argue that a diaspora is like a "nation which envisions a people with a common past ... who may or may not at any one time have its own state"[46] Therefore, instead of calling a dispersed people group a diaspora which usually connotes a relationship with a homeland or nation-state, Basch and her colleagues propose the term "deterritorialized nation-state" since "wherever its people go, their state goes too."[47] This dispersion model is consistent with the European Jewish diaspora before the creation of the modern state of Israel.

---

44 Okamura, "Filipino American Diaspora," 390.
45 San Juan, quoted in Okamura, *Imagining the Filipino American*, 13.
46 Basch, Schiller, and Blanc, *Nations Unbound*, 269.
47 Basch quoted in Okamura, *Imagining the Filipino American*, 18; see also Camroux, "Nationalizing Transnationalism?"

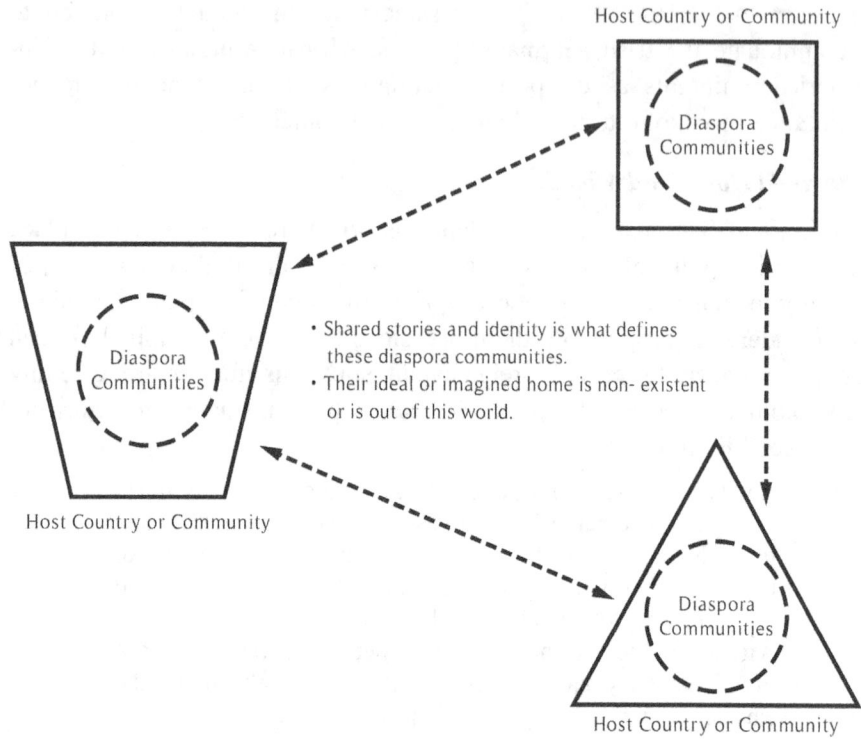

Figure 7.5: Imagined Homeland Model

In figure 7.5, one would notice that the diaspora communities exhibit the same shape, but none conform to any of the host countries. Thus, in this model, the notion of a homeland is just imagined by the community. In San Juan's model, the nation-state or homeland is not the defining factor of a Filipino diaspora, rather the defining factor is the Filipino collective shared identity and social concern for each other. He argues,

> Diasporic groups are historically defined not only by a homeland but also by a desire for eventual return and a collective identity centered on myths and memories of the homeland. The Filipino diaspora, however, is different. Since the homeland has been long colonized by Western powers [Spain, United States] and remains neo-colonized despite formal and nominal independence, the Filipino identification is not with a fully defined nation but with regions, localities, and communities of languages and traditions.[48]

---

48 San Juan, "Trajectories of the Filipino," 229.

Rather than the notion of homeland or even a return to homeland, the collective concern of Filipinos for each other is the essence of the Filipino diaspora. Filipino migrant groups are diasporic communities since they share the same personal dreams, heartaches, and aspirations. San Juan argues,

> The Filipino diaspora here is defined by the Filipinas' social interaction and its specific differentiated geography, an interaction characterized by family/kinship linkages as well as solidarity based on recursive acts of mutual aid and struggle for survival ... This is not postcolonial ambivalence or hybridity because it is centered on the organic bonds of experience with oppressed compatriots; Nelly's affiliation with Vicky is tied to a web of shared stories of intimacy, dehumanization, and vulnerability.[49]

San Juan's argument is consistent with the notion that a homeland could be something "imagined," meaning that a homeland does not need to have political or geographic attributes. It only needs to exist in the collective shared memory of its people.

There was a time in Jewish history when the state of Israel did not exist. Yet, these Jewish communities could keep their ethnic ideals alive simply because of a shared, imagined, collective memory of their story as people of Yahweh. Despite the absence of a geographic space, the nation existed among its people.[50] San Juan's model is intriguing since it closely represents the Christian community. Our ideal and imagined home is out of this world. Yet, Christians across the ages share similar collective experiences as one community, all looking forward to the day that our real home is revealed. As the author of Hebrews affirms,

> All these people were still living by faith when they died. They did not receive the things promised; they only saw them and welcomed them from a distance, admitting that they were foreigners and strangers on earth. People who say such things show that they are looking for a country of their own. If they had been thinking of the country they had left, they would have had opportunity to return. Instead, they were longing for a better country—a heavenly one. Therefore God is not ashamed to be called their God, for he has prepared a city for them.[51]

These models show how complex a diaspora community can be. Apart from such models, it would be imprudent to lump all diaspora communities into one particular definition and apply the same missiological approach, thinking they all behave the same way.

---

49 San Juan, 235.
50 Grotein, *Mediterranean Society*; Clifford "Diaspora(s)."
51 Heb 11:13–16 (NIV); see also 1 Pet 2:11 (NIV).

Theological and Missiological Implications

The previous models of diaspora communities would undoubtedly change how we do diaspora ministry and mission. What then are the implications of these models to our theological and missiological understanding of diaspora communities?

Diaspora Communities in the Biblical Narratives Behave Differently from Each Other

For instance, the Jewish diaspora during the Babylonian captivity behaved differently from the New Testament diaspora communities. During Jeremiah's life, the Jewish community was bent on returning home. This diaspora community closely resembles Safran's homeland-diaspora model and Cohen's victim model. Their desire to return and reconstruct their homeland was so strong that Jeremiah needed to warn them that, for the moment, that was not God's purpose for them. The Lord instructed Jeremiah to tell the Jews to:

> Build houses and settle down; plant gardens and eat what they produce. Marry and have sons and daughters; find wives for your sons and give your daughters in marriage, so that they too may have sons and daughters. Increase in number there; do not decrease. Also, seek the peace and prosperity of the city to which I have carried you into exile. Pray to the LORD for it, because if it prospers, you too will prosper.[52]

Jeremiah dealt with any form of "ambivalence" among the exiled Jewish community. They were to live out their faith under subjugation within their host society. Revising Safran's model, the Jewish diaspora of Jeremiah's time would have looked like this.

---

52 Jer 29:5–7 (NIV).

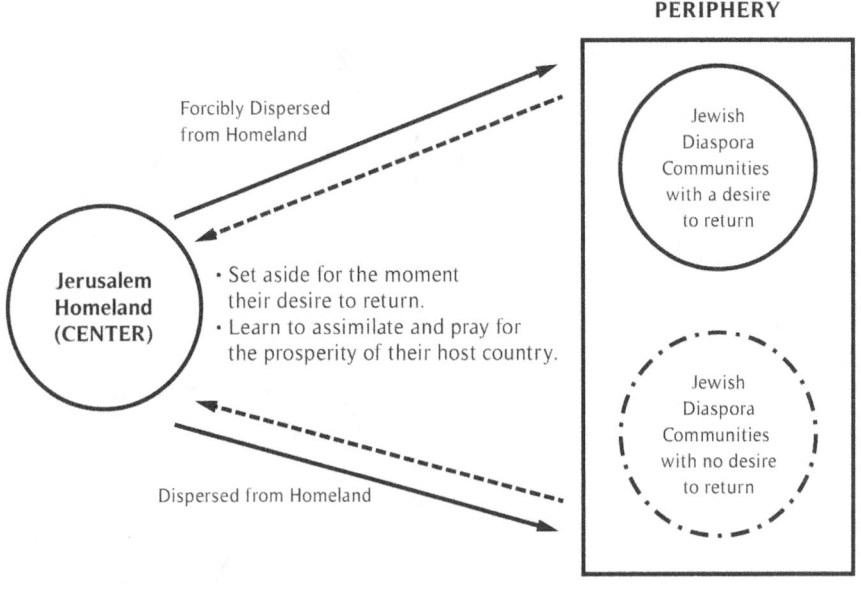

Figure 7.6: Applying Safran's Homeland-Diaspora to the Jewish Babylonian Exiles

Soon, those born and assimilated into their host country remained there. Not all the Jews went home. Many stayed in their host country. Although Nehemiah went back, it is not hard to imagine that many people like him who have a stable and rewarding life preferred to stay in Babylon or Persia. Nehemiah is one classic example of a migrant experiencing ambivalence. He was a cupbearer for the king, but his heart no doubt longed for Jerusalem. At this point, it is safe to assume that the Jewish diaspora attitude has become more consistent with Safran's homeland model.

In contrast, the diasporic Jewish community of the New Testament period, particularly during the Pentecost event, starkly contrasts with the Babylonian diaspora. By this time, countless Jewish communities across the Roman Empire have no desire to go home. Their travel was limited to festivities and ritual obligations. Even their language evolved. Diasporic Jews exclaimed, "How is it that each of us hears them in our native language?" (Acts 2:8).

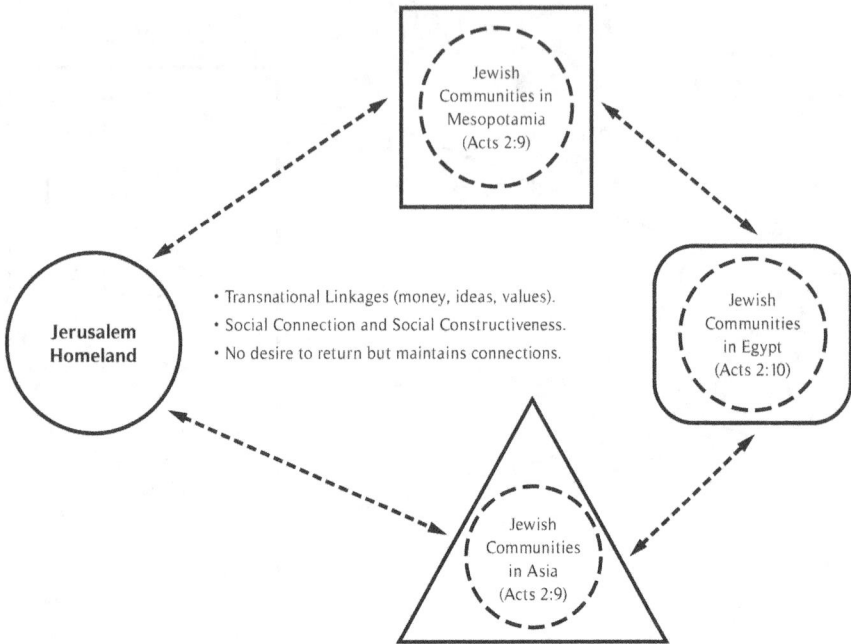

Figure 7.7: Applying Okamura's Transnational Linkages Model in Understanding the Jewish Diaspora Communities of the Acts 2 Pentecost Event

The behavior of the New Testament diasporic Jews resembles Okamura's transnational-linkages model. These accounts show that Jewish diasporic communities behaved differently, and each diasporic community is distinct.

Some Diaspora Communities Are More Effective in Evangelization than Others

As we have seen previously, each diaspora community is different. Yet, one of the significant differences has to do with their engagement with their host society. Let us take the Babylonian-captivity model, for example, and compare it with what I call the *Pentecost-diaspora model*, which refers to the Acts 2 Pentecost phenomenon. During the Babylonian captivity, the Jews were generally seen as second-class citizens. Animosity and tensions between the Jewish community and their host society have always been high. As a result, the diaspora community became introverted. They preserved their ethnic identity and kept it to themselves. Evangelization was held at a minimum. Some people were drawn to their way of life (centripetal action), but for the most part, they focused on their kin group and their survival.

This type of diaspora community has minimal influence on mainstream society. Overseas Filipino Workers (OFWs) in the Middle East and other restricted countries behave this way. Yet, they are very effective in evangelizing and raising Filipino missionaries and church leaders who eventually return home and continue their ministry. There are a few stories of Filipino domestic helpers who are able to influence and convert their employers and host families, but these stories are infrequent.

In comparison, the Pentecost-diaspora model behaves differently than the Babylonian-captivity model. As we know, Jews from every nation would take annual trips to Jerusalem for the festivities. Many of these ethnic Jews were raised in their host societies and were "dual-citizens." Acts 2 shows the vast array of Jewish diaspora communities across the Greco-Roman world:

> Parthians, Medes and Elamites; residents of Mesopotamia, Judea and Cappadocia, Pontus and Asia, Phrygia and Pamphylia, Egypt and the parts of Libya around Cyrene; and visitors from Rome (both Jews and converts to Judaism); Cretans and Arabs—we hear them declaring the wonders of God in our *own* tongues![53]

These Jews spoke a different mother tongue, were accustomed to, and were well assimilated into their host countries. One great example is the Apostle Paul, who was not only a full-blooded Jew but was also a full-fledged Roman citizen espousing dual citizenship. As a result, it was easier for him to penetrate the Gentile society (centrifugal action) than it was for the Jewish diaspora to influence the Persians during the Babylonian captivity.

Thus, Pentecost-diasporas models are more effective in doing "missions *beyond*" their kin group than the first-generation migrants. On the other hand, the first generation is more effective in doing "mission *to*" and among their kin group.

Filipino Christian churches in the United States, with many first-generation migrants, behaved similarly.[54] They are very effective in ministering among their kin but not to their American neighbors. Generally, Filipino churches in the US are incapable of penetrating mainstream American society. On the other hand, second and third-generation Filipino-Americans have a better chance of reaching the mainstream society than their parents since they have been acculturated into their host country.

This fact shows that some diaspora communities may exhibit centrifugal behavior; that is, they can reach out to those outside their community, while others are more effective in reaching out to fellow Filipinos (centripetal action).

---

53 Acts 2:9–11 (NIV – emphasis added).
54 Tan, "Diaspora Within," 241.

First-Generation Christian Migrants Behave Differently from Second- or Third-Generation Christians

Based on my observation, most second- or third-generation Filipino-American migrants are more assimilated into their host society than their parents. As a result, they identify more with their host culture than with their ethnic culture.[55]

Immigrant churches in Europe or the US are more effective in reaching out to new migrants in the area and among their kin. However, they could also prepare their children or the next generation for future ministry among the mainstream population.

The Apostle Paul was a second-generation Jewish migrant, a Roman citizen from Tarsus. Thus, he was a child of both worlds. This fact gave him the ability to engage both Hebrews and Gentiles. In the same way, children born in host countries will be more effective in engaging the mainstream society than their parents. The downside is that migrant churches risk losing the next generation to mainline churches in the host society unless they deliberately create programs that minister to the next generation.

Migrant churches should be aware of their task of reaching out to their kin groups and preparing the next generation to be more effective in engaging mainstream society.[56] However, one of the significant issues migrant churches face is the need for ministry workers. Most of these churches tend to hire pastors from their own countries. However, this practice often creates generational gaps between the old and the younger generation. If not resolved, this gap will only drive the younger generation away from the church community.

Conclusion

The models show that we need to identify carefully which kind of diaspora community we are dealing with before we can apply any mission strategy. Roger Rouse affirms, "We live in a ... world of crisscrossed economies, intersecting systems of meaning, and fragmented identities. Suddenly, the comforting, modern imagery of nation-states and national languages, of coherent communities and consistent subjectivities, of dominant centers and distant margins no longer seems adequate.... . We have all moved irrevocably into a new kind of social space."[57]

---

55 Tan, 242.
56 For a more nuanced treatment of the issue, read Tan's, "Diaspora Within."
57 Rouse, "Mexican Migration," 8.

We need to bear in mind three things:

Firstly, diaspora communities are not always objects of mission; there are times when they are agents of mission working in partnership with the local churches in their homeland. Some even serve as a link that allows for the flow of ideas from their homeland to the diaspora communities and the flow of monetary resources from the diaspora communities to their homeland. This reality is exemplified by numerous stories of Filipinos sending repatriation or financial support to church planting projects back home.

Second, social migration has opened opportunities for more people to be exposed to the gospel; however, we should be careful not to glamorize it or valorize it. Millions of people are often forced to flee or leave their homeland due to unimaginable abuse and violence. The global church must be sensitive when dealing with and working with migrant churches and churches with diaspora communities. We must not promote the "kingdom" agenda at the expense of their pain and suffering. We have a tendency to be triumphalist and to valorize the stories coming from the diaspora communities and present them as the new "heroes" of the modern missionary church. However, these stories may blunt the profound pain, sacrifices, and persecution these communities are currently facing. The global church must be as sensitive to the needs of these communities as it is committed to the mission of God, for they are the object of the *missio dei*.

Third, local churches in societies with high immigrant traffic have an obligation to help new immigrants adjust to their new environment. This service is in keeping with God's concern for the welfare of aliens and foreigners living among the people of God (Ps 146:9; 1 Tim 5:10; Heb 13:2; 3 John 1:5). Although this command concerns all the church, the diaspora Christian community is most attuned to the needs of the sojourners, for they too are strangers of the land. Churches among these people groups would do well to begin by addressing their primary needs—namely belonging, identity, family relations, and political rights.

Fulfilling the diaspora mission mandate involves carefully studying a migrant community if we are to advance missions to, for, and beyond the community. These diaspora models hope to move the discussion forward.

Bibliography

Basch, Linda, Nina Glick Schiller, and Cristian Szanton Blanc. *Nations Unbound: Transnational Projects, Postcolonial Predicaments and Deterritorialized Nationstates.* New York: Routledge, 1994.

Camroux, David. "Nationalizing Transnationalism? The Philippine State and the Filipino Diaspora." *Centre D'etudes et de Recherché Internationals Sciences* 152 (2008): 1–39.

Choy, Catherine Ceniza. *Empire of Care: Nursing and Migration in Filipino American History.* North Carolina: Duke University Press, 2003.

Clifford, James. "Diasporas." *Cultural Anthropology* 9, no. 3 (1994): 302–38.

Clifford, James. *The Ethnicity Reader: Nationalism, Multiculturalism and Migration.* Edited by Montserrat Guibernau and John Rex, 283–90. Cambridge, UK: Polity Press, 1997.

Cohen, Robin. *Global Diasporas: An Introduction.* Seattle: University of Washington Press, 1997.

Constable, Nicole. "At Home but Not at Home: Filipina Narratives of Ambivalent Returns." *Cultural Anthropology*, 14 no. 2 (1999): 203–28.

Crouchett, Lorraine J. *Filipinos in California: From the Days of the Galleons to the Present.* El Cerrito, CA: Downey Place, 1982.

Espiritu, Yen Le. "The Intersection of Race, Ethnicity and Class: The Multiple Identities of Second-Generation Filipinos." *Identities* 1, nos. 2, 3 (1994): 249–73.

Espiritu, Yen Le. *Filipino American Lives.* Philadelphia: Temple University Press, 1995.

Goitein, Solomon Dob. *A Mediterranean Society: The Jewish Communities of the Arab World as Portrayed in the Documents of the Cairo Geniza.* 6 vols. Berkeley: University of California Press, 1967–93.

Ignacio, Emily Noelle. *Building Diaspora: Filipino Community Formation on the Internet.* New Jersey: Rutgers University Press, 2005.

Im, Chandler H., and Tereso C. Casiño. *Global Diasporas and Mission*, edited by Chandler H. Im and Amos Yong. Oxford: Regnum Books, Oxford Centre for Mission Studies, 2014.

Levy, André, and Alex Weingrod. *Homelands and Diasporas: Holy Lands and Other Places.* Stanford, CA: Stanford University Press, 2005.

Mendoza, S. Lily. *Between the Homeland and the Diaspora: The Politics of Theorizing Filipino and Filipino American Identities.* Edited by Franklin Ng. New York: Routledge, 2002.

Mercy Corps. "The World's 5 Biggest Refugee Crises." Mercy Corps, updated July 2, 2020. https://www.mercycorps.org/blog/worlds-5-biggest-refugee-crises.

Moo, Douglas J. *The Letters of James.* Grand Rapids, MI: Eerdmans, 2000.

Okamura, Jonathan Y. "The Filipino American Diaspora: Sites of Space, Time, and Ethnicity." In *Privileging Positions: The Sites of Asian American Studies*. Edited by Gary Y. Okihiro, Marilyn Alquizola, Dorothy Fujita Rony, and K. Scott Wong. Pullman, WA: Washington State University Press, 1995.

Okamura, Jonathan Y. *Imagining the Filipino American Diaspora: Transnational Relations, Identities, and Communities*. New York: Garland Publishing, 1998.

Okamura, Jonathan Y. *Ethnicity and Inequality in Hawaii*. Philadelphia: Temple University Press, 2008.

Operational Data Portal. "Ukraine Refugee Situation." *ODP*. Updated February 15, 2023. https://data.unhcr.org/en/situations/ukraine.

Pantoja, Luis, Jr., Sadiri Joy Tira, and Enoch Wan. *Scattered: The Filipino Global Presence*. Manila: Lifechange Publishing, 2004.

Parrenas, Rhacel Salazar. "Transgressing the Nation-State: The Partial Citizenship and 'Imagined (Global) Community' of Migrant Filipina Domestic Workers." *Signs* 26, no. 4 (2001): 1129–54.

Rouse, Roger. "Mexican Migration and the Social Space of Postmodernism." *Diaspora: A Journal of Transnational Studies* 1, no. 1 (1991): 8–23. doi:10.3138/diaspora.1.1.8.

Safran, William. "Diasporas in Modern Societies: Myths of Homeland and Return." *Diaspora: A Journal of Transnational Studies* 1, no. 1 (1991): 83–99.

San Juan, E., Jr. "Fragments from a Filipino Exile's Journal." *Amerasia Journal* 23, no. 2 (1997): 117–33.

San Juan, E., Jr. *Toward Filipino Self-determination: Beyond Transnational Globalization*. New York: State University of New York, 2009.

San Juan, E., Jr. "Trajectories of the Filipino Diaspora." *Ethnic Studies Report* (2000): 221–38.

Santos, Narry F. "Survey of the Diaspora Occurrences in the Bible and of Their Contexts in Christian Missions." In *Scattered: The Filipino Global Presence*, edited by Luis Pantoja Jr., Sadiri Joy Tira, and Enoch Wan, 53–66. Manila: LifeChange Publishing, 2004.

Schmidt, Karl Ludwig. *Theological Dictionary of the New Testament*. Vol. 2. Grand Rapids, MI: Eerdmans, 1962.

Strobel, L. M. "Born-Again Filipino: Filipino American Identity and Asian Panethnicity." *Amerasia Journal* 22, no. 2 (1996): 31–53.

Strobel, L. M. "Coming Full Circle: Narratives of Decolonization among Post-1965 Filipino Americans." In *Filipino Americans: Transformation and Identity*, edited by M. P. P. Root, 62–79. Thousand Oaks, CA: Sage, 1997.

Tan, Jason Richard. "A Diaspora Within: The Marginalization of Local Filipino Churches." In *God at the Borders: Globalization, Migration, and Diaspora*, edited by Charles R. Ringma, Karen-Hollenbeck-Wuest, and Athena O. Gorospe, 240–525. Manila: OMF Literature and Asian Theological Seminary, 2015.

Tira, Sadiri Joy, and Stuart Lightbody. "A Cyclical, Glocal Diaspora Congregation: A Case Study of the First Filipino Alliance Church from 1984–2007." *Diaspora Study* (2009): 1–4.

Tolentino, Roland B. "Bodies, Letters, Catalogs: Filipinas in Transnational Space." *Social Text* 48 (1996): 49–76.

Tololyan, K. "Rethinking Diaspora(s): Stateless Power in the Transnational Movement." *Diaspora* 5, no. 1 (1996): 3–36.

Tsuda, Mamoru, ed. *Filipino Diaspora: Demography, Social Networks, Empowerment and Culture*. Philippines: Philippine Migration Research Network and Philippine Social Science Council, 2003.

Tyner, James A. *The Philippines: Mobilities, Identities, and Globalization*. New York: Routledge, 2009.

Walls, Andrew F. "Mission and Migration: The Diaspora Factor in Christian History." *Journal of African Christian Thought* 5, no. 2 (2002): 3–11.

Walls, Andrew F. "Migration and Evangelization: The Gospel and Movement of Peoples in Modern Times." *The Covenant Quarterly* 63, no. 3 (2005).

Walls, Andrew F. *Mission and Migration: The Diaspora Factor in Christian History*. Global Diasporas and Mission, edited by Chandler H. Im and Amos Yong. Oxford: Regnum Books, Oxford Centre for Mission Studies, 2014.

Wan, Enoch. *Diaspora Missiology: Theory, Methodology, and Practice*. Portland, OR: Institute of Diaspora Studies, Western Seminary, 2011.

Wan, Enoch, and Michael Pocock. *Missions from the Majority World: Progress, Challenges, and Case Studies*. Littleton, CO: William Carey Library, 2009.

Wan, Enoch, and Sadiri Joy Tira. "The Filipino Experience in Diaspora Missions: A Case Study of Mission Initiatives from the Majority World Churches." In *Missions from the Majority World: Progress, Challenges and Case Studies*, edited by Enoch Wan and Michael Pocock, 387–411. Pasadena, CA: William Carey Library, 2009.

Weingrod, Alex, and André Levy. "Paradoxes of Homecoming: The Jews and Their Diasporas." *Anthropol* 79, no. 4 (2006): 691–716.

Chapter 8
Rural Migration and Diaspora Missions

Matt Cook

A 2022 report from the International Organization for Migration, which is sanctioned by the United Nations, reveals that the number of international migrants has increased from 173 million in 2000 to 281 million in 2020.[1] The United States hosts 50.6 million international migrants—the highest number in the world, and more than three times higher than Germany, which hosts the second highest number of immigrants.[2] The authors and readers of this book likely agree that God's people must not stand idly by and do nothing about this phenomenon. Fortunately, over the past twenty years, diaspora missiology has emerged as a legitimate subfield of missiology to help the church thoughtfully respond to global immigration.[3] Diaspora missiology studies occur at the intersection of missiology and migration theory, with an emphasis on strategies to minister to and through the diaspora populations of the world.[4]

Understandably, the focus of diaspora missiologists has been on urban gateway cities, where the majority of immigrants live.[5] This focus on urban immigration is not isolated to diaspora missiology. Policy advocates for the Center for American Progress similarly note that immigration scholars "traditionally approach it as an urban phenomenon: first, detailing how immigrants live and work in traditional receiving communities such as New York, Los Angeles, and Boston... . However, less research is dedicated to studying how immigrants who move to sparsely populated rural areas live in those communities and how those communities adapt to these newcomers."[6]

A friend recently lamented in an email, "Very little is written about rural ministry from a scholarly viewpoint. Scholarly work on rural immigration and diaspora work is the rarest of all." But does it have to be this way? While urban areas in the United States do draw the majority of immigrants, small towns and rural areas are impacted by immigration as well. I live in a small town in a rural Tennessee county and just through interactions at businesses and youth

---

1 McAuliffe and Triandafyllidou, *World Migration Report 2022*, 10.
2 McAuliffe and Triandafyllidou, 24.
3 Tira and Yamamori, *Scattered and Gathered*; Tira and Uytanlet, *Hybrid World*; Im and Yong, *Global Diasporas and Mission*; Pocock and Wan, *Diaspora Missiology*.
4 Tira and Yamamori, *Scattered and Gathered*, 633–38.
5 Rijnhart, "World's Least Reached."
6 Mathema, Svajlenka, and Hermann, "Revival and Opportunity."

sports practices, I know of residents from Laos, India, China, the Philippines, Mexico, Guatemala, Thailand, Yemen, New Zealand, and Pakistan, not including international students at the Christian university where I teach. Small towns in rural areas across the United States have similar realities with represented nationalities that span the globe. Visits to evangelical churches in rural areas, however, indicate that the foreign-born membership of churches in these areas does not match the foreign-born population. Diaspora missiology, then, can not only assist in reaching the larger diaspora populations of urban centers, but it can also stimulate the concern of churches in small towns and rural areas for their foreign-born neighbors.

Migration to rural areas of the United States, though less prevalent than migration to urban gateway cities, is a growing phenomenon. In this chapter, I propose that rural churches can and should utilize the principles of diaspora missiology to reach their diaspora neighbors. While global gateway cities are vitally important to scholarship in migration studies and diaspora missiology, the least-reached are also living in rural areas as business owners, agricultural workers, and soccer moms. In this chapter I will begin by exploring the demographic realities of rural migration. Second, I will explain the rather positive results of my dissertation (2019) and follow-up research (2022) that explored the experience of Asian diaspora populations in rural, southern, evangelical contexts. Third, I will briefly propose some reasons for the positive results of the research. Finally, I will explore how the principles and best practices of diaspora missiology can be used by predominantly white, rural churches in order to take a more missional posture toward their immigrant neighbors. The principles of diaspora missiology are not only for churches in global gateway cities with larger immigrant populations to serve. These principles can be contextualized and applied in non-urban settings as well.

Demographics of Rural Migration in the United States

Immigration statistics are constantly changing, so researchers can only report what is relevant in that moment. The demographics of rural migration in the United States are especially difficult to determine because the data is not only constantly changing, it is also scarce and dependent on the researcher's definition of rural. For example, Pew Research Center estimates that 4 percent of rural residents are foreign-born.[7] Researchers at the University of New Hampshire, however, report that 4.8 percent of rural residents are

---

7 Parker et al., "What Unites and Divides."

foreign-born.[8] In my opinion, the most comprehensive set of data on rural migration comes from the US Census Bureau. According to the US Census Bureau, while urban counties in the United States draw the majority of immigrants (14.8 percent of urban county residents are foreign born), the foreign-born population of rural counties is 2.6 percent.[9] The difference in numbers is the result of differing definitions of urban-rural classifications. The US Census Bureau provides added help by providing a downloadable spreadsheet listing every county in the United States and the number of rural residents and urban residents in each county.[10] This allows for detailed examination of each county in the United States based on its rural or urban classification. Unfortunately, this data was produced in 2015 and is based on 2010 census data. However, new urban-rural classifications and data from the 2020 census were announced in December of 2022.[11] For the purposes of this chapter, we will assume that approximately 3 percent of rural residents are immigrants, meaning that the principles of diaspora missiology can definitely serve rural churches as they minister to these immigrants.

Though 3 percent may seem statistically insignificant, rural immigrants create population growth in rural areas that would be declining otherwise. One study indicated that rural areas experienced a 4 percent decline in overall population, which would have been far more pronounced had it not been for the 130 percent growth they experienced among immigrants.[12] This same study stated, "In the 873 rural places that experienced population growth, more than 1 in 5, or 21 percent, can attribute the entirety of population growth to immigrants."[13] These growing immigrant populations bring economic growth and vitality, providing what Johnson and Lichter call "a demographic lifeline."[14] Though demographics on rural immigration are not thorough, they do present sufficient evidence to warrant participation by rural church scholars in research that will contribute to the church's ability to minister effectively to immigrants. Rural immigration sparked my interest in such research.

---

8   Schaefer and Mattingly, "Demographic and Economic Characteristics."
9   Gryn, "Foreign-Born by Urban-Rural Status."
10 The United States Census Bureau offers a "Country Classification Lookup Table."
11 United States Census Bureau, Areas FAQs.
12 Mathema, Svajlenka, and Hermann, "Revival and Opportunity," 2.
13 Mathema, Svajlenka, and Hermann, 3.
14 Johnson and Lichter, "Rural Depopulation."

2019 and 2022 Research among Asian Americans in Rural Counties in Tennessee

My 2019 dissertation[15] endeavored to make a small contribution to the literature gap in rural diaspora missions. It explored the experiences of Asian Americans in rural counties in Tennessee.[16] Interestingly, the Asian American population grew faster than any other major racial or ethnic group between 2000 and 2019, and Asian Americans "are projected to become the largest immigrant group in the country, surpassing Hispanics in 2055."[17] The United States Census Bureau estimates that 22.9 million Asians lived in the United States in 2019.[18]

I conducted research in four major steps.[19] First, a thorough literature review in the field of diaspora missiology was conducted. Second, concurrently with the bibliographic research, twenty-three Asian Americans who lived in mostly and completely rural counties in Tennessee were interviewed using qualitative interviews.[20] Third, the data was analyzed through coding processes that facilitated the discovery of themes that, in turn, informed the theories that were developed. Fourth, these theories were combined with the best practices of diaspora missiology to form missiological implications that could inform the ministry of evangelical churches to diaspora populations in rural counties in the research area. Having compiled and coded the data gathered through qualitative interviews with twenty-three individuals, five theories were developed as a result of selective coding.[21]

Theory 1: Asian Americans Sensed Mistreatment in Rural Areas in the Past

Until the close of the twentieth century, Asian Americans in rural counties of Tennessee felt as if mistreatment was more common because of their ethnicity. Three interviewees experienced this mistreatment, and each noted that a change had occurred and that by 2019, mistreatment was less common and less severe. Another interviewee described a certain level of mistreatment that he endured as a child in the 1970s, but also noted that he

---

15 Cook, "Diaspora Missions among Asian."
16 Gryn, "Foreign-Born by Urban-Rural Status."
17 Budiman and Ruiz, "Key Facts about Asian Americans."
18 United States Census Bureau, "Asian American and Pacific."
19 Pew Forum, "Religious Landscape Study."
20 Rubin and Rubin, *Qualitative Interviewing*.
21 Creswell, *Qualitative Inquiry and Research*, 150.

has experienced no level of mistreatment as an adult in the rural county in which he lived. Some of the Millennials who were interviewed also seemed to realize that a previous generation endured more mistreatment than their own generation. This realization that things were at one time worse than they are now, though perhaps an assumption that most Americans would make, became a prevalent theme in the interviews.

Theory 2: Asian Americans Mostly Feel Positively about Treatment in Rural Counties in Tennessee

Connected to the first theory, and perhaps in spite of the rural South's reputation for racism, the Asian Americans I interviewed felt mostly positively about the way they were treated in rural counties in Tennessee in 2019. Twenty-two of the twenty-three individuals interviewed for this research described their treatment in positive terms. They seemed to be genuinely thankful for their experience, their place in the community, and their home in rural areas. This theory was surprising to me, and as the interviewees reflected on the reality of what they were describing, they were surprised as well. In the dissertation prospectus, I expressed a fear that I would discover that the research population was consistently mistreated in rural areas. That fear proved to be unfounded.

Theory 3: Small-Scale Mistreatment of Asian Americans Is Still a Reality

Though the research population was positive in their description of how they have been treated, several of them acknowledged some small-scale mistreatment. The mistreatment they experienced was more likely to be caused by children, teenagers, or the elderly.[22] Further, foreign-born Asian Americans who speak English with an accent were more likely to experience mistreatment than those who do not speak with an accent. Also, Christian Millennials were more likely to say that they were not bothered by what they described as "joking" about their ethnicity.

Theory 4: Asian Americans Feel Positively about Churches and Christians in Rural Counties

The interviews strongly indicated that Asian Americans in rural counties of Tennessee feel positively about churches and Christians in rural counties. Twenty-two of the twenty-three interviewees viewed the church and Christians in a positive light. Several of those who spoke positively about their experience with churches tried intently to think of something negative

---

22 Weeks, "Age-Old Problem."

and were unable. Those who were not evangelical Christians unanimously viewed Christians positively. Additionally, those who were not evangelical Christians had nothing negative to say about the Christians in their communities.

Theory 5: Some Have Negative Experiences in Rural Churches

Though the majority spoke positively about their experience with the church, a minority described negative experiences. Seven of the interviewees, all evangelical Christians, described negative experiences with churches. The four interviewees who seemed to take these negative experiences most seriously were also foreign-born and spoke English with some level of an accent, therefore adding the causal condition to Theory 5 that the foreign-born who speak with an accent were more likely to have had negative experiences.

2022 Research

Just four months after defending this dissertation however, COVID-19 changed the world, changed diaspora missions, and changed the Asian American experience. I wondered if the results of my research would be different in 2022 than they were in 2019. The pandemic's interruption to the life of Asian Americans was even more significant than for others as the media reported that the city of Wuhan, China was the original epicenter of the virus. Further, former US President Donald Trump repeatedly referred to COVID-19 as the "China virus" and the "kung flu."[23] Immediately, a rise in hate incidents against Asian Americans was reported and these incidents have continued. As would be expected, the response against Asian American hatred has been strong. Notably, Asian American theologians developed the Asian American Christian Collaborative. The Coalition's "Statement on Anti-Asian Racism in the Time of COVID-19"[24] has collected over ten thousand signatures, "including from Asian and non-Asian leaders at the National Association of Evangelicals, Fuller Theological Seminary, Princeton Theological Seminary, Yale Divinity School, Emory's Candler School of Theology, Claremont School of Theology, and *Sojourners*, and *Christianity Today*."[25] The tragic increase of hatred and violence toward Asian Americans has jolted our culture into awareness of their long-lasting challenges as a diaspora people in the United States.

---

23 Campbell, "Anti-Asian Hate Crimes."
24 Asian American Christian Collaborative, "Statement on Anti-Asian Racism."
25 Yoshiko, "Fuller Picture of God," 27.

In a small follow-up research effort in early 2022, I sought to communicate digitally with some of the interviewees from my dissertation to see if their experience had changed in the previous two years. Though most of the news about hatred toward Asian Americans was coming from urban areas, I assumed that the interviewees from my dissertation would also have experienced a change, or at least heightened awareness of the racism they had endured but perhaps had not acknowledged. With this in mind, I reached out via Facebook messenger, text message, or email to thirteen of the twenty-three interviewees from my dissertation. Of the ten that were excluded, four had moved to an urban location near the beginning of COVID, and I did not have contact information for the remaining six. The thirteen that remained still lived in a rural area of Tennessee during at least part of the pandemic. Only one of the thirteen did not respond to my message, and two responded quickly that they wanted to think about their response, but then never responded again. That left ten who responded to my message.

In the message, I thanked them again for their help with my dissertation and told them how pleasantly surprised I was that the results of the interviews were mostly positive. I noted that the world had changed significantly since 2019, especially for Asian Americans, and then asked them the following questions: "In the past two years during the pandemic, have you experienced any change in the way you have been treated as an Asian American? Has anything changed in the way you've been treated in church? If so, what have those changes been like?" Obviously, this research was not as thorough as my initial research. Further, this study is limited by the same factors in my dissertation as described above.

Shockingly, all ten stated in clear terms that there had been no change in their experiences in their rural Tennessee communities or in their churches. Multiple respondents were extra clear that this had not been a problem at church, almost indicating that they could not imagine such a thing happening at their church. One noted that she had paid close attention to the news and was heartbroken by it, but thankful that she had not experienced mistreatment. Another respondent said that she thought her experience would be worse in a more urban area. Another noted that nothing had changed for him, but he knew that his Japanese American friends had negative experiences. One had split time between West Virginia and Tennessee and noted that her experience had become much more negative in rural West Virginia, but there had been no changes in Tennessee. None of these expressed any concern about potential racism. Two of them, however, stated that they had close family members who had warned them to be careful.

As was the case with my dissertation, I was very surprised by these results. How is it that racism toward Asian Americans has spiked dramatically in the past two years, but all ten of my respondents had not experienced anything negative? The contrast is clear between the current data and these individuals. I had assumed that re-questioning these individuals would contradict the findings of my dissertation, but that was not the case.

Potential Reasons for the Positive Results of My Research

This research encouraged me concerning the state of rural churches. I am a product of the rural church. Other than my time as a church planter in Peru, I have been a member of churches in rural counties in Tennessee and West Virginia. I have personally witnessed racist attitudes, and I expected to find that rural Christians in Tennessee had failed miserably in their interactions with Asian Americans, and that I would be the one to set them straight. I am thankful, at least in the case of the individuals I interviewed, that I was mostly wrong. But, racism in the United States (especially the rural United States) and the increase in anti-Asian hate is undeniable, so what is going on here? Why did the rural immigrants in my research respond in mostly positive ways about their experience in rural settings and churches? My expertise is in missiology, so I am not qualified to analyze this too deeply, but here are some possible reasons that these individuals reported fairly positive experiences.

1. The respondents have abnormal experiences, and my sample size is too small to highlight a diverse set of circumstances. According to one Kaiser Family Foundation study, one in three Asian American immigrant respondents reported "that they have personally felt more discrimination based on their racial/ethnic background since the COVID-19 pandemic began in the US."[26] Perhaps my respondents simply did not fall into the one in three category.

2. The respondents are giving the answers they think the interviewer wants, also called response bias. While I suspect that this may have come into play in two of the families I interviewed for my dissertation, my follow-up research respondents were friends who had been very transparent and believe in the importance of this research.

3. The interviewer subconsciously created interviewer bias by influencing the responses of the interviewee. While this is always possible, I pushed in the opposite way. In both sets of research, I expected to

---

26 Artiga, Hill, Corallo, and Tolbert, "Asian Immigrant Experiences."

hear and specifically asked for instances of mistreatment as a way to honor those experiences, but I heard very few.

4. The respondents are unintentionally participating in the "model-minority" (the intelligence, hard work, and success of Asian Americans) stereotype and have unconsciously perpetuated and internalized it.[27] In an effort to stay positive and continue to project the "model-minority" stereotype, perhaps my respondents refuse to complain.

5. Small town living actually permits a more positive experience than an urban one. Two factors come into play here:

- In small towns, where there are only a handful of Asian families, Yale sociologist Grace Kao suggests people feel less threatened. In an urban area, people may become uncomfortable with the growing Asian American population and then lash out negatively. This, she argues, is unlikely to happen in a small town.[28]

- Small towns allow for more "meaningful proximity" than urban areas. Benya Kraus writes, "At its worst, this lack of meaningful proximity and shared friendship is replaced with blame, hateful assumptions, and threatened entitlement—some of the forces driving the most recent (though not new) waves of anti-Asian violence happening across our country."[29] Describing rural life, she adds: "I am, indeed, a racial minority in my rural community.... But the thing is: there is an opportunity for real proximity, to have your landlord be your bartender, your police officer does downward dog at yoga with you. If we choose to drown out the fearful media and politics, we can deploy a childhood curiosity that turns our rural proximity into transformative relationships: the kind that sees and values difference, with an affection so profound that we cannot realize our own humanity without fighting for yours as well."[30]

While one should not idealize rural living, perhaps a combination of reasons one, four, and five contribute to their reporting of mostly positive experiences.

Diaspora Missiology for Rural Churches

While my research was narrowly focused on the experience of Asian Americans in rural Tennessee, it indicated that this particular group views

---

27 Hwang, "Demystifying and Addressing Internalized," 597.
28 Rao, "What Anti-Asian Sentiment."
29 Kraus, "View: Asian Americans."
30 Kraus.

rural life and rural churches fairly positively. This fact is good news for the rural church, and by extension it should awaken rural Christians to the possibility of reaching their immigrant neighbors, regardless of their nation of origin, with the good news of Jesus. As stated previously, the principles of diaspora missiology are not only for churches in urban centers with larger immigrant populations to serve. The principles of diaspora missiology can be contextualized and applied in non-urban settings as well, and these principles can help to increase engagement between predominantly white, rural, evangelical Christians and the diaspora populations in their communities. Below, I will offer four possible suggestions for rural churches to utilize the best practices of diaspora missiology. Though these ideas are not innovative and have often been emphasized by diaspora missiologists, their impact may be profound in some non-urban churches.

First, in rural churches, awareness must be raised concerning the realities and opportunities of diaspora and the negative experiences of immigrants. Additionally, teaching on racism should occur more regularly. In *Scattered to Gather*, the third step for engaging in diaspora missions is for a church to explore its neighborhood. Some rural churches still need to take this vital step.[31] A connected point is that when church leaders have intentionally provided educational opportunities on diversity, a natural result should be a discussion of the inspiring opportunity that the local church has to reach the nations for Christ, even in rural areas. Even though diversity in urban areas is greater, some level of diversity exists in rural areas. Global missions, therefore, can occur in a rural church's "backyard" as it reaches out to diaspora people in its community.[32]

Second, rural Christians should be more intentional about building relationships with diaspora people. If it is true in my research that rural Asian Americans feel fairly positively about their experiences, then fear should not prevent relationship building. Unfortunately, Christians have not always been effective in this area. On an international scale, Johnson and Zurlo note that 86 percent of Muslims, Buddhists, and Hindus "do not personally know a Christian."[33] In rural areas, especially in the southern United States where evangelicals represent a higher percentage of the population, immigrants will more than likely interact on a regular basis with evangelicals through work and business associations, school, or neighborhood interactions. Lee suggests that because a "relational emphasis permeates their lives," if an

---

31 Tira and Yamamori, *Scattered to Gather*, 33.
32 Payne, *Strangers Next Door*, 128.
33 Johnson and Zurlo, "Global Christianity and Global Diasporas," 55.

Asian American connects with a church, this connection will likely occur because of relationships, not traditional marketing. She expounds:

> For today's Asian American Christians this relational emphasis permeates their lives and, by extension, their choices and preferences with regard to their church. They look for churches that demonstrate the importance of community, whose members assist one another in tangible, concrete ways and, more importantly, whose relationships reflect healthy attitudes and practices.... For most Asian American churches, effective marketing usually has nothing to do with traditional business methods.... In other words, effective marketing occurs through the Asian American grapevine, a very community-oriented approach befitting the target audience's cultural tendencies.[34]

One may infer, then, that although an immigrant "grapevine" is a less likely reality in a rural area, traditional church marketing through social media and attractive graphics will not be the key to reaching immigrants. Relationships will be the key.

In Western culture, though, Wan observes "a lack of 'relational reality.'"[35] He explains that this lack of relational reality can be seen in the "high mobility in general and high density of population in urban centers," the abundance of dysfunctional families, "the prevalence of virtual relationship over actual personal interaction," the church's emphasis on programs over relationships, and the popularity of prosperity theology.[36] Because Westerners are increasingly less relational, Western Christians must be intentional about relationship building instead of falling into the non-relational habits of Western culture. Rural Christians, however, may have an advantage if Kraus is right that rural living provides more opportunity for more "meaningful proximity," as mentioned previously.[37]

Third, and closely related to relationship building, hospitality is a key way that rural Christians can serve the immigrant population. Admittedly, anyone who takes hospitality seriously has struggled with its safe but biblical practice in light of COVID-19. Even before the pandemic, though, hospitality was not a strength of the American church. The Immigration Coalition estimates that "eighty-five percent of immigrants to the USA have never been invited into an American home."[38] Van Rheenen, however,

---

34 Lee, "Hospitable Households: Evangelism," 125.
35 Wan, "Relational Paradigm for Practicing," 192.
36 Wan, 192.
37 Kraus, "View: Asian Americans."
38 Treviño, "7 Practical Steps."

argues that "gracious hospitality" must be central to the life of missional churches. He believes that this type of hospitality "forms the character of our communities—both in our worship gathering and in our missional communities." He notes, "Gracious hospitality leads us to invite people into our lives to 'come and see' the presence of God."[39] Unfortunately, though hospitality is a biblical value and a cultural value for many non-Westerners, hospitality "is not a big part of our culture" and Christians must be reminded of its importance.[40] Though the art of hospitality may not be lost, as former Muslim, Baptist pastor, and author Thabiti Anyabwile observes, "it does need some resuscitation, to be freshly modeled and taught."[41] If hospitality is biblical, then it must be revived, even if it is counter-cultural.

Of all of the strategies that might be used to minister to immigrants in rural areas, especially in the South, hospitality should come the most naturally. "Southern hospitality" is a well-known maxim and assumption. *Southern Living* magazine recently published an article with the subtitle, "Because Southern hospitality isn't just a catchphrase, it's a way of life below the Mason Dixon."[42] Others, like Anthony Szczesiul in his 2017 book published by the University of Georgia, claim that Southern hospitality is a myth that served to advance the social and political ideologies of Southern exceptionalism.[43] Regardless of whether Southern hospitality is a reality or a myth, rural Christians have the opportunity to demonstrate the biblical value of hospitality to immigrants living in their communities. They have the opportunity to provide affirmative answers to Szczesiul's probing questions, "Can the regional ideal of southern hospitality serve as a meaningful frame of reference for a South and for southerners faced with the demands and pressures of globalization? In other words, can southern hospitality develop … into a discursive practice oriented toward the challenges of the future, one that calls for an ethical response to the foreigner, the stranger, and the risk of the unknown?"[44]

Fourth, rural churches can utilize the best practices of holistic ministry to serve the immigrants in their communities. From the early stages of the diaspora missiology movement, Enoch Wan has called for diaspora missions to focus on holistic ministry.[45] Diaspora people face a myriad of challenges.

---

39 Van Rheenen, "Is Missional a Fad?"
40 Wilch, "Organizational Models–Hospitality," 111.
41 Anyabwile, *Gospel for Muslims*, 70.
42 Darrisaw, "The 6 Qualities."
43 Szczesiul, *Southern Hospitality Myth*, 2.
44 Szczesiul, 27.
45 Wan, "Phenomenon of Diaspora," 112.

These challenges, however, can be seen by Christians as opportunities to demonstrate the love of God. Diaspora missiologists have been passionate about the expression of this sentiment. Rogers writes, "The challenges of immigration are open doors of opportunity for the church to step through and help people who need help. Stepping through the door the Lord has opened for us may not be easy, but few worthwhile endeavors are. We need to begin seeing the challenges of immigration as opportunities to serve and make a difference in people's lives, just as Jesus did during his ministry."[46]

Schaefer and Mattingly report that "rural immigrants are poorer and have lower educational attainment than their urban counterparts."[47] Writing from a political perspective about rural immigrants, Mathema, Svajlenka, and Hermann note, "The most critical services for immigrant families often revolve around language learning, educational access, and social inclusion."[48] Undoubtedly, these are services that churches can help to provide. Though holistic ministry is often referenced in urban ministry, rural churches should also pay close attention to opportunities to minister to immigrants holistically.

While holistic ministry opens up a plethora of possibilities, language teaching and meeting vocational needs could be especially significant among rural immigrant populations. Churches have been ministering to immigrants through language acquisition classes for multiple decades. In rural areas, this service could be an especially useful ministry because rural areas often lack adequate English as a second language instruction opportunities and bilingual services.[49]

Rural churches are also especially equipped to help with vocational needs. Churches in rural areas often include members that are very connected in the local government and economy. They will be aware of job opportunities in the community and can assist immigrants in their search for a job. If the immigrant already owns a business, then Christians can be intentional about frequenting the business and helping to spread the word about it in smaller towns where successful marketing can be achieved by word of mouth. I minister in a rural church with a membership that includes multiple medical professionals, teachers at every level of education, a Christian counselor and social worker, financial planners, insurance agents, electricians, plumbers, construction workers, speech pathologists, volunteer

---

46 Rogers, *Evangelizing Immigrants*, 47.
47 Schaefer and Mattingly, "Demographic and Economic Characteristics," 1.
48 Mathema, Svajlenka, and Hermann, "Revival and Opportunity," 4.
49 Mathema, Svajlenka, and Hermann, 25.

firefighters, a mayor, a football coach, a college admissions counselor, business owners, an international business broker, and caterers. It is a small church, but its membership could meet nearly any need that an immigrant might have; and if the need cannot be met directly, its wide net of influence could be used to find a way to meet the need. Churches in rural counties are equipped by God to participate in holistic ministry to diaspora people, for the glory of God.

Conclusion

Though the explosion of literature over the past twenty years in the field of diaspora missiology is encouraging, more research is needed on how rural churches can participate in this vital subfield of missiology. The data gathered from interviewees in my research points to the potentially significant impact that the rural church can have on diaspora populations. The rural church must be prepared to come alongside what God is doing through the opportunities that he has given it through diaspora groups. American churches, both urban and rural, must be aware of the "unprecedented need and opportunity"[50] that global immigration provides. The rural church's ministry to diaspora populations is one opportunity among many through which the church might point the nations to Jesus, "in order that the Gentiles might glorify God for his mercy" (Rom 15:9 ESV).

Bibliography

Adeney, Miriam. "Colorful Initiatives: North American Diasporas in Mission." *Missiology* 69, no. 1 (2011): 5–23.

Anyabwile, Thabiti. *The Gospel for Muslims: An Encouragement to Share Christ with Confidence*. Chicago: Moody Publishers, 2010.

Artiga, Samantha, Latoya Hill, Bradley Corallo, and Jennifer Tolbert. "Asian Immigrant Experiences with Racism, Immigrant-Related Fears, and the COVID-19 Pandemic." *Kaiser Family Foundation*, June 18, 2021. https://www.kff.org/coronavirus-covid-19/issue-brief/asian-immigrant-experiences-with-racism-immigration-related-fears-and-the-covid-19-pandemic/.

Asian American Christian Collaborative. "Statement on Anti-Asian Racism in the Time of COVID-19." 2022. https://www.asianamericanchristiancollaborative.com/read-statement.

Bernard, H. Russell. *Research Methods in Anthropology: Qualitative and Quantitative Approaches*. 5th ed. Lanham, MD: AltaMira, 2011.

---

50 Adeney, "Colorful Initiatives," 6.

Budiman, Abby, and Neil G. Ruiz. "Key Facts about Asian Americans, a Diverse and Growing Population." *Pew Research Center*, April 29, 2021. https://www.pewresearch.org/fact-tank/2021/04/29/key-facts-about-asian-americans/.

Campbell, Josh. "Anti-Asian Hate Crimes Surged in Early 2021, Study Says." *CNN*, May 5, 2021. https://www.cnn.com/2021/05/05/us/anti-asian-hate-crimes-study/index.html.

Cha, Peter, Steve Kang, and Helen Lee. *Growing Healthy Asian American Churches: Ministry Insights from Groundbreaking Congregations*. Downers Grove, IL: IVP Books, 2006.

Cook, Matthew E. "Diaspora Missions among Asian Americans in Rural Counties in Tennessee." PhD diss., Southern Baptist Theological Seminary, 2019. https://hdl.handle.net/10392/5982.

Creswell, John W. *Qualitative Inquiry and Research Design: Choosing among Five Traditions*. Thousand Oaks, CA: Sage Publications, 1998.

Darrisaw, Michelle. "These Are the 6 Qualities That Really Define Southern Hospitality." *Southern Living*. Updated January 5, 2023. https://www.southernliving.com/culture/southern-hospitality.

Gryn, Thomas. "The Foreign-Born by Urban-Rural Status of Counties: 2011–2015." *United States Census Bureau*, December 8, 2016. https://www.census.gov/newsroom/blogs/random-samplings/2016/12/the_foreign-bornby.html.

Hwang, Wei-Chin. "Demystifying and Addressing Internalized Racism and Oppression among Asian Americans." *American Psychologist* 76, no. 4 (2021): 596–610. https://doi.org/10.1037/amp0000798.

Im, Chandler H., and Amos Yong, eds. *Global Diasporas and Mission*. Regnum Edinburgh Centenary Series 23. Oxford: Regnum Books, 2014.

Johnson, Kenneth M., and Daniel T. Lichter. "Rural Depopulation: Growth and Decline Processes over the Past Century." *Rural Sociology* 84, no. 1 (2019): 25. https://doi.org/10.1111/ruso.12266.

Johnson, Todd M., and Gina A. Zurlo. "Global Christianity and Global Diasporas." In *Global Diasporas and Mission*, edited by Chandler H. Im and Amos Yong, 38–56. Regnum Edinburgh Centenary Series 23. Oxford: Regnum Books, 2014.

Kraus, Benya. "View: Asian Americans in Rural America." *Minnesota Women's Press*, March 18, 2021. https://www.womenspress.com/view-asian-americans-in-rural-america/.

Lausanne Movement and Global Diaspora Network. *Scattered to Gather: Embracing the Global Trend of Diaspora*. Rev. ed. Vernon Hills, IL: Parivar International, 2017.

Lee, Helen. "Hospitable Households: Evangelism." *Growing Healthy Asian American Churches: Ministry Insights from Groundbreaking Congregations*, edited by Peter Cha, Steve Kang, and Helen Lee, 122–44. Downers Grove, IL: IVP Books, 2006.

Mathema, Silva, Nicole Prchal Svajlenka, and Anneliese Hermann. "Revival and Opportunity: Immigrants in Rural America." *Center for American Progress*, September 2, 2018. https://www.americanprogress.org/article/revival-and-opportunity/.

McAuliffe, M., and A. Triandafyllidou, eds. *World Migration Report 2022*. International Organization for Migration, 2021. https://worldmigrationreport.iom.int/wmr-2022-interactive/.

Oksnevad, Roy, and Dotsey Welliver, eds. *The Gospel of Islam: Reaching Muslims in North America*. Wheaton, IL: Evangelism and Missions Information Service, 2001.

Parker, Kim, Juliana Menasce Horowitz, Anna Brown, Richard Fry, D'Vera Cohn, and Ruth Igielnik. "What Unites and Divides Urban, Suburban, and Rural Communities." *Pew Research Center*, May 22, 2018. https://www.pewresearch.org/social-trends/2018/05/22/demographic-and-economic-trends-in-urban-suburban-and-rural-communities/.

Payne, J. D. *Strangers Next Door: Immigration, Migration, and Mission*. Downers Grove, IL: IVP Books, 2012.

Pew Forum. "Religious Landscape Study: Evangelical Protestants." *Pew Research Center*, 2015. http://www.pewforum.org/religious-landscape-study/.

Pocock, Michael, and Enoch Wan, eds. *Diaspora Missiology: Reflections on Reaching the Scattered Peoples of the World*. Evangelical Missiological Society Series 23. Pasadena, CA: William Carey Library, 2015.

Rao, Naina. "What Anti-Asian Sentiment Looks Like in Smaller, Rural Areas, and Why It Matters." Wyoming Public Radio, April 12, 2021. https://www.wyomingpublicmedia.org/open-spaces/2021-04-12/what-anti-asian-sentiment-looks-like-in-smaller-rural-areas-and-why-it-matters.

Rijnhart, Charles. "The World's Least Reached Are on Our Streets." *Lausanne Global Analysis* 9, no. 6 (2020). https://lausanne.org/content/lga/2020-11/the-worlds-least-reached-are-on-our-streets.

Rogers, Glenn. *Evangelizing Immigrants: Outreach and Ministry among Immigrants and Their Children*. Bedford, TX: Mission and Ministry Resources, 2006.

Rubin, Herbert J., and Irene S. Rubin. *Qualitative Interviewing: The Art of Hearing Data*. 2nd ed. Thousand Oaks, CA: Sage, 2005.

Schaefer, Andrew P., and Marybeth J. Mattingly. "Demographic and Economic Characteristics of Immigrant and Native-Born Populations in Rural and Urban Places." *The Carsey School of Public Policy at the Scholars Repository*, October 5, 2016. https://dx.doi.org/10.34051/p/2020.273.

Szczesiul, Anthony. *The Southern Hospitality Myth: Ethics, Politics, Race, and American Memory*. The New Southern Studies Series. Athens: University of Georgia Press, 2017.

Tira, Sadiri Joy, and Juliet Lee Uytanlet. *Hybrid World: Diaspora, Hybridity, and Missio Dei*. Littleton, CO: William Carey Publishing, 2020.

Tira, Sadiri Joy, and Tetsunao Yamamori, eds. *Scattered and Gathered: A Global Compendium of Diaspora Missiology*. Rev. Ed. Carlisle, UK: Langham Global Library, 2020.

Treviño, Rondell. "7 Practical Steps We Can Take to Engage Immigration Issues." *The Immigration Coalition*, 2018. https://theimmigrationcoalition.com/7-practical-steps-we-can-take-to-engage-immigration-issues/.

United States Census Bureau. "Asian American and Pacific Islander Heritage Month: May 2021." *United States Census Bureau*, April 19, 2021. https://www.census.gov/newsroom/facts-for-features/2021/asian-american-pacific-islander.html.

United States Census Bureau. Areas FAQs. *United States Census Bureau*, 2020.

United States Census Bureau. "Country Classification Lookup Table." https://data.census.gov/table?q=United+States&table=DP05&tid=ACSDP1Y2017.DP05&g=010XX00US&lastDisplayedRow=29&vintage=2017&layer=state&cid=DP05_0001E.

Van Rheenen, Gailyn. "Is Missional a Fad?" *Missio Dei: A Journal of Missional Theology and Praxis* 7 (2016). http://missiodeijournal.com/issues/md-7/authors/md-7-van-rheenen.

Wan, Enoch, ed. *Diaspora Missiology: Theory, Methodology, and Practice*. 2nd ed. Portland, OR: Institute of Diaspora Studies, 2014.

Wan, Enoch. "The Phenomenon of Diaspora: Missiological Implications for Christian Missions." In *Scattered: The Filipino Global Presence*, edited by Luis L. Pantoja, Sadiri Joy Tira, and Enoch Wan, 103–21. Manila, Philippines: LifeChange Publishing, 2004.

Wan, Enoch. "Relational Paradigm for Practicing Diaspora Missions in the 21st Century." In *Diaspora Missiology: Theory, Methodology, and Practice*, edited by Enoch Wan, 191–98. 2nd ed. Portland, OR: Institute of Diaspora Studies, 2014.

Weeks, Linton. "An Age-Old Problem: Who Is 'Elderly'?" *NPR*, March 14, 2013. https://www.npr.org/2013/03/12/174124992/an-age-old-problem-who-is-elderly.

Wilch, Gerhard. "Organizational Models–Hospitality." In *The Gospel of Islam: Reaching Muslims in North America*, edited by Roy Oksnevad and Dotsey Welliver, 111–19. Wheaton, IL: Evangelism and Missions Information Service, 2001.

Yoshiko, Caitlin. "A Fuller Picture of God: Confronting Anti-Asian Racism in the Church." *The Christian Century*, November 4, 2020. https://www.christiancentury.org/article/features/asian-american-christian-collaborative-s-efforts-confront-anti-asian-racism-church.

Chapter 9
Embracing the Refugees in Canada through Hospitality

Craig C. Kraft

This chapter explores the biblical hospitality mandate in the context of modern society with a focus on the potential for hospitality to bring revitalization to local churches and fruitful discipleship to refugees. The author conducted grounded research on Canadian evangelical congregations and their interactions with Syrian refugees between 2015 and 2019. This case study demonstrated the critical importance of biblical hospitality in the life of a local church and in missional engagement with refugees. Churches engaged with refugees indicated improved vitality, stronger community, and intentional mission as a result of their reciprocal hospitality with the Syrian people. Refugee ministry is an effective method for revitalizing churches and making disciples. The chapter concludes with five practical recommendations for a contextual understanding and fruitful practice of biblical hospitality with refugees today.

A friend of mine described the journey from Kiev to the Polish border like something you would see in a Hollywood production. The signs of war are everywhere. People gather what they can fit in their car or carry in their arms and start a journey to an unknown destination. A trip of a few hours stretches into days as the tidal wave of people surges into surrounding countries, flooding hotels, hostels, homes, and churches, straining all available resources. Some Ukrainians have found shelter with relatives here in Vancouver, BC, over eight thousand kilometers away from their homes. Like so many others, they arrive at the airport broken, dislocated, and homeless. They are refugees.

Two Syrian men arrived in Vancouver at the same time. One received a government sponsorship and was placed on Vancouver Island, the other was sponsored by a church. These two men met a few years later and shared their experiences. The man who received government sponsorship had a very bad experience. He was isolated from other Syrians. He and his wife thought Canada was unfriendly and racist. They moved to Vancouver and then to Surrey, looking for a place to fit in. The second man was sponsored by a church. He experienced a warm welcome, caring people, appropriate resources, and a place where he could connect with others in meaningful relationships. Both had arrived at the same time, to the same place, but had very different experiences. One loves his new home, and one wants to leave.

Connections are one of the greatest needs of refugees. They need friends, people who will develop relationships with them. Pastor Jack Taylor in Vancouver has worked with hundreds of refugees. His church provides housing and resources and helps immigrants learn English and find jobs. Taylor states, "These people are looking for a welcoming community, a place where they can find peace, housing, education, and opportunities. We show hospitality to them from the moment they arrive. We provide community and help them get connected."[1]

Hospitality is a powerful practice, with the potential to bring restoration and revitalization to souls in need. It is a virtue espoused in Scripture from God's earliest interactions with the patriarchs right through the teachings of Jesus and the apostles. Often misunderstood in our modern context, hospitality rediscovered allows hosts and guests to experience a taste of God's love and grace through their interactions with each other and opens the door for disciple-making relationships.

Hospitality and the Gospel

The Bible is full of hospitality. From the provision of clothing for Adam and Eve in Genesis to the final Marriage Supper of the Lamb in Revelation, one cannot study Scripture without encountering themes, stories, and teaching on hospitality. The biblical understanding of hospitality is the demonstration of love for strangers, as illustrated in the Luke 10 story of the good Samaritan. Hospitality is a spiritual discipline found all through the pages of Scripture. Christine Pohl writes, "Hospitality is central to the meaning of the gospel … and a practice by which we can welcome Jesus."[2] Amy Oden adds, "The astounding range and depth of the evidence tells us that hospitality as a practice and as a virtue held a central place in the early Christian life. Indeed, there is hardly a place we can look where we will not see traces of it."[3] When Christians practice the command to love one another, they are reflecting the hospitality of God.

The Old Testament is a story of God's hospitality toward the people he has chosen to make into a nation. When God delivers the Hebrews from slavery in Egypt, he initiates a great wave of refugees who are pilgrims and strangers in a land that belongs to him. They experience God's loving care and are commanded to show the same hospitality toward others (Lev

---

[1] Taylor, "Homes and Meals," 16.
[2] Pohl, *Making Room*, 2.
[3] Oden, *You Welcomed Me*, 27.

19:33–34; Num 9:14). By the end of the Old Testament, love for strangers is expanded to include widows, orphans, the poor, and even the physically disabled. In the closing book of the Old Testament, we receive a warning that those who fail to care for the widows and fatherless, and those who deprive the sojourners, will be judged severely by God (Mal 3:1–5).

The New Testament is also ripe with hospitality. Jipp sees it as more than just a spiritual discipline but as "the heart of the Christian faith."[4] Sutherland defines hospitality in this way: "In the light of Jesus' life, death, resurrection, and return, Christian hospitality is the intentional, responsible, and caring act of welcoming or visiting, in either public or private places, those who are strangers, enemies, or distressed, without regard for reciprocation."[5]

Willis and Clements write: "Any time we practice hospitality, we put human flesh on this gospel story. The Apostle Paul made this idea clear when he wrote, 'Welcome one another as Christ has welcomed you, for the glory of God'"[6] (Rom 15:7 ESV).

It is difficult to find a page in the New Testament where we do not see hospitality. Commands to love one another permeate the Gospels, and we learn that being a good neighbor to those living among and around us is what it means to be the people of God.

Hospitality is modeled by God, personified in Christ, and should be imitated by his followers. The story of the good Samaritan effectively illustrates biblical hospitality. Love your neighbor, even if he or she is a stranger.[7] In this way, followers of Jesus reflect the hospitality of God toward those who were once strangers but are now children and heirs of God, and citizens of heaven. Sharing the gospel with the broken, dislocated, and homeless begins with hospitality.

Canadian Hospitality

Canada is a nation of immigrants. Apart from our indigenous people, all our Canadian ancestors were immigrants from somewhere, and the trend continues. Statistics Canada states that over 401,000 immigrants arrived in Canada in 2021, the most newcomers Canada has ever welcomed in a single year.[8] The 2016 census identified the Philippines, India, China, Iran, and Pakistan as the top five countries of origin but in recent years we have seen

---

4 Jipp, *Saved by Faith*, 7.
5 Sutherland, *I Was a Stranger*, xiii.
6 Willis and Clements, "*Simplest Way to Change*," 41–42.
7 Yong, "Spirit of Hospitality," 61.
8 Immigration, Refugees, and Citizenship Canada, "Canada Welcomes the Most Immigrants."

new waves from Syria, Afghanistan, Mexico, and Ukraine.[9] Many of these people have come as refugees, and Canadian churches have responded with sponsorships and hospitality.

In 2019 I examined how Canadian evangelicals responded to the wave of over sixty-four thousand Syrian refugees. My research focused on a survey of 176 evangelical churches. I conducted interviews with select pastors and church members from five provinces and eleven denominations. I observed how churches practiced hospitality and how it impacted their congregations. I concluded that almost every time a church engaged with refugees, the church provided necessary care for the immigrant and the interaction had a positive impact on the congregation.

Observable Impact of Hospitality in Canadian Churches

It is natural to be suspicious of people who are different than us. A Canadian couple from Regina shared how their first response to the wave of Syrian refugees was anger. They felt that this would be bad for Canada. Still, after praying about it, they started to study about the Syrian diaspora and develop connections with some of the Syrians arriving in their community. Their hearts were dramatically changed. Their connections grew into deeper friendships and offered opportunities for them to share the gospel and invite the new arrivals to visit their church.[10] They experienced a transformation and concluded, "God is sending the mission field to us; we must love them." They see their love for the Syrians as an expression of the mission of God.

Faith Fellowship Baptist Church in Vancouver shared a similar story. In 2004 they started serving local refugees. Since then, they have welcomed more than six hundred refugees from sixty countries. Pastor Taylor states that serving refugees has changed their congregation: "It changed the way we prayed, the way we raised resources, even how we did baby showers. It changed our senior's meetings because the refugees adopted our senior ladies as their Canadian mothers, who, in turn, adopted refugee women as their daughters. It changed the whole dynamics of how church functioned."[11]

These examples are consistent with what I repeatedly heard in my interviews with Canadian pastors. Every church I interviewed spoke about how their interactions with Syrian refugees had changed them. Most of their observations fell within four categories: transformed attitudes, expanded relationships, spiritual development, and missional focus.

---

9 Canadian Heritage, "Annual Report on the Operation of the Canadian Multiculturalism Act."
10 Lutzer, "Muslim Outreach."
11 Taylor, "Homes and Meals," 16.

Transformed Attitudes

Many interviewed hosts spoke of fears or concerns when they first heard about the Syrian Muslims who were coming to Canada. They also shared how those fears were mitigated through their interactions with the Syrian people. God was clear about his expectations for the people of Israel.

> When a stranger sojourns with you in your land, you shall not do him wrong. You shall treat the stranger who sojourns with you as the native among you, and you shall love him as yourself, for you were strangers in the land of Egypt: I am the LORD your God. (Lev 19:33 ESV)

In the New Testament, Jesus commands us to "make disciples of all nations" (Matt 28:19 ESV), and the author of Hebrews writes: "Let brotherly love continue. Do not neglect to show hospitality to strangers, for thereby some have entertained angels unawares" (Heb 13:1–2 ESV).

I found that when Christians engage with immigrants, they experience a transformed attitude toward people who are different. As we saw above, friendship replaced fear. This reflects a biblical perspective regarding strangers.

Expanded Relationships

In addition to the transformed attitudes outlined above, I observed that practicing hospitality leads to the expansion of relationships and partnerships outside of the local church, resulting in the development of more significant unity among Christians.

The research identified five different types of partnerships: partnerships with denominations and sponsorship agreement holders, with other churches in the community, with missionaries, with the Muslim community, and with other resource providers. Concerning building unity among Christians, I found that by partnering with other churches and missionaries, the churches were, in fact, building unity in the body of Christ.

A church in British Colombia developed a partnership with other churches in the city to reach out to the local Muslim community and provide sponsorship to additional Syrian families. Refugee sponsorship often creates the need for partnerships, which, in turn, leads to new levels of cooperation and unity between local Christian congregations and resource providers.

The relationship between churches and their missionaries also developed into significant partnerships. In some instances, missionaries serving in the Middle East were proactively engaged in helping their denomination and individual churches to connect with families in refugee camps. These missionaries helped to establish communication between the family and sponsoring church during the lengthy application period. These church-missionary partnerships provided strategic assistance to the church in developing relationships with the families hosted and offered coaching for effective resettlement.

Several of the churches interviewed also identified partnerships with local missionaries who were retired or on a home assignment. COVID-19 displaced a lot of missionaries who were unable to travel between 2019 and 2022. Some of these missionaries helped their Canadian churches to cross some cultural barriers. Missionaries can provide significant assistance to churches in the hosting of refugee families. Professionals, with cross-cultural experience and language skills, can coach congregations in their interactions with their guests. Pastors indicate that these local missionaries are a vital part of their successful cooperation with refugees and working with them enhances their experience as hosts.

Engaging in hospitality with refugees enhances existing partnerships between churches. It leads to new partnership development with churches, organizations, and missionaries, providing opportunities to build collaboration, cooperation, and unity among Canadian believers.

Spiritual Development

My research demonstrates that when we practice hospitality with the broken, dislocated, and homeless, we experience spiritual renewal. Interviews noted that hospitality is seen as an act of obedience to God, which was usually accompanied by a sense of joy and fulfillment. If we agree that spiritual vitality may be measured by the presence of spiritual fruit, then it was evident from my interviews that the hosting churches were experiencing spiritual vitality. Ninety-three percent of the churches interviewed indicated that they felt spiritually healthier as a result of their interactions with immigrants. They described their interactions with words and phrases that highlighted the presence of spiritual fruit, particularly love and kindness. Interviews indicated that individuals associated their acts of hospitality with a greater appreciation of God and his love for people. One woman stated, "It adds to our overall sense of God's hospitality, talking to people who are different from you, and hearing their stories. I think it just encourages people to keep fostering that." I find that churches engaged in acts of hospitality toward marginalized individuals, are likely to experience a realignment of some of their views and to recognize spiritual fruit, both personally and corporately.

I also found that hospitality led to a personal renewal in the individuals interviewed. Six of the individuals interviewed spoke of how they have become more welcoming of all immigrants because of their experiences with extending hospitality toward refugees. Several indicated that their interactions with refugees had changed their views and perceptions about people who are different. "We have lost our fear of Muslims. We have learned to love them." Interviews also indicated that people who created space in their lives to include interaction with strangers also experienced a renewed sense of spiritual vitality. They described their renewed vitality with enthusiasm: "It's been energizing for the church ... I see people who didn't know that this was their calling or even their passion. They got involved, and for these people, it has been so life-giving."

The findings from the interviews indicated a renewal of the attitudes and spiritual practices of Canadian evangelical hosts. Eighty-eight percent of the interviewed hosts spoke of their love for the refugees. Seventy-six percent indicated they saw their interactions with refugees as a direct expression of their commitment to missions.

At a time when North Americans are being torn apart by the history and persistence of racism, my research demonstrates that the practice of biblical hospitality is an effective way to build intercultural bridges. Engaging and building relationships with "strangers" removes the strangeness and allows the host and guest to relate to one another as friends. "Refugees are looking for a safe place to be with others. They have left their communities and are looking for new community. Generations of racial barriers are torn down through new friendships."[12]

Missional Focus

An African proverb states: "Western society has the watch and the clock, but Africans have the time." The proverb refers to Western society's preoccupation with time, schedules, and calendars, while Africans are more concerned with people and relationships.

The practice of biblical hospitality focuses on relationships and the pursuit of seeing people as God sees them. Loving strangers and engaging with them as God mandates is participation in the mission of God. Evangelical Christians and the church have been criticized as being largely irrelevant to their cultural contexts.[13] Biblical, missional, hospitality builds bridges and aligns the beliefs and actions of the church in a way that is relevant to the particular needs of the community. It will not be Syrian immigrants in every situation, but in every situation, and in every nation, there are strangers in need of loving relationships. Missiological hospitality brings missiological relevance to Christian congregations. I found that practicing biblical

---

12 Pastor Alan Hiller, personal conversation, 2022.
13 Roxburgh, *Structured for Mission*; Penner et al., "Hemorrhaging Faith"; Kinnman and Hawkins, *You Lost Me*.

hospitality brought a new awakening to the church's mission, realities, and opportunities, resulting in action and the presence of spiritual fruit.

In "Widening Our Welcome," an article in a recent issue of *Faith Today*, Renée James looks at how God breathes new spiritual life into people through hospitality. James shares the stories of Lis Lam, David and Cathy Phillips, and Aaron and Cherie White, illustrating how the practice of hospitality has brought new meaning into their lives and into the lives of the people they host. She quotes Lam, "There's an exchange that happens. You have a meal with someone, and at the end of the day you're changed"[14]

Park spoke of hospitality evangelism within a broken and suffering community. He reflects, "The good news was not new to them; it rather had to be proved good and true. Without genuinely caring about them and seeking to serve them as whole persons, without practicing biblical hospitality, we could not communicate God's redeeming love in Christ with credibility."[15]

As a follow-up to my interview data, the final survey of 176 churches also demonstrated that churches that have been engaged in hospitality with marginalized people in the last five years consistently describe themselves as being healthier than those churches that only identify as "foyer friendly."[16] Hospitable churches welcome new people as guests and seek to develop meaningful relationships with them. Less hospitable churches or "foyer friendly" churches tend to treat new people as visitors who show up for a visit and then go on their way. The results of the survey supported the findings of the narrative interviews.

The survey demonstrated that hospitable churches are missional churches. They exhibit more growth, more outreach, more people developing and using their spiritual gifts, more community outreach, more cross-cultural outreach, a more robust experience of community, and more engagement with marginalized people in their community.

In 1990, Canadian missionary Arnel Motz wrote: "I would like to suggest that if we are going to reverse the present trends in Canada, we must trust God to bring us three winds of change: revitalization, reformation, and relevance."[17]

While it is hard to determine the cause of spiritual fruit in an individual or believer, every church in the sample that was practicing biblical hospitality was also exhibiting spiritual fruit. I can conclude that spiritual fruit and hospitality accompany each other. I believe that practicing hospitality flows

---

14 James, "Widening Our Welcome."
15 Park, *Hospitality as Context*, 392.
16 *Foyer friendly* is a term used by the author to refer to churches that focus their hospitality on the welcoming of visitors to their church on a Sunday morning.
17 Motz, *Reclaiming a Nation*, 257.

out of spiritual maturity, but it can also lead to spiritual maturity. It is the age-old question of the chicken and the egg, and my research is unable to identify which comes first, but in every church that I interviewed, they existed together. I believe that the spiritual disciplines, of which hospitality is one, lead toward the progressive development of spiritual fruit and vitality in individuals and congregations. It is my interpretation that the discovery and practice of a contextual theology of hospitality should lead to spiritual reformation.

It is evident in the interviews that hospitality with Syrians has had a profound impact on the attitudes, perceptions, and feelings of Canadian Christians toward Syrians. The replacement of fear with friendship and favor is evidence of relational renewal.

I believe that hospitality is central to the mission of God. Churches that seek to be "missional" should thus seek to practice biblical hospitality. Hospitality is one way that Canadian evangelicals can reclaim a point of relevance with society outside their doors. Hospitality can connect us with the people who need to experience Jesus.

I conclude that a biblically informed, contextual theology and practice of hospitality contributes toward the revitalization, reformation, and relevance of the church in Canada. Hospitality toward strangers and outsiders can spark renewal in evangelical churches.

Fruitful Practices for Canadians

The art of biblical hospitality has been lost in modern Western society. Replaced long ago by a complex system of hospitals, hotels, and social programs, the church's role as host has changed. But there are still ways for the church to rediscover this ancient practice.

One way that Canadian churches may experience revitalization is through a contextually relevant practice of biblical hospitality. It is evident that Canadian churches practicing biblical hospitality also experience higher levels of spiritual vitality than churches that do not. Dreher argues that, as in Benedict's day (referring to the church in the early sixth century as addressed by Saint Benedict), the modern church has lost its place and influence in society and needs to look back to its roots to discover meaning, purpose, and relevance.[18] Hospitality is not optional. Guided by the Gospels, Jipp concludes that, "Hospitality to strangers was not an optional practice for the church, but is something that is deeply related to salvation … hospitality is a tangible testimony to our wholehearted embrace of Jesus's person and message."[19]

---

18 Dreher, *Benedict Option*, 1–5.
19 Jipp, *Saved by Faith*, 7.

The following are five recommendations to assist Canadian churches in developing a contextual theology and practice of hospitality.

Rediscover Biblical Hospitality

A review of Scripture and precedent literature paints a bright and colorful picture of the centrality of hospitality in the biblical narrative, the gospel, and the establishment of the church. Hospitality was a core discipline of the early church that served the rapid expansion of Christianity in the early centuries and made the gospel accessible to people who were previously outsiders, foreigners, and strangers. The practice of hospitality in most modern, Western churches is a faint shadow of the vivid picture portrayed in the early church. Genuine hospitality has become a lost art. My first recommendation is for Canadian churches to study and understand the theology of hospitality as a spiritual discipline and vivid reflection of the nature and mission of God.

Welcome Strangers

The early church grew and flourished through the discipline of hospitality. Worshipping in homes, hosting traveling pastors and missionaries, and welcoming strangers were significant in the rapid expansion of the church. The church today is in decline in many Western nations. Evangelicals and mainline congregations are asking why. I propose that one of the contributors to the decline of Christianity has been the loss of genuine hospitality in our culture. Many churches aspire no further than to be foyer friendly, extending a warm greeting, handshake, and perhaps a welcome package to visitors. But biblical hospitality is proactive. "Practicing hospitality is quite difficult and arduous. It involves our whole being, not just a part, and demands all we have, not just a portion."[20]

Today the church must move outside its walls and be involved in the community. Churches that only focus on the care and nurture of their members are irrelevant and unbiblical. My second recommendation is for churches to be proactive in reaching out to people in the community, offering a warm welcome to people who are different. A hospitable church will not create barriers based on age, appearance, language, color, culture, gender, or other visible difference. Hospitable churches will welcome strangers.

Faith Baptist Church in Vancouver is a radiant example of what the church can be. They celebrate sixty nations celebrating together under one roof. This church is currently sponsoring twenty refugees from various locations, and they are building communities of trust. Through these relationships people

---

20 Park, *Hospitality as Context*, 392.

are choosing to study the Bible, learn about Jesus, and become disciples. The whole church is involved in their refugee ministry, and it has brought new life to their congregation.

Be Known for Our Love

Observing the ministry of Jesus, Paul, Peter, and others, we see that hospitality was not confined to the home or the church setting. Hospitality was observed on the road and in the community. People crowded Jesus on the road and the hillsides, but he made space for them. Despite all that was going on, he paused and paid personal attention to those he healed, those he visited, and those he called to follow him. He demonstrated love for people who were different. Peter and Paul faced hostility as they entered some cities, and yet they expressed love and concern for those they met, even when the meeting was adversarial. We observe *philoxenia*, brotherly love toward strangers. My third recommendation for churches is that they need to be known for their love for others rather than their judgment. Far too many people identify Christianity by what it is against than by what it is for (Christians are identified as judgmental, phobic, intolerant, condescending, and irrelevant rather than being known for our love—John 13:35).

Hope Central in Winnipeg loves refugees. Through acts of kindness and providing furniture and other basic needs, they have become a safe place and trusted friends to many new residents in Winnipeg. Acts of love and kindness are the open end of the funnel that draws people toward understanding the love of God in Jesus. Through discovery Bible studies, friends are becoming brothers and sisters in Christ.

Know Our Neighborhood

Between November 4, 2015, and April 30, 2019, almost sixty-four thousand Syrians entered Canada as refugees.[21] There has been a large number of Syrians entering Canada, but they have not been disbursed evenly into every community. Many communities will have no Syrian refugees present. But this fact does not mean that those communities do not need the rediscovery of hospitality.

On the contrary, Syrian refugees are just one highly visible minority group which has been prominent in the media. Canada is a nation of immigrants. From 2018 to 2019 the Canadian population grew by 531,497 people, representing a 1.4 percent growth rate, the largest of any of the G7

---

21 Britten, "Canadians May Not Be."

countries. Eighty-two percent of that growth was through immigration.[22] Syria ranked seventh behind the Philippines, India, China, Iran, Pakistan, and the United States as the top countries of birth of recent immigrants in the 2016 census. While Syrians are a notable group of immigrants in Canada, they are by no means the largest group. My fourth recommendation to churches is that they must be intentional in learning who their neighbors are. Canadian information is easy to obtain through Outreach Canada or WayBase. A local church can quickly identify the demographics of their community by visiting with people in the neighborhood. There is no reason for a church not to know the ethnic demographics of their neighborhood.

In Montreal, Pastor Gus discovered that there were many Iranian refugees arriving in his city. They arrived with little English and no French which is a monumental barrier to settlement in Quebec. Gus and his team have been providing language study classes and orientation to the unique culture of Quebec. They have learned that many Iranian refugees are curious about Christianity. Hospitality has become an effective way for them to build relationships and introduce Jesus. Many refugees have joined Bible studies and Alpha groups[23] to learn more about Christianity and as a result, people are being saved, discipled, and baptized.

Repent and Pray

Knowing who lives next door is a big step toward recognizing their needs and finding opportunities for connections. We don't have to sponsor a refugee to be hospitable. We can show hospitality to people who are already here in our neighborhoods. As we have seen in Scripture, hospitality was not just for the foreigner or stranger, but also the widows, orphans, prisoners, and the sick. There are people in every neighborhood who need to experience God's hospitality through the local church. My fifth recommendation for churches and followers of Christ is to repent of our fear and pride and pray that God will give us a vision for what hospitality must look like in our immediate context. One size does not fit all. Each church must discern what God has called it to do in its own community. There will be contextual expressions of hospitality in each community that will be unique from other communities across Canada or around the world.

---

22 Statistics Canada, "Canada's Population Estimates."
23 Alpha is an eleven-week, small-group Bible study that introduces people to faith, Scripture, and Jesus. https://alphacanada.org.

Bibliography

Britten, Liam. "Canadians May Not Be as 'Obsessed' Over Immigration This Election, but It Remains a Key Issue for Parties." *CBC News*, October 7, 2019. https://www.cbc.ca/news/canada/british-columbia/refugees-2019-election-1.5310154.

Canadian Heritage. "Annual Report on the Operation of the Canadian Multiculturalism Act 2016–2017." Date modified November 11, 2018. https://www.canada.ca/en/canadian-heritage/corporate/publications/plans-reports/annual-report-canadian-multiculturalism-act-2016-2017.html.

Carroll R., M. Daniel. *The Bible and Borders: Hearing God's Word on Immigration*. Grand Rapids, MI: Brazos Press, 2020.

Dreher, Rod. *The Benedict Option: A Strategy for Christians in a Post-Christian Nation*. New York: Sentinel, 2017.

Immigration, Refugees, and Citizenship Canada. "Canada Welcomes the Most Immigrants in a Single Year in Its History." December 23, 2021. https://www.canada.ca/en/immigration-refugees-citizenship/news/2021/12/canada-welcomes-the-most-immigrants-in-a-single-year-in-its-history.html.

James, Renée. "Widening Our Welcome." *Faith Today*, July 6, 2020. http://www.faithtoday.ca/Magazines/2020-Jul-Aug/Widening-our-welcome.

Jipp, Joshua W. *Saved by Faith and Hospitality*. Grand Rapids, MI: Eerdmans, 2017.

Kinnaman, David, and Aly Hawkins. *You Lost Me: Why Young Christians Are Leaving Church—and Rethinking Faith*. Grand Rapids, MI: Baker Books, 2011.

Lutzer, Harold. "Muslim Outreach." March 5, 2017. Harvest Bible Chapel Kelowna. https://www.youtube.com/watch?v=PbtsZ2rJ1Hg.

Motz, Arnell. *Reclaiming a Nation: The Challenge of Re-evangelizing Canada by the Year 2000*. Richmond, VA: Church Leadership Library, 1991.

Oden, Amy. *And You Welcomed Me: A Sourcebook on Hospitality in Early Christianity*. Nashville: Abingdon Press, 2001.

Ott, Craig, and Juan Carlos Tellez. "The Paradox of American Evangelical Views on Immigration: A Review of the Empirical Research." *Missiology: An International Review* 47, no. 3 (2019): 252–68.

Park, Joon-Sik. "Hospitality as Context for Evangelism." *Missiology* 30, no. 3 (2002): 385–95.

Penner, James, Rachael Harder, Erika Anderson, Bruno Desorcy, and Rick Hiemstra. "Hemorrhaging Faith: Why and When Canadian Young Adults Are Leaving, Staying and Returning to Church." hemorrhagingfaith.com.

Pohl, Christine D. *Making Room: Recovering Hospitality as a Christian Tradition*. Grand Rapids, MI: Eerdmans, 1999.

Roxburgh, Alan J. *Structured for Mission: Renewing the Culture of the Church.* Downers Grove, IL: IVP Books, 2015.

Statistics Canada. "Canada's Population Estimates: Age and Sex, July 1, 2019." https://www150.statcan.gc.ca/n1/daily-quotidien/190930/dq190930a-eng.htm.

Sutherland, Arthur. *I Was a Stranger: A Christian Theology of Hospitality.* Nashville: Abingdon Press, 2006.

Taylor, Jack. "Homes and Meals for Refugees." *Faith Today*, February 3, 2020. https://www.faithtoday.ca/Magazines/2020-Jan-Feb/Homes-and-meals-for-refugees.

Willis, Dustin, and Brandon Clements. *The Simplest Way to Change the World: Biblical Hospitality as a Way of Life.* Chicago: Moody Publishers, 2017.

Yong, Amos. "The Spirit of Hospitality: Pentecostal Perspectives toward a Performative Theology of Interreligious Encounter." *Missiology* 35, no. 1 (2007): 55–73.

Chapter 10
Understanding and Ministering to Survivors of Sex Trafficking

Valerie Geer

What informs a contextualized, Christ-centered ministry to sex trafficking survivors? This chapter will begin to answer this question by offering a two-part, contextualized approach for Christian workers whose personal ministry, church outreach, or parachurch organization focuses on people experiencing sexual exploitation. Part one will detail the relational system of trafficking, i.e., the dynamics of traffickers/pimps, victims/survivors, and johns/clients/purchasers of sex. Part two will offer a scripturally informed hermeneutic for those working with survivors in a ministry setting. While this chapter assumes the reader is somewhat familiar with the widespread, global slave trade that is sex trafficking, it is important to point to a few reliable sources of information before jumping into the contextualized approach for ministry described in this chapter.

- The Trafficking in Persons (TIP) Report—Published annually by the US Department of State
- The Trafficking Victims Protection Act (TVPA)
- "Trafficking & Slavery"—International Justice Mission
- "Recognizing Sex Trafficking"—Polaris Project
- "Human & Migrant Smuggling"—The United Nations

Part One: Relational Dynamics of Sex Trafficking

There are a number of lenses we could don when focusing our vision on understanding sex trafficking. We could don an economic lens to see sex trafficking as a global, billion-dollar industry fueled by supply and demand. We could don the lens of justice to examine sex trafficking as modern-day slavery and how this injustice stands in stark contrast to biblical ethics. These perspectives are important—even essential. However, this chapter will focus on the relational dynamics of the key players in sex trafficking because ministry to sex trafficking victims/survivors is relational, and understanding their relational history in trafficking is absolutely necessary in order to come alongside them in Christ's kindness, grace, and love.

Understanding the Traffickers

There are numerous types of pimps (traffickers), each characterized by a different relationship to victims and different strategies for controlling them. Robin Miller identifies three kinds of pimps that she sees in her work as a case manager of New Options for Women at LifeWorks Northwest in Portland, Oregon.[1] *Gorilla pimps* are those who use violence and intimidation to control victims. For example, an American Indian woman from Minnesota who was trafficked into prostitution in 2011 reported: "A pimp ... took me to someone's place and he said this guy ... [is] interested in you. Then he started hitting me after I said no. I was so scared I just did it. After that I kept doing it because I was afraid to get hit."[2] Sophie Hayes is another example of a survivor who was controlled by a gorilla pimp. After meeting her in a club and taking her on a date, her pimp isolated her and used brutal terror, physical beatings, and extreme violence to control and prostitute Sophie.[3]

Romeo pimps, on the other hand, are men who act like boyfriends or lovers, but exploit the victims. A Romeo pimp uses psychological manipulation, false declarations of love, gift-giving, and other strategies to exploit his victim, leading the female to believe that he cares about her and that they have a special relationship. For example, a Romeo pimp might fake romantic relationships with females online. He creates an emotional connection over time, convincing her that they are boyfriend/girlfriend, eventually moving from the online world to the real world. He gains her trust before forcing her or asking her to engage in commercial sex acts, at which point he functions as her pimp.[4] He may use manipulation, such as stating that she has to prove her love for him by doing what he asks or convincing her it is safe. He isolates her from friends and family, and she becomes dependent on him for food, housing, money, and security.

Sponge pimps are men who live off the income of a woman working in the commercial sex industry. For example, he uses or takes the pay the victim makes working in a strip club, creating a scenario in which the woman does not have full access to the income she generates through men purchasing her sexual services. Sponge pimps are often the victim's boyfriend, but

---

[1] Miller, "Counseling Sex Trafficking Survivors." Conference on Counseling Sex Trafficking Survivors: Understanding and Treating Complex Trauma. Western Seminary. Portland, OR. March 11, 2016.

[2] Behnke, *Up for Sale*, 34.

[3] Hayes, *Trafficked: My Story*.

[4] Behnke, *Up for Sale*, 37.

they can also be family members or any other significant person in her life. The difference between a Romeo pimp and a sponge pimp is that the Romeo pimp directly pimps his victim out to men, whereas the sponge pimp does not; he simply takes the earnings she makes from stripping or prostitution. Survivor Rachel Lloyd, founder of GEMS (Girls Education Mentoring Services), is an example of a sexually exploited woman who had a sponge pimp. In Rachel's case, her live-in boyfriend was a drug addict who, often by force, took Rachel's earnings from her employment at a strip club.[5] He did not directly arrange for men to use her, like a Romeo pimp would, but he pressured her to keep working as a stripper and earn more money so that he could take it to purchase drugs.

In addition to gorilla, Romeo, and sponge pimps, there are *family pimps* and *gang-based pimps*. Family pimps are typically the victim's mother or father (or both), or possibly an extended family member, such as an uncle or cousin. In this scenario, sex trafficking income makes up part or the entirety of the family income. In fact, the family may even be operating a larger sex trafficking ring made up of family and non-family victims. The family pimp forces or coerces the young females (and males) of the family into the family business by selling them for sex. For example, survivor Savannah Parvu was sold to men for sex by her drug-addicted mother.[6] Savannah's mother would often take Savannah with her to buy drugs from dealers, and Savannah remembers her mother prostituting herself when she didn't have enough money to buy drugs. On one such occasion, the man who was to purchase Savannah's mother for sex wanted 11-year-old Savannah instead. Her mother did not hesitate but pimped her out then and many times thereafter.

Gang-based pimps exist in high numbers, particularly in urban settings where gangs thrive. A gang-based pimp might employ Romeo or gorilla pimp strategies, but the difference is that he is connected to a larger, organized crime system in which many gang members participate. In fact, this type of pimp is the kind that is glorified in pop culture and music, as evidenced by rapper 50 Cent's hit song "Pimp" in which he brags about being a gangster making a lot of money from his "hoes" and "bitches."[7] There is even a so-called "Players' Ball" that takes place annually in various cities across the US celebrating and glorifying the gangster-pimp lifestyle.[8]

---

5 Lloyd, *Girls Like Us*.
6 Washington, "Woman Sold into Sex Trafficking."
7 For full lyrics to the song, see "P.I.M.P." by 50 Cent.
8 Cohen, "Dazzling Look Inside."

No matter the type of pimp or trafficker, the relationship to the victim is characterized by extreme abuse, psychological manipulation, shame, and degradation. To those who do not understand the relational dynamics of sex trafficking, it can appear that victims are women who stay because they make bad choices to fuel their unhealthy lifestyles. This could not be further from the truth. According to the *Trafficking in Persons Report*: "An adult's consent to participate in prostitution is not legally determinative: if one is thereafter held in service through psychological manipulation or physical force, he or she is a trafficking victim and should receive benefits outlined in the Palermo Protocol and applicable domestic laws."[9]

In her article, "Aftercare for Survivors of Human Trafficking," Dr. Becca C. Johnson calls the seeming compliance of victims to their pimp's demands the Silence Compliance Model.[10] In this model, Johnson explains how victims experience coercion, collusion, and contrition. In the coercion stage, victims experience fear stemming from the pimp's manipulation, cruelty, brutality, and torture. He will threaten to harm the victim and/or her loved ones, or will threaten to deport the victim or have her arrested. The pimp might withhold food, drugs (often the very drugs that he used to hook the victim and keep her under his control), or other life necessities to the point that the victim is unable to identify any solutions, help, or escape. Prostitution research expert Melissa Farley states: "Pimps and customers use methods of coercion and control like those of other batterers: minimization and denial of physical violence, economic exploitation, social isolation, verbal abuse, threats and intimidation, physical violence, sexual assault, and captivity. The systemic violence emphasizes the victim's worthlessness except in her role as a prostitute."[11]

The coercion stage of the Silence Compliance Model leads to the collusion stage in which victims live in survival mode. For example, the pimp has caused the victim to be dependent on him for emotional needs, drugs, and finances, leaving the victim isolated and helpless, doing whatever she must do in order to get what she needs from her pimp. The extent of the psychological manipulation causes the victim to feel confused and uncertain about what is or isn't real or true. Rather than looking to others for help, such as police or friends, the victim looks to the pimp because he has convinced her that no one will believe her, that she'll be considered unworthy of help, that it's her fault, or that she'll be arrested.

---

9 US Department of State, *Trafficking in Persons Report*.
10 Johnson, "Aftercare for Survivors."
11 Farley, "Prostitution Is Sexual Violence."

Subsequently, the victim experiences contrition—a sense of shame, guilt, remorse, and self-blame. She believes she is worthless, that her situation is hopeless, and that she has dishonored her family (if she had previous positive connections with her family). Once contrition sets in, it is very unlikely that a victim would leave her pimp. She believes no one wants her but him and that survival is not possible without what he provides.

Understanding the Johns/Clients/Purchasers

"John" is the term commonly used to refer to a man[12] who purchases sexual services. It should be noted that in popular usage, "John" or "John Doe" is simply a generic name used to refer to any average man, thus the appropriation of the term "john" in the context of sex trafficking communicates that it is simply normal, average men who purchase women for sex. While it is certainly true that men who purchase sex come from every racial, ethnic, socioeconomic, and professional background, it is horrendous to imply that purchasing women for sex is merely a normal, everyday activity expected of any man.

Men who purchase females for sex do so, in part, because they do not affirm females as full and equal humans. In his article "Keeping Up with the Johns: Why Men Pay for Sex, and What Happens When They Do," Jay Dixit reports that one of the reasons men purchase sex is "to act out fantasies they couldn't with their wives or girlfriends."[13] Dennis Hof, infamous pimp and proprietor of legal brothels in Nevada, gives numerous detailed accounts of all kinds of men, especially married men, who purchase prostitutes because they want to do sexual acts or role-play fantasies they would never presume to do with their wives.[14] In both of these examples, the underlying idea is that the women men marry are respectable and fully human, but the women they purchase are not dignified with the same human status. Feminist theologian Karen Peterson-Iyer makes the point that women who are purchased for sex are devalued by the men who buy them, as well as by the broader culture. This devaluation, this rejection of the *imago Dei*, is evidenced in the very language used to talk about these women, such as: whore, slut, bad girl, and ho.[15]

---

12 While it is certainly not unheard of for women to purchase sex acts, and it is definitely well-known that women recruit and traffic victims, men remain far and above the main purchasers of sexual services. It is also worth noting that women or girls who recruit other victims are often under the control of a pimp/trafficker themselves.
13 Dixit, "Keeping Up," 47.
14 Hof, *Art of the Pimp*.
15 Peterson-Iyer, "Prostitution: A Feminist Ethical," 20.

Sex trafficking survivors experience multidimensional aspects of trauma both prior to and during their sexual exploitation. They may "suffer ongoing mental and emotional issues from trauma, including nightmares, anxiety, depression, a sense of having no future, a sense of loss of safety and trust, drug and alcohol addiction, and PTSD."[16] Victims experience being hunted down, dominated, sexually harassed, and assaulted, resulting in depression, lethal suicidality, mood disorder, anxiety disorders (including PTSD), dissociative disorders, and chemical dependence. Dissociation is a response in which the mind detaches from one's current emotional or physical state, and occurs among prisoners of war who are tortured, children who are sexually assaulted, battered women, and women who are raped and prostituted.

Considering the relational dynamics within sex trafficking reveals that services for sex trafficking survivors must be trauma-informed—an adjective describing the type of care or environment provided to victims of various types of trauma, including sexual trauma. Caregivers cultivate awareness and sensitivity to maximize the comfort level and physical, emotional, and mental safety of the victim, with the goal of minimizing potential actions or environments that may trigger a trauma-response in a victim. A therapeutic environment, program, relationship, or community providing support to victims of trauma can be considered "trauma-informed." Specifically, psychologists Elliot, Bjelajac, and Fallot offer ten principles for trauma-informed services, as seen below.[17]

Principles of Trauma-Informed Services

- Principle 1: Recognize the impact of violence and victimization on development and coping strategies.
- Principle 2: Identify recovery from trauma as a primary goal.
- Principle 3: Employ an empowerment model.
- Principle 4: Maximize a survivor's choices and control over her recovery.
- Principle 5: Base services in relational collaboration.
- Principle 6: Create an atmosphere that is respectful of survivors' needs for safety, respect, and acceptance.
- Principle 7: Emphasize survivors' strengths, highlighting adaptations over symptoms and resilience over pathology.

---

16 Behnke, *Up for Sale*, 42.
17 Elliot, Bjelajacm, and Fallot, "Trauma-Informed," 461–77.

- Principle 8: Minimize the possibilities of re-traumatization.
- Principle 9: Service providers strive to be culturally competent and to understand each person in the context of her life experiences and cultural background.
- Principle 10: Solicit the input of survivors in designing and evaluating services.

Taking seriously the implementation of trauma-informed aftercare is important when ministering to survivors of sex trafficking.[18]

Part Two: Scripturally Informed Hermeneutic

When survivors are ready and willing to learn more about Christ and the teachings of the Bible, where should a teacher begin? What are scriptural principles about sexual exploitation and sexual violence? Are there certain texts that would resonate better with survivors than others? Are there any texts that should be avoided when introducing the gospel to survivors because they may take on an unintended meaning in light of the survivors' background? The answers to these questions are complex and will be discussed in the remainder of this chapter.

The Bible contains many references to prostitution, prostitutes or harlots, and adulterous women, but these passages involve serious matters of interpretation and application. It is important that a contextualized approach to ministry of the word to sex trafficking survivors be scriptural, not merely biblical. Biblical is "that which is found in the Bible and is of descriptive, precedent or cultural/temporal in nature." Scriptural is "that which is taught by the Bible and is prescriptive, principle and transcultural/eternal in nature."[19] For example, consider John 8:1–11, the passage containing Jesus's interactions with a woman who was allegedly caught in the act of adultery. A biblical approach might look to this passage and tell sex trafficking survivors to "leave your life of sin" (v. 11), indicating that the primary fault and responsibility for their exploitation is a matter of choice and that she has the power to opt in or out of the system. A scriptural approach, however, would likely focus on Jesus's gracious, personal interaction with the woman (he did not condemn her in v. 11), and recognize that Jesus regularly interacted with the powerless and marginalized of his day in this manner. A scriptural approach might also highlight Christ's redefining of the adulterous woman's exploitation by focusing on her accusers' role and the broader, unjust context

---

18 Youth.Gov, "SAMHSA's Concept of Trauma and Guidance"; see also Gerassi and Nichols, *Sex Trafficking and Commercial Exploitation*.
19 Wan, "Critique of Charles Krafts' Use/Misuse," 123.

in which the exploitation occurred. The overarching point is that a scriptural hermeneutic, rather than a biblical one, must guide contextualization.

Three problematic types of biblical texts that can create potential barriers to the gospel message for survivors include: texts that depict Christ as One who buys/purchases humans; texts that normalize slavery or emphasize gender-based subordination; and texts that seem to dehumanize prostitutes or express revulsion toward them. An example of the first type is 1 Corinthians 6:19b–20 (NIV), "You are not your own; you were bought at a price. Therefore, honor God with your bodies." These verses depict Christ as one who purchases human beings' bodies. The fact that this type of language is common in gospel presentations making an appeal for the unsaved to receive Jesus should give us pause to consider the impact it might have on survivors of sex trafficking. Survivors' lived reality, sometimes for years on end, is that men purchase their bodies; men pay a price to have access to their bodies in sexually violent ways. Therefore, when Jesus is presented in language that is similar to survivors' painful experiences of having been bought by men, it can repel them from Christ or cause them to associate meanings and imagery with Jesus that they do with the men who exploited them. A different metaphor would be better used, such as the one in Romans 8:15 that emphasizes our spiritual adoption and inclusion into the family of God.

The second type of biblical texts that could cause harm and be inappropriate to use with survivors are those emphasizing the submission and subordination of slaves and women. Without a proper understanding of the cultures of the Ancient Near East and of the Greco-Roman world, interpreting and applying the slave and women passages is very difficult, even for an advanced student of the word. If these types of texts are used without proper care and sensitivity, they can feel like weapons wielded to oppress women, people of color, servants, and slaves.[20] Take Ephesians 6:5 (NIV) as an example: "Slaves, obey your earthly masters with respect and fear, and with sincerity of heart, just as you would obey Christ." Slaves obeying their masters is likened to obedience to Christ. For today's modern-day slaves, including victims of sex trafficking, this passage might leave them feeling confused, belittled, and under the impression that God is not for their freedom from slavery. 1 Peter 2:18 (NIV) goes even further to exhort slaves to submit to abusive or violent masters: "Slaves, in reverent fear of God submit yourselves to your masters, not only to those who are good and considerate, but also to those who are harsh." For survivors who have regularly had to submit to harsh masters (pimps and clients), this passage

---

20 Pierce, Groothuis, and Fee, *Discovering Biblical Equality*.

functions as traumatic and abusive. Similarly, 1 Corinthians 11:3 (NIV) has been used to teach women's inferiority to men: "Now I want you to realize that the head of every man is Christ, and the head of the woman is man, and the head of Christ is God." 1 Timothy 2:12–14 (NIV) has been misused in a similarly oppressive way: "I do not permit a woman to teach or to assume authority over a man; she must be quiet. For Adam was formed first, then Eve. And Adam was not the one deceived; it was the woman who was deceived and became a sinner." At the very root of sex trafficking is gender-based oppression, therefore passages that seem to support the devaluing of women and extol the authority of men are harmful texts that should be avoided when working with survivors of sex trafficking.[21]

Finally, a third barrier to be avoided is the seeming degradation of and disgust with prostitutes in the Bible. For example, within 1 Corinthians 6, Paul teaches believers to refrain from sexual sin, and expresses disgust at the notion of a Christian having sex with a prostitute (1 Cor 6:15). Ephesians 5:5 (NIV) says, "For of this you can be sure: no immoral, impure, or greedy person—such a person is an idolater—has any inheritance in the kingdom of Christ and of God." Similarly, 1 Corinthians 6:9–10 states:

> Or do you not know that wrongdoers will not inherit the kingdom of God? Do not be deceived: neither the sexually immoral, nor idolaters, nor adulterers, nor men who have sex with men, nor thieves, nor the greedy, nor drunkards, nor slanderers, nor swindlers will inherit the kingdom of God.

Old Testament law speaks negatively of prostitutes: "You must not bring the earnings of a female prostitute or of a male prostitute into the house of the LORD your God to pay any vow, because the LORD your God detests them both" (Deut 23:18 NIV). Leviticus 21:9 (NIV) states it even harsher: "If a priest's daughter defiles herself by becoming a prostitute, she disgraces her father; she must be burned in the fire."

Israel's unfaithfulness to God is regularly depicted as prostitution in Old Testament prophetic literature (Jer 2:20–24; 3:2, 3; Ezek 23:9–20; Hos 9:1). Furthermore, in the book of Revelation (chs. 17, 18), grotesque evil, apostasy, and abomination is depicted as a prostitute. These are just a few New and Old Testament examples about prostitution and sexual sin that could very easily lead a survivor to believe God hates her, is disgusted with her, and desires to punish her. Consequently, teaching survivors about sexual ethics by highlighting these passages is neither wise nor responsible in a contextualized approach.

---

21 Pierce, Groothuis, and Fee.

If the above biblical texts are problematic for survivors, then it is necessary to offer Scriptural teaching about sexual exploitation, oppression, abuse, and sexual violence so that they may come to understand more accurately God's loving, gracious character. There are three scriptural principles that need to be established. First, God is grieved and displeased by all injustice, including sexual violence. The following table, synthesized from Deirdre Brouer's article "Voices of Outrage against Rape: Textual Evidence in Judges 19," offers a summary of how Old Testament biblical writers viewed rape:[22]

Table 10.1. God's Disapproval of Sexual Violence in the Old Testament

OT Legal texts	OT Prophetic texts	OT Narrative texts
Rape is equivalent to murder. (Deut 22:26)	Rape is physically and psychologically traumatic.	Rape is an outrage (*nebalah*), which also means godlessness and abomination. Examples include the rapes of Dinah, Tamar, and the "concubine from Bethlehem" (Judges 19).
Pressuring a woman physically into sexual intercourse is wrong. (Deut 22:25–27)	Rape is used as a metaphor to convey the horror, trauma, and desolation of foreign invasion and warfare. (Ezek 16)	Rape is a serious threat to the life and wellbeing of an individual, community, and nation.
Pressuring a woman psychologically into sexual intercourse is wrong. (Deut 22:28–29)		Tamar's outcry in 2 Samuel 13:19–20 reveals that rape was understood as physically, socially, and psychologically devastating, resulting in desolation.
The consent and voice of the woman is valued and her innocence is assumed. (Deut 22:27–29)		1 Samuel 2:22–25 portrays the wicked abuse of power in the rape of the women who served at the entrance to the Tent of Meeting. The rapists, Eli's sons, are called wicked, and their sin is not only against the women and their families, but against the LORD.

---

22 Brouer, "Voices of Outrage," 24–28.

Rape threatens the social and economic survival of the woman. (Deut 22:29; Exod 22:16–17)			
Rape is a violation of the woman and of her family. (Deut 22:29; Exod 22:16–17)			

Second, God challenges the systems that support the sexual exploitation and devaluation of women, and intervenes graciously on the victim's behalf. When social norms called for the exclusion of women whose sexual morals were in question, Jesus regularly included them in his circle. When social norms called for the exclusion of individuals who were deemed bodily unclean, Jesus regularly included them in his ministry, extolled them for their faith, and considered them to be part of the family of God. The following table offers several instances that demonstrate God's inclusion of women who had been sexually violated or individuals who would have been considered bodily unclean and excluded from the family of God.

Table 10.2. Summary of Inclusion into the Family of God of Those Deemed Inappropriate

Name	Text	Insights
Hagar	Genesis 16 and 21	An Egyptian slave sexually exploited by Sarah and Abraham. God converses with her. She names God. God gives her a promise/blessing to make her son into a great nation.
Rahab	Joshua 2; 6:22, 23; Matthew 1:5; Hebrews 11:31; James 2:25	Prostitute from Jericho who believed God, hid Hebrew spies, and in so doing saved her entire family. Commended for her faith and included in the lineage of Christ.
Bathsheba	2 Samuel 11; Matthew 1:6	Wickedly taken by a lustful David who slept with her, got her pregnant, and killed her husband. Included in the lineage of Christ.
Esther	Esther	A godly Hebrew woman taken into the king of Persia's custody to be groomed for sexual service to the king. God favored her, she became queen and risked her life to save the Jewish people. Esther means "star" and is considered to be a type of Christ.

Sinful woman	Luke 7:36–50	Criticized by Simon the Pharisee, but commended by Jesus for her act of loving service and her faith. Forgiven and saved.
Woman with issue of blood	Matthew 9:20–22	Jesus touched a perpetually unclean woman, healed her, and commended her faith.
Crippled woman	Luke 13:10–17	On the Sabbath, Jesus heals a woman who had been crippled for eighteen years. Calls her a "daughter of Abraham" when only "son of Abraham" was considered a valid term of inclusion into God's family.
Woman caught in adultery	John 8:1–11	Jesus forgives and does not condemn a woman accused of adultery. He releases her and, instead, challenges her accusers.

Undoubtedly, the Scripture provides a consistent witness to God's gracious and merciful interactions with women who were at the mercy of their culture's narrow view of their bodies and sexual histories.

Third and finally, a scriptural witness to sex trafficking survivors depicts God as one who removes the shame associated with the female body and replaces it with honor. Listening to survivors and reading their stories reveals their shared sense of feeling dirty, violated, ashamed, and repulsed as a result of being prostituted. The actions committed against them caused deep shame associated with their bodies. Consequently, it is important to establish the ways God relates to women to take away their bodily shame and replace it with honor. In the Ancient Near East a woman's ability or inability to bear offspring was the source of either honor or shame. Therefore, when we read of God's decision to miraculously make fertile a female body that was infertile, we should understand that he removed their disgrace and replaced it with honor. Sarah (Gen 21:1–2), Hannah (1 Sam 1:19–20), and Elizabeth (Luke 1:23–25) are all examples of God intervening to move a female body from shame to honor. Elizabeth declared: "The Lord has done this for me ... In these days he has shown his favor and taken away my disgrace among the people" (Luke 1:25 NIV). Furthermore, the body—both literal/physical and metaphorical—is associated with nurture (Eph 5:29), love (1 John 4:7–8), purity/cleanliness (Matt 8:2), mutuality (1 Cor 12; Acts 4:32–37), protection (John 15:13), and fellowship (Gal 2:9; 1 John 4:7) in the New Testament. Ministering the truth of God as one who brings honor and care to bodies is an important scriptural concept for survivors of sex trafficking.

This chapter has offered a two-part, contextualized approach to ministry among victims/survivors of sex trafficking, taking into account the relational dynamics of the system and a scriptural hermeneutic. My concluding prayer is that the Holy Spirit will lead you as you engage in contextualized ministry to people involved in sexual exploitation. I hope that some of the resources, information, and perspectives shared in this chapter will be both foundational and useful for my fellow co-laborers in the gospel of Jesus in today's world.

Bibliography

Behnke, Alison. *Up for Sale: Human Trafficking and Modern Slavery.* Minneapolis: Twenty-First Century Books, 2015.

Brouer, Deirdre. "Voices of Outrage Against Rape: Textual Evidence in Judges 19." *Priscilla Papers* 21, no. 1 (Winter 2014). https://www.cbeinternational.org/resource/voices-outrage-against-rape/.

Cohen, Adam Jason. "A Dazzling Look Inside the Don 'Magic' Juan Payer's Ball." *Chicago Magazine*, December 5, 2017. https://www.chicagomag.com/style-shopping/december-2017/players-ball-2017/.

Dixit, Jay. "Sex Ed: Keeping Up with the Johns." *Psychology Today*, November 1, 2009. https://www.psychologytoday.com/intl/articles/200911/sex-ed-keeping-the-johns.

Elliott, Denise, Paula Bjelajacm, and Roger Fallot. "Trauma-Informed or Trauma Denied: Principles and Implementation of Trauma-Informed Services for Women." *Journal of Community Psychology* 33, no. 2 (July 2005): 461–77.

Farley, Melissa. "Prostitution Is Sexual Violence." *Psychiatric Times* 21, no. 12 (October 1, 2004). https://www.psychiatrictimes.com/view/prostitution-sexual-violence.

Gerassi, Lara B., and Andrea J. Nichols. *Sex Trafficking and Commercial Exploitation: Prevention, Advocacy and Trauma-Informed Practice.* New York: Springer Publishing Company, 2017.

Hayes, Sophie. *Trafficked: My Story of Surviving, Escaping, and Transcending Abduction into Prostitution.* Naperville, IL: Sourcebooks, Inc, 2013.

Hof, Dennis. *The Art of the Pimp.* New York: Regan Arts, 2015.

Johnson, Becca C. "Aftercare for Survivors of Human Trafficking." *Social Work & Christianity* 39, no. 4 (Winter 2012): 370–89.

Lloyd, Rachel. *Girls Like Us: Fighting for a World Where Girls are Not for Sale.* New York: Harper Collins, 2011.

Miller, Robin. Conference on Counseling Sex Trafficking Survivors: Understanding and Treating Complex Trauma. Western Seminary. Portland, OR. March 11, 2016.

Peterson-Iyer, Karen. "Prostitution: A Feminist Ethical Analysis." *Journal of Feminist Studies in Religion* 14, no. 4 (Fall 1998): 19–44. https://www.jstor.org/stable/25002334.

Pierce, Ronald W., Rebecca Merrill Groothuis, and Gordon D. Fee, eds. *Discovering Biblical Equality: Complementarity without Hierarchy.* Westmont: InterVarsity Press, 2005.

Trafficking in Persons Report. Washington, DC: United States Department of State, 2015. 5 December 2015. http://www.state.gov/documents/organization/245365.pdf.

Wan, Enoch. "A Critique of Charles Krafts' Use/Misuse of Communication and Social Sciences in Biblical Interpretation and Missiological Formulation." In *Missiology and the Social Sciences.* Pasadena, CA: William Carey Library, 1994. http://ojs.globalmissiology.org/index.php/english/article/view/120/349.

Washington, Eryka. "Woman Sold into Sex Trafficking for $10 at Age 11 Shares Her Story." *News 6*, September 21, 2016. http://www.clickorlando.com/news/investigators/woman-sold-into-sex-trafficking-for-10-at-age-11-shares-her-story.

Youth.Gov. "SAMHSA's Concept of Trauma and Guidance for a Trauma-Informed Approach." https://youth.gov/feature-article/samhsas-concept-trauma-and-guidance-trauma-informed-approach.

Chapter 11

Examining Ourselves
Working for Freedom in a World of Exploitation[1]

Marion L. S. Carson

There are millions of victims of trafficking all over the world, and many Christians are involved in rescuing and caring for them. But how can Christians help prevent such suffering in the first place? The antebellum Quakers, inspired by the Golden Rule, were able to stand up against the religious and cultural norms of their day and play a crucial part in the abolition movement. Today, we too can speak out against slavery, but are we willing to challenge the prevailing norms, even within our own faith communities? If our message is to be credible, we must first examine ourselves.

The Story of a Victim

He had arrived in Glasgow via London on the overnight bus. Over a hot cup of coffee in our city center drop-in, and with the aid of a volunteer who could speak his language, he told us some of his story.[2] He had left Africa for Europe in order to escape terrorism and warfare and had managed to find his way to Belgium. He had hoped that he would be able to claim asylum, acculturate, and make a life for himself in Europe. But like so many others he found himself vulnerable to exploitation. He was delighted when a Belgian farmer offered him employment, and he worked hard for him for many weeks. He was given very basic accommodations along with some others, and was provided with food. At first it seemed to be a good arrangement, but it soon became obvious that the farmer had no intention of paying him. When he asked for his wages, he was given a short shrift. He decided to leave—but where could he go? He opted for the UK and eventually arrived in Glasgow—knowing no one and speaking no English. After several nights sleeping rough, he was exhausted, hungry, and bewildered.

Victims of exploitation and trafficking are found all over the world. They work in the hospitality sector, on construction sites, in private homes

---

1 An expanded version of this chapter was previously published as an ebook, *Freedom from Exploitation: Christian Responses to Modern-Day Slavery*, William Carey Publishing, 2023.
2 The author serves as Chaplain at Glasgow City Mission in Glasgow, Scotland.

as domestic servants, in beauty salons and in brothels.[3] Although the work they do is varied, they have this in common: they have been tricked or coerced into working for people who have no intention of paying them, or of allowing them freedom to live their lives. Human traffickers exploit the most vulnerable in society—those in poverty, the displaced, and the young. Many victims have been exploited while escaping religious or ethnic persecution, or, like this man (I'll call him Thierry), fleeing war and terrorism. And their numbers are increasing. As I write, nearly seven million people, mostly women and children, have had to leave Ukraine as a result of the invasion of their country by Russian forces. According to the United Nations Office on Drugs and Crime, "over 13,000 unaccompanied and separated children from Ukraine were registered in the European Union (EU) as of 6 May 2022, a subgroup of whom were orphaned due to the war, or were already orphans in institutional care."[4] In their displacement and desperation, they are highly vulnerable to exploitation by human traffickers who know whom to target. Early in the war it was reported that many children had gone missing on the Ukrainian-Polish border.[5]

At our drop-in center, it is our privilege to be able to work with victims of exploitation, to learn something of their stories, and help them as best we can. We are able to offer a safe space, hot meals, English language classes, and assistance in the lengthy and complex United Kingdom asylum process. We can also provide a temporary community for making friends and learning new skills, such as computing. Working alongside social workers, housing officers, and other charitable organizations we can ensure that displaced persons are given safe accommodation as well as financial, medical, and psychological help. In Thierry's case, we were able to help him find the right support, and I am happy to report that life has turned around for him. He has started the long journey of learning how to live with the trauma of his past and in hope for a more stable life.[6]

I say it is our privilege to work with people like Thierry, and indeed it is. But we are very much aware that we are only scratching the surface of what is a tragic situation for millions of people throughout the world. Many more will remain enslaved for years, hidden from view, robbed of the hope of freedom, and in physical danger from those who exploit them. We are also very aware that we are dealing with the damage done by those who exploit others—serving people whose lives have been wrecked by criminals who

---

3 Kara, *Modern Slavery*.
4 United Nations Office on Drugs and Crime, *Conflict in Ukraine*.
5 Mitchell, "Thousands of Vulnerable Children."
6 Hemmings, Jakobowitz, Abas, et al., "Responding to the Health Needs."

saw them only as commodities. Those who do manage to escape are likely to suffer from psychological wounds which will affect them for years to come. They will need a great deal of help to learn to live in freedom without becoming isolated or exploited all over again.

Our ministry at Glasgow City Mission, like so many others, works with the victims of exploitation and human trafficking. We are able to do so through the generous financial support of churches and individuals and by many dedicated volunteers who give up their time to pray, listen to, and walk alongside people like Thierry. We would much rather, however, that such exploitation did not happen at all. And we believe that it is the responsibility of Christians not only to work with victims but to help prevent such suffering in the first place.

But how can individual Christians and church communities do this? For many, it might feel like a problem that is "out there," well divorced from our everyday experience. Most of us are unlikely to come across enslaved people in our daily lives, and we can feel ill-equipped to do anything. We know there are people like Thierry, and we would love to prevent further suffering, but what can we do about such a huge problem which affects millions throughout the world?

Learning from History

Christians can learn a great deal from the Quakers of antebellum America, who did so much to speak out against the injustice of slavery.[7] In their time, slavery was the norm, and very few people had ever questioned it. Most Christians took it for granted that they should be able to own slaves, and found support for their view in Scripture. For example, it was argued on the basis of texts such as Leviticus 25:44–46 that slavery was commanded by God and part of the correct ordering of society.[8] The Bible also was used to teach those who were enslaved that they should obey their masters as a matter of divine command: "Let all who are under the yoke of slavery regard their masters as worthy of all honor, so that the name of God and the teaching may not be blasphemed" (1 Tim 6:1).

The Quakers, however, began to challenge this—how could slave ownership be compatible with the biblical principles of freedom and equality? They began to stand up against the values and norms of the prevailing culture, both within the church and in society as a whole. They were well aware of the biblical texts which could be used to support slavery, but as they

---

7 Carey and Plank, *Quakers and Abolition*; Soderlund, *Quakers and Slavery*.
8 Irons, *Origins of Proslavery Christianity*; Tise, *Proslavery: A History*.

considered the matter, the so-called Golden Rule became crucial to their thinking: "So in everything, do to others what you would have them do to you, for this sums up the Law and the Prophets" (Matt 7:12 NIV). For them, Jesus's words encapsulated all that was necessary to grasp that slavery must be against the will of God. They realized that they themselves would not want to be enslaved, and so they could not inflict this on others. Inevitably, their stance drew criticism and hostility, in particular from Christians who found support for slave-holding in the biblical writings.[9] Nevertheless, they stood up against the prevailing culture, both in society and amongst Christians, and played a large, crucial part in the story of abolition.

For us, too, the maxim "Do unto others what you would have them do to you," can be the impetus to do something about modern-day slavery. Perhaps the most obvious way is to support and be involved in services which enable people like Thierry to build up new lives for themselves. By volunteering in charities like Glasgow City Mission, we can bring God's love into the lives of those who have experienced years of exploitation and of being treated as commodities. We can help ensure that their immediate needs are met and draw alongside them as they become used to freedom and all that it entails. We can support such work with our financial resources and faithful prayer. We can welcome the victims of trafficking into our church communities and help them to rebuild their lives.[10]

There is also much that we can do to ensure that exploitation and enslavement are unacceptable in our societies.[11] Like the Quakers, we can join the prophetic tradition of seeking justice and mercy in our communities, in business, and from our lawmakers. Like the Quakers, we can campaign against the injustice that is human trafficking and become involved in awareness-raising. We can speak out against the commodification of human beings, and lobby people in power, not just in the churches but the political world too. We can boycott those companies whose goods are produced by people who are being exploited. We can support charities worldwide which work to rescue those who are enslaved, and encourage collaboration amongst the many organizations engaged in this work.[12]

So far so good—but it is not enough to identify and treat the signs and symptoms of any disease—it is important also to tackle the causes. The causes of human trafficking are varied and complex. They include the lack

---

9 Carson, *Human Trafficking, the Bible*.
10 Pratt, *Slavery-Free Communities*.
11 Bales, *Ending Slavery*.
12 Christian Organisations against Trafficking Network.

of opportunity, capitalism, inequality (racial, social, religious, and gender).[13] These are political matters, of course, and there are many Christians who are involved in trying to change things at this level. But very often, the root cause lies much deeper. People find themselves exploited because of human failings—greed for wealth and lust for power over others. On this point Christians do have something to say; the prophetic tradition which makes itself heard throughout our canon of Scripture, and in which Jesus himself stands, warns us against these very things.[14]

What about Us?

However, if our message is to be credible, we must first, undertake some self-examination. Are we modeling the kind of living that we are demanding of others? First, we must ask ourselves about our priorities as Christian communities. Do we really want to work for justice and mercy for the most vulnerable in our societies or are we more concerned with preserving our own way of being Christians? The Old Testament prophets railed against those who were more concerned with their own comfort than with exposing corruption and oppression in society (e.g., Jer 22:13–19; Mal 3:5; Amos 5:12–15), and Jesus himself made it very clear that compassion and mercy should take precedence over observance of the law (e.g., Luke 13:10–17). Christians cannot be inward looking—real worship must always result in a concern for the poor both in our own communities and in society as a whole. Second, are we in any way colluding with the values which are at the root of human trafficking? This means that we must ask ourselves about our attitude to money and possessions. Are we driven by love of money or love of God? Jesus's words are unequivocal—you cannot serve both God and mammon (Matt 6:24). For Christians living in consumerist cultures, this issue can be particularly hard to face. It can be easy to fall into the trap of materialism and the desire to accumulate wealth, while being blind to the powers that drive us.[15]

The exploitation of human beings is not only rooted in economics, however, which brings us to a third question. What is our attitude toward others, in particular those who are different from ourselves? It is much easier to exploit someone if we believe that they are inferior to us because of race, religion, social status, or gender. Much commercial sexual exploitation of women, for example, comes about because they are seen merely as objects, and many people are treated as commodities because they are considered

---

13 Enrile, *Ending Human Trafficking*, 51–70.
14 Gushee and Stassen, *Kingdom Ethics*.
15 Welby, *Dethroning Mammon*.

to come from an inferior race or religion.[16] So, we must examine ourselves about these too. Attitudes towards race, religion, social status, and gender are very much culture-bound, and throughout our history Christians have wrestled with when we should adhere to the norms of the prevailing culture and when we should challenge them. Sometimes this has caused great problems within the church itself, as in the case of slavery. Scripture attests to this in the early church itself as, for example, in the letter to the Galatians. In Galatia, the church was being assailed with demands from people that they should conform to certain religious practices amid assertions that those who did not conform were to be considered religiously inferior. Paul argued strongly against this capitulation and insisted that it was an attempt to place the Galatians under a "yoke of slavery" (Gal 5:1). He objected to the idea that believers from pagan, rather than Jewish, backgrounds were inferior Christians. Moreover, he widened the parameters of his argument and declared that in baptism *all* become equal: "There is no longer Jew or Greek, there is no longer slave or free, there is no longer male and female" (Gal 3:28). These famous words do not mean that Paul is saying that racial, social, and gender differences be disregarded altogether. He is saying that the cultural and religious presuppositions which can govern our thinking, and whose influence we may not necessarily be aware of, can come to dominate our communities to the extent that our ability to love one another can become compromised (Gal 5:6).[17]

A Challenge to Ourselves

It is a privilege to be part of Thierry's life, and to see hope restored to him. But important as practical and emotional support for him and those like him may be, our responsibilities do not stop there. As followers of Jesus, we are called to "proclaim release to the captives, and recovery of sight to the blind, to let the oppressed go free" (Luke 4:18). We therefore have an obligation to tackle the causes of human trafficking by being a prophetic voice against the values and norms which allow it to flourish.[18] However, if our voice is to be effective, we must first be willing to examine our own values and ask how far our own communities live up to the standards that we advocate for. The prophetic tradition demands that our communities be characterized by compassion and mercy rather than complacent insularity. Jesus himself challenges us to follow him rather than dedicate ourselves to the accumulation of wealth; Paul's words

---

16 US State Department, "Trafficking in Persons Report."
17 Horrel, *Solidarity and Difference*, 124–49.
18 Pratt, *Slavery-Free Communities*.

in Galatians challenge us to reflect on our own attitudes with regard to race, gender, and social status in our churches.

All these voices in the Scripture challenge us to ask ourselves how far we prioritize our cultural and religious norms at the expense of the freedom to love and serve each other as Christ's new creation. These can be difficult questions for churches to acknowledge, let alone address, but we ignore them at our peril, for if our communities do not model what we want to advocate for the rest of the world, our prophetic voice in wider society can only be weakened. It is vital that we Christians willingly, prayerfully, and humbly examine our attitudes regarding money and possessions, social status, and differences of gender, ethnicity, and religion (including our own theological differences) if we are to be credible witnesses for social justice in our world. At the very least, we must be willing to acknowledge our own weaknesses and prejudices as we try to understand where our cultures, both religious and secular, have compromised our ability to love our neighbors, even within our own communities. It takes courage, as the Quakers well knew, to challenge accepted norms, even, and perhaps especially within the church—but if we are to have a prophetic voice in this world and help prevent the enslavement and exploitation of people like Thierry, we must first examine ourselves.

Bibliography

Bales, Kevin. *Ending Slavery: How We Free Today's Slaves*. Berkeley: University of California, 2007.

Carey, Brycchan, and Geoffrey Plank, eds. *Quakers and Abolition*. Champaign: University of Illinois Press, 2018.

Carson, Marion L. S. *Human Trafficking, the Bible and the Church: An Interdisciplinary Study*. Eugene, OR: Cascade, 2016.

Christian Organizations against Trafficking Network. Homepage. Accessed September 12, 2022. https://www.coatnet.org/.

Enrile, Annalisa V. *Ending Human Trafficking and Modern-Day Slavery: Freedom's Journey*. Thousand Oaks: Sage Publications, 2018.

Gushee, David P., and Glen H. Stassen. *Kingdom Ethics: Following Jesus in Contemporary Context*. 2nd ed. Grand Rapids, MI: Eerdmans, 2006.

Hemmings, S., S. Jakobowitz, M. Abas, et al. "Responding to the Health Needs of Survivors of Human Trafficking: A Systematic Review." *BMC Health Services Research* 16:320 (2016). https://bmchealthservres.biomedcentral.com/counter/pdf/10.1186/s12913-016-1538-8.pdf.

Horrell, David G. *Solidarity and Difference: A Contemporary Reading of Paul's Ethics*. London: T&T Clark, 2005.

Irons, Charles F. *The Origins of Proslavery Christianity: White and Black Evangelicals in Colonial and Antebellum Virginia*. Chapel Hill: University of North Carolina Press, 2008.

Kara, Shiddharth. *Modern Slavery: A Global Perspective*. New York: Columbia University Press, 2017.

Mitchell, Sue. "Ukraine: Thousands of Vulnerable Children Unaccounted For." *BBC*, March 11, 2022. https://www.bbc.com/news/world-europe-60692442.

Pratt, Dan, ed. *Slavery-Free Communities: Emerging Theologies and Faith Responses to Modern Slavery*. London: SCM, 2021.

Soderlund, Jean R. *Quakers and Slavery: A Divided Spirit*. Princeton: Princeton University Press, 2016.

Tise, Larry A. *Proslavery: A History of the Defense of Slavery in America 1701–1840*. Athens: University of Georgia Press, 1987.

United Nations Office on Drugs and Crime. "Conflict in Ukraine: Key Evidence on Risks of Trafficking in Persons and Smuggling of Migrants." Updated December 22, 2022. https://www.unodc.org/documents/data-and-analysis/tip/Conflict_Ukraine_TIP_2022.pdf.

United States Department of State Office to Combat Trafficking in Persons. "2022 Trafficking in Persons Report." Accessed September 18, 2022. https://www.state.gov/reports/2022-trafficking-in-persons-report/.

Welby, J. *Dethroning Mammon: Making Money Serve Grace*. London: Bloomsbury Continuum, 2016.

Chapter 12

Missional Transnationals

Coming Full Circle

Sadiri Joy Tira

I had the pleasure of representing the Jaffray Centre for its "Foundation for Global Ministry" series in Davao City, Philippines from July 13–31, 2012. I taught two courses: Issues in Twenty-First Century Christian Mission at the Koinonia Theological Seminary (KTS), and the other with a team headed by Dr. Charles Cook of Ambrose University College and Seminary at Christian Colleges of Southeast Asia, Alliance Graduate School (CCSA-AGS).

My hosts while in Davao were members of the Ang family, a Chinese-Filipino family, who like me, are Canadian citizens. The first generations of the Ang family left the Philippines at the height of the Marcos Martial Law regime. Disillusioned by the political situation in their homeland, engineer Michael Ang Sr. and his wife left their thriving business in the Philippines to settle down in Canada. They quickly set up shop in Canada and slowly and steadily grew their Canadian business venture. Their children were raised in Western Alberta and were university-educated in the Canadian system. Decades after putting down roots in Canada, Mr. and Mrs. Ang, along with their grown children and grandchildren, embarked on an international missions initiative that crossed Philippine and Canadian borders by operating in both places simultaneously.

I was encouraged by the Ang's initiative to provide Filipinos with quality theological education through Canadian theological educators and hosting visiting professors like myself in their home during their teaching ministries in Davao. I was also quite intrigued by their weekly tradition of hosting Wednesday night dinners for distinguished members of the Davao city community for their outreach program.

In the Philippines it is difficult to reach out to the upper echelon of the society. But the Angs have been successfully inviting and hosting hundreds of people for weekend fellowships in their natural way for almost twenty years. The global scope of their mission as a family is more than inspiring and only eternity will reveal the impact of their hospitality.

The Ang family is a diaspora family who has come full circle—from leaving the Philippines to returning to their homeland, to make a "difference" while maintaining their Canadian roots. Their missions' activities are what I would call transnational, or transcending national borders. They are members of a growing group of what my mentor, former International Director of the Lausanne Committee for World Evangelization Dr. Ted Yamamori, refers to as missional transnationals.

In May 2012 while visiting Ukraine for the opening of the Diaspora Center at the Ukrainian Evangelical Theological Seminary (UETS), I asked Dr. Yamamori, what he meant by *missional transnationals*. His reply was "I don't know exactly, but if I find some time in the future, I will write about this subject. So why don't you write about it now?" My response was that I had no idea whether people were already writing about these missional transnationals, but I determined to attempt to describe what we both meant.

The term *transnationalism* was originally used to describe a part of the economic globalization process. Joseph Stiglitz provides the definition: "The closer integration of the countries and peoples of the world which has been brought about by the enormous reduction of costs of transportation and communication, and the breaking down of artificial barriers to the flows of goods, services, capital, knowledge, and (to a lesser extent) people across borders."[1] Geographers, historians, sociologists, anthropologists, and political scientists were quick to adopt the term. It was then further refined by sociologists Luis Eduardo Guarnizo, Alejandro Portes, and William Haller: "Transnationals are a new class of immigrants, economic entrepreneurs, or political activists who conduct cross-border activities on a regular basis."[2]

On the other hand, and in line with the topic of this chapter is the term *transmigrant*, developed by anthropologist Nina Glick Schiller, referring to "immigrants whose daily lives depend on multiple and constant interconnections across international borders and whose public identities are configured in relationship to more than one nation-state."[3]

For our purposes, *missional transnationals* would refer to "migrants whose missions initiatives regularly transcend borders." This is an ongoing, cross-border missions involvement. This involvement goes beyond the intermittent short-term missions (STM) trips. I am referring specifically to Christians such as the Angs who are simultaneously doing ongoing missions "here" and "there." I have some other friends like them.

Like the Angs, Ro and Cecille Euroba immigrated to Canada in the 1970s. They established themselves in Canada as successful professionals—Ro as a mechanical engineer, and Cecille as a nurse. As they built and developed their Canadian identities, they continued to maintain close cultural and

---

1 Stiglitz, *Globalization and Its Discontents*, 9.
2 Guarnizo, Portes, and Haller, "Assimilation and Transnationalism," 1213.
3 Schiller, "From Immigrant to Transmigrant," 48.

family ties to the Philippines. They read up on local news, regularly visited the homeland, and supported missions causes when opportunities arose.

After raising their two daughters, quintessential second-generation Filipino-Canadians, Ro and Cecille celebrated early retirement from their jobs. However, as soon as they had retired, they embarked on a new transnational ministry. They set up a school in their hometown in the Philippines and devoted themselves to providing the townsfolk with courses on health, public safety, evangelism, and discipleship. Today, they spend half of the year in the Philippines and the other half in Canada.

The Angs and the Eurobas are what I call *missional transnationals*. Transnationals are on the rise as scattered people become established in new lands and return "home" to make a difference. Imagine if we could motivate and mobilize these transnationals to join the missional transnational force?

I want to give you an example of what could be. Despite the geographic proximity between Cuba and the United States (Cuba being only about one hundred miles from the coast of Florida), the two countries continue to have strained relations, and free travel between them is limited. What would happen if the borders between these two countries were opened and the Cuban transmigrants or transnationals flood "back home?" Imagine the massive trans-border movements that would ensue. Can you imagine what opportunities could arise if the Americans of Cuban descent are reached, discipled, and strategically trained in evangelism and discipleship? Imagine their roles in kingdom building, theological education, leadership development, holistic missions, church planting, and even in the political arena as proponents of transformative legislations.

Now think of the Chinese, the South East Asian, the African, Korean, Latino, Japanese, Slavic, Arab, and Jewish transnationals?

The Lausanne Movement seeks to bring the whole gospel to the whole world, and is motivating, equipping, and mobilizing the transnationals among the scattered people to take part.

Bibliography

Guarnizo, Luis Eduardo, Alejandro Portes, and William Haller. "Assimilation and Transnationalism: Determinants of Transnational Political Action among Contemporary Migrants." *American Journal of Sociology* 108, no. 6 (2003): 1211–48.

Schiller, Nina Slick. "From Immigrant to Transmigrant: Theorising Transnational Migration." *Anthropological Quarterly* 68, no. 1 (January 1995): 48–63.

Stiglitz, J. E. *Globalization and Its Discontents*. New York: W.W. Norton & Co., 2002.

Chapter 13
Rooted in Spirituality, Committed to Missions
My Tribute to the Late Dr. Thomas Wang

Juno Wang

As you approach the end of this book, I would like to pay tribute to the late Dr. Thomas Wang. His spiritual life led him to global diaspora missions as a person of the Chinese diaspora in the US. I pray that his example will encourage believers in Jesus Christ to get involved in today's diaspora missions to everyone and everywhere.

One day, after a church service, I picked up a mission newsletter. I saw a photo of Dr. Thomas Wang standing in a bread line in Russia. As a new believer, I was not familiar with who he was or what missions were all about. I could not understand why he would go to one of the countries of the former Soviet Union right after its dissolution. Little did I know then that he would eventually become my boss for nearly eighteen years and later my godfather. I was led by God to work in his office, but I did not meet him until he returned from a short-term mission trip to Russia a month later. Upon their return, the entire team was sick with a bad case of flu, but they were rejoicing over the great response to the gospel that resulted from the trip.

Gradually, through handling his correspondence, I discovered Wang's global leadership through his writings and photos with global leaders, including the late Dr. and Mrs. Billy Graham, with whom he was a guest. The late Dr. Ralph Winter, was also a very supportive friend of Dr. Wang. In fact, our office was once located in his university campus in Pasadena, California.

Why would a person who was part of the Chinese diaspora in the US get involved in diaspora missions and make an impact in missions as a global leader? This article will be a brief exploration of this question, with a focus on Dr. Wang's life and global diaspora missions. Due to space limitations, names and years will be omitted. Additionally, I will share a few insights from my personal experience. But first and foremost, I would like to express my gratitude to every leader and supporter of Dr. Wang around the world. As Dr. Wang often told the staff, his ministry was a team effort with people like us—for God's kingdom and glory.

His Journey of Dispersion

Dr. Wang was born in Beijing, China, to a third-generation Christian family. His parents were leaders in Mr. Wang Ming-Dao's church. Wang was fluent in both English and Mandarin due to his American schooling from elementary to high school and his Chinese home tutoring during his childhood. He came to Christ at the age of eleven while attending an evangelical meeting led by Dr. John Sung. Both Mr. Wang and Dr. Sung had a very profound influence on Dr. Wang's life and ministry to be faithful and obedient to God and to be transparent despite criticism and opposition.

In his late teens, Thomas Wang was internally displaced to Inner China during the Sino-Japanese War. Several years after the war, Wang was externally displaced by the Communists to Hong Kong and then Taiwan. He was repeatedly forced out of his home and comfort zone. After graduating from a seminary in Taiwan, he was an itinerant evangelist in Europe for a time. Later, Wang and his family immigrated to the US for seminary training and ministry opportunities. As a part of the diaspora in foreign lands, the biblical teachings Wang received from childhood to adolescence instilled in him a strong identity in Christ and the kingdom. He used his bicultural skills and migrant experience for missions to all peoples.

Wang did not permanently settle in the US. Instead, he moved his family to Hong Kong for a decade and traveled the world for missions until his passing. His more than fifty years of global diaspora missions began with his service with the Chinese Christian Mission (CCM), Chinese Coordination Center for World Evangelization (CCCOWE), and later with the Lausanne Committee for World Evangelization, AD2000 and Beyond Movement, Great Commission Center International (GCCI), Back to Jerusalem Movement (BTJ), and America, Return to God Movement (ARTG).

Did he not get tired from traveling, jet lag, sleep problems, and other related issues? I noticed that he struggled more as he got older, but he persevered for the kingdom. During my time working with Dr. Wang, the phrase which I heard him say the most was "Kingdom mindset."

A Leader with a Kingdom Mindset

Thomas Wang was a catalyst and a visionary who had very different leadership gifts and anointing from God that many Christians leaders often misunderstood. He was recognized for his gift of mission leadership and was a man with a big heart.

Dr. Wang seized many ministry opportunities presented to him, guided by his certainty of God's wisdom. He remained steadfast in his vision despite human opposition. When faced with criticisms, Wang would seek the largeness of heart, similar to what God gave to King Solomon (1 Kgs 4:29 KJV), in order to keep his focus on God and his kingdom as the main thing. His kingdom mindset transcended his cultural and ethnic boundaries, and he urged Chinese churches to grow and take on the responsibility of world missions.

Chinese churches can be difficult to partner with if they lack a kingdom mindset, as they may be egocentric and ethnocentric; leaders may be narrow-minded, self-exalted, and pursuing power.[1] Wang called on the churches to work in unity, regardless of labels, organizations, or self-imposed divisions, to call all peoples to repentance and return to God's kingdom. For Dr. Wang, it was kingdom missions and kingdom partnership for the kingdom growth that mission leaders should strive for.[2] It was his desire to see the Chinese church grow up from being a mission field to being a missionary. He believed that every believer should bear the responsibility of world missions. As the spirituality continues to develop, the commission for missions becomes greater.[3]

Integration of the Great Commission with the Great Commandments

At GCCI, where I worked under Dr. Wang, the motto was "rooted in spirituality, committed to missions." GCCI was a pioneering missions agency that emphasized spiritual formation and called the church back to the biblical mandate[4] to expand God's kingdom by integrating the Great Commission with the two greatest commandments. Wang received vision and strength from the Lord through his vertical relationship with God, and then through his horizontal relationships to carry out missions to all peoples.

Thomas Wang was an evangelical who sought the empowerment of the Holy Spirit in all aspects of life—his being, doing, and knowing. He recognized that there is a battle for authority and principalities. He also recognized the urgent need for the church to depend profoundly on the Holy Spirit's strength. This led Thomas Wang to his final movement; to call America to return to God. And call her people towards love for God and obedience to him. Dr.

---

1 Wang, 中華民族最後的轉捩點 [The Last Turning Point of the Chinese Race], 16–17.
2 Thomas Wang, *Kingdom Story*, iv.
3 Leung, "Rev. Thomas Wang."
4 Chan, "Great Commission Center International," 9 (under "Publication").

Wang expressed his deep gratitude for American missionary efforts in China in the past and as a Chinese diaspora missions leader in the U.S., he engaged himself in missions among the Chinese in the USA.

He and the staff always began the day with a morning group devotion, and I often saw him bow his head to pray when I walked into his office. As a leader, Wang constantly reminded himself to be humble and vigilant against his flesh of being prideful. He was a person of prayer, integrity, and faith.

Dr. Wang frequently emphasized the importance of taking action in accordance with one's faith. He drew inspiration from the biblical account of the priests carrying the ark, who had to step into the Jordan River before the waters parted (Josh 3:13). Wang believed that we must leap by faith with actions rather than be a passive bystander. I have learned from his life that it took faith to plant a church where the gospel has not been preached, and it took more faith to stand up and stand firm for God and to finish well. What motivated him for lifelong involvement in missions was to serve God and bring the gospel to the world in obedience to his mandate to men to proclaim the gospel and make disciples of men.

He believed that Jesus was the creditor, and he was the debtor, and that the method of paying off this debt was through his deep involvement in evangelism and missions. What motivated him for his lifelong involvement in missions was to pay back the "gospel debt," similar to the apostle Paul who felt indebted to everyone who had not yet heard the gospel (Rom 1:14). Therefore, the apostle became his example of being a missionary, and the feeling of paying back the gospel debt grew stronger.[5] Wang obeyed the commandments to fulfill the Great Commission.

Global Diaspora Missions Involvements

The early church practiced four types of diaspora missions: missions to the diaspora (Acts 1–7), missions through the diaspora (Acts 8–12), missions by and beyond the diaspora (Acts 13–28), and missions with the diaspora (Acts 11–20).[6] Dr. Wang was involved in these four types for his global diaspora missions, which included evangelism, mobilization, networking, partnership, publication, spiritual formation, and training for the gospel debt.

Wang began his global missions to Chinese and all peoples while he was dispersed in Taiwan. This section will focus on his global diaspora missions after leaving Taiwan, which can be categorized into three major stages based on the organizations and movements he served.

---

5 Gospel Herald, "緬懷王永信牧師:一輩子只為還福音的債" [Remembering Rev. Thomas Yung-Hsin Wang].

6 Wan, "Practice of Diaspora Missions" (under "Archives").

CCM and CCCOWE

Wang founded CCM in the US and Taiwan[7] after receiving a vision to proclaim the gospel to Chinese people worldwide. CCM ministered to members of Chinese diaspora communities through evangelism, and then discipled them to become worshipping communities and congregations.

Fifteen years later, Wang helped to establish CCCOWE based in Hong Kong, which was the only organized ethnic and spiritual movement in the world at that time. The movement mobilized and empowered local Chinese diasporic individuals and congregations to reach out to their kinsmen through networks of communication in host countries, their homelands, and abroad. It is also a vision for world evangelization among Chinese diaspora churches.[8]

Lausanne and AD 2000

Wang served two terms at CCCOWE before being invited to serve as the executive director of the Lausanne Committee of World Evangelization, and later as the international director of Lausanne II in Manila. While serving at Lausanne, Wang wrote an article titled "By the Year 2000: Is God Trying to Tell Us Something?"[9]—he received overwhelming responses from global leaders. This led him to found and chair the AD 2000 and Beyond Movement. The movement, led by Wang and other third-world leaders, brought the third-world and American mission efforts together.[10] Ralph Winter stated that "motivate" and "network" were the two key words of AD 2000, and it was a marvelous networking movement which expanded around the world.[11] Since that time, the doors for Wang's global diaspora missions were opened wide.

GCCI, BTJ, and ARTG

After retiring from Lausanne, Wang founded GCCI. The organization's policy was to pass the baton when other organizations or local people can take up the responsibility of a certain ministry. GCCI consistently followed this policy.[12]

---

7 馮文莊 and 錢志群, "不能忘卻的懷念—追記王永信牧師的事奉人生"[Unforgettable Memories].
8 Wang, "Our Origin and Development."
9 Wang, "By the Year 2000."
10 Wood, "The AD2000 Movement."
11 Winter, "Mysterious Tension in Missions Today" (under "Past Issues").
12 Chan, 大使命中心感恩紀念特刊 [GCCI Thanksgiving Memorial Special Issue].

GCCI expanded its missions to Chinese diasporas in Hungary, the Pacific Islands, the Persian Gulf, Spain, Russia, and scholars in North America. Additionally, God led GCCI to minister in the form of pre-evangelistic social services among a group of survivors of the Chinese Muslim (Hui people) rebellion who fled from China to Kazakhstan and Kyrgyzstan during the Qing Dynasty.[13]

For global ethnic diaspora missions, GCCI motivated and mobilized diaspora Christians who have acquired the language and are adjusted to the host culture with the shared migrant experience for cross-cultural missions to other ethnic groups in their host countries, homelands, and abroad. It also mobilized non-diasporic Christians, both individually and institutionally, to partner with diasporic groups and congregations.[14]

Wang and GCCI were invited to organize the first training for Nepali churches after the country opened up in 1991. Following this, two Himalayan Conferences of Evangelism were held, with participants from the Himalayan region. The churches were encouraged to unite and evangelize the entire region with the motto "Himalayan people, mission people." Today, this has become a mission movement among Nepalis both within and outside of Nepal.[15]

Furthermore, GCCI rekindled the Back to Jerusalem Movement, a vision God gave to a group of Chinese Christians that was disrupted in 1949. GCCI held the first International Consultation for networking and partnership and promoted the movement outside of mainland China. Since the majority of the population from West China to Jerusalem consists of Jews and Muslims, GCCI mobilized Chinese churches for missions among them through conferences, seminars, and publications for the movement.[16] Wang later retired from GCCI, but he never retired from the gospel debt.

In his late 80s, Wang embarked on his last global diaspora missions to the Roma people (Gypsies) in eight Eastern European countries. He made several trips for this large group of unwelcomed people in Europe to address their desperate physical and spiritual needs.[17] His final movement was to call the West to evangelize the immigrants and diaspora and be involved as instruments of God to show salvation and love to these dispersed people.

Wang mobilized Chinese Christians to express love and concern to America, the nation that has sent missionaries to Chinese people for the

---

13 Chan.
14 Wan, "Practice of Diaspora Missions in Local Congregation."
15 Chan, 大使命中心感恩紀念特刊 [GCCI Thanksgiving Memorial Special Issue].
16 Chan, "Ministry Highlights of the Great Commission."
17 Chan, 大使命中心感恩紀念特刊.

past 200 years. He called for America to return to the faith of her founders through publications, annual letter campaigns to the President and top leaders, and holding prayer rallies. In fact, the last person Wang led to Christ was an American who attended a Christmas evangelistic event that he had organized a few weeks before he passed away.

As Wang awaited to face the Lord whom he had served without any reservations or regrets, I noticed his eyes were filled with faith when I said my final farewell. Like King David, he had served his own generation by the will of God for global missions, and then he fell asleep (Acts 13:36). The baton of missions is now passing on to every believer, and Thomas Wang's life and ministry offer valuable insights for today's missions.

Implications for Today's Missions

Nowadays, people are on the move in all directions, blurring the boundaries between local and global. Our world has become glocal, so must our missions. Diaspora missions encompasses both local and global aspects.

Glocalization with Tides of Opportunities

In 2020, it was estimated that there were around 281 million international migrants worldwide, meaning that 1 in 30 people in the world is a migrant.[18] Glocalization refers to the interdependent relationship between the local and the global. Global realities shape local contexts,[19] and therefore, local missions have a rippling effect on global missions. Thus, the tide of diaspora mission opportunities is glocal.

Traditional Missions vs. Diaspora Missions

Traditional mission is polarized or dichotomized in focus and territorial with a sharp distinction between here and there; and movement is linear, meaning it goes one way. It is geographically divided and compartmentalized as a discipline.[20] In contrast, diaspora missions focus on holistic missions and contextualization integrating evangelism and social concern. It is deterritorialized and simultaneously local and global conceptually. In perspective, it is not geographically divided but borderless—it is transnational and global.[21] Dr. Enoch Wan calls everyone to engage in diaspora missions and to integrate the Great Commission with the great commandments relationally.[22]

---

18 International Organization for Migration, "World Migration Report 2022."
19 Hill, *Global Church*, 26–7.
20 Hesselgrave, *Paradigms in Conflict*, 348.
21 Wan and Tira, "Diaspora Missiology," 11 (under "Diaspora Studies").
22 Wan, "Global People and Diaspora Missiology" (under "Conference Details").

The Great Commandments for Gospel Debt

The two greatest commandments that Jesus spoke are to love God and to love our neighbors. In addition, we are sent to invite all peoples to enter his diverse kingdom. When we do that in obedience, we glorify the One who sends us because of our absolute obedience to his will and lordship. Diaspora missions requires us to practice strategic stewardship for our relational accountability to God and the unsaved[23] for our gospel debt. It is missions to every person outside his kingdom everywhere, and it supplements traditional missiology.[24]

Identities and Transformation

How to maintain the identity of culture, family, and religion, while at the same time learning and adapting to the culture of the new land, is a significant challenge for most diasporic people. Diasporic people look at acculturation differently (depending on their age when they migrated, their life cycle, other issues[25]) than those who are born in the host country to parents of first- or second- generation diasporas.[26] We need to be like the apostle Paul to embrace and use our bicultural diasporic roots for today's diaspora missions.[27] The shared migrant experience helps ethnic diaspora Christians not only to empathize and understand diasporic people, but also to help them find their new identity in Christ and the kingdom. Once we understand that our identity in the kingdom transcends beyond any worldly identities, we will be transformed into disciples and missionaries.[28]

People are unimpressed by mere talk, but they are in need of seeing personal transformation by the Spirit and genuine love expressed corporately.[29] Our transformation comes from the transcendental Triune God who is graciously active in our relational reality of being, belonging, and becoming.[30] We should see diasporas from God's perspective.

---

23 Wan, "Rethinking Missiology in the Context of the 21st Century" (under "Journal Publications").
24 Wan and Tira, "Diaspora Missiology."
25 McIntosh and McMahan, *Being the Church in a Multi-Ethnic Community*, 126.
26 Dunaetz, "Three Models of Acculturation," 130–31.
27 Caldwell, "Diaspora Ministry in the Book of Acts," 103.
28 Nussbaum, *A Reader's Guide to Transforming Mission*, 23.
29 Green, *Evangelism in the Early Church*, 19–20.
30 Wan and Raibley, "Introducing Relational Interactionism," in *Transformational Change in Christian Ministry*, edited by Wan and Raibley, 13.

Conclusion

What is God communicating to us through the rising tides of opportunities? Loving those from the diasporas, whether similar to us or not, requires us to draw upon the Spirit's power. It frees us from our comfort zones, disobedience, fear, limitations, and all forms of weakness. With humility and obedience, we place our trust in the Lord to enact his will through us by his grace and might. Our spirituality must be deeply rooted, and our commitment to diaspora missions resolute, as we strive to reach every non-believer across the globe. Seize these opportunities and, with a leap of faith, strive to repay the gospel debt for the sake of God's kingdom and his glory, following the example set by Dr. Wang. Are you truly listening—and discerning?

Bibliography

Caldwell, Larry W. "Diaspora Ministry in the Book of Acts: Insights from Two Speeches of the Apostle Paul to Help Guide Diaspora Ministry Today." In *Diaspora Missiology: Reflections on Reaching the Scattered Peoples of the World*, edited by Michael Pocock and Enoch Wan, 91–105. Evangelical Missiological Society Series 23. Pasadena, CA: William Carey Library, 2015.

Chan, Sharon. "Great Commission Center International—A Ministry of Integration of Spirituality with Mission." *Great Commission Quarterly* 20 (August 1998): 9–14. http://globalmissiology.org/gcci/Chinese/b5_publications/GCB/1998/GCB_2.pdf.

Chan, Sharon. *Ministry Highlights of the Great Commission Center International (GCCI): 1993–2017*. Great Commission Center International. http://globalmissiology.org/gcci/index_EN.html (accessed December 17, 2023).

Chan, Sharon. 大使命中心感恩紀念特刊: 1993–2017 [Great Commission Center International Thanksgiving Memorial Special Issue:1993–2017]. http://globalmissiology.org/gcci/pdf/GCCI%20Special%20Issue.pdf.

Dunaetz, David R. "Three Models of Acculturation: Applications for Developing a Church Planting Strategy among Diaspora Populations." In *Diaspora Missiology: Reflections on Reaching the Scattered Peoples of the World*, edited by Michael Pocock and Enoch Wan, 129–45. Evangelical Missiological Society Series 23. Pasadena, CA: William Carey Library, 2015.

Gospel Herald, The. "緬懷王永信牧師: 一輩子只為還福音的債" [Rev. Thomas Yung-Hsin Wang: A Life of Paying Back the Gospel Debt]. January 8, 2018. https://chinese.gospelherald.com/articles/26370/20180108/緬懷王永信牧師-一輩子只為還福音的債.html.

Green, Michael. *Evangelism in the Early Church*. Rev. ed. Grand Rapids, MI: Eerdmans, 2003.

Hesselgrave, David J. *Paradigms in Conflict: 10 Key Questions in Christian Missions Today*. Grand Rapids, MI: Kregel, 2005.

Hill, Graham. *Global Church: Reshaping Our Conversations, Renewing Our Mission, Revitalizing Our Churches*. Downers Grove, IL: InterVarsity Press, 2016.

International Organization for Migration. "World Migration Report 2022." https://worldmigrationreport.iom.int/wmr-2022-interactive/.

Leung, Luke. "Rev. Thomas Wang: 'World Missions Is the Responsibility of Chinese Church.'" *Gospel Herald*, December 3, 2007. https://www.gospelherald.com//article/missions/44032/rev-thomas-wang-world-missions-is-the-responsibility-of-chinese-church.html.

McIntosh, Gary L., and Alan McMahan. *Being the Church in a Multi-Ethnic Community: Why It Matters and How It Works*. Indianapolis, IN: Wesleyan Publishing, 2012.

Nussbaum, Stan. *A Reader's Guide to Transforming Mission: A Concise, Accessible Companion to David Bosch's Classic Book*. Maryknoll, NY: Orbis, 2005.

Wan, Enoch. "Global People and Diaspora Missiology." Plenary paper, Tokyo 2010 Global Mission Conference, Tokyo, Japan, May 11–14, 2010. http://tokyo2010.org/resources/Tokyo2010_Plenary_Enoch_Wan.pdf.

Wan, Enoch. "The Practice of Diaspora Missions in Local Congregation: From Beginning to Base." Evangelical Missiological Society National Conference, GIAL, Dallas, Texas, October 14–16, 2016. http://ojs.globalmissiology.org/index.php/english/article/view/1951.

Wan, Enoch. "Rethinking Missiology in the Context of the 21st Century: Global Demographic Trends and Diaspora Missiology." *Great Commission Research Journal* 2, no. 1 (Summer 2010). http://journals.biola.edu/gcr/volumes/2/issues/1/articles/7.

Wan, Enoch, and Jon Raibley, eds. *Transformational Change in Christian Ministry*. Portland, OR: Western Academic Publishers, 2022.

Wan, Enoch, and Sadiri Joy Tira. "Diaspora Missiology and Mission in the Context of the 21st Century." *Global Missiology English* 1, no. 8 (October 2010). http://ojs.globalmissiology.org/index.php/english/article/viewFile/383/994.

Wang, Thomas. "By the Year 2000: Is God Trying to Tell Us Something?" *World Evangelization* (June 1987). Reprinted by *International Journal of Frontier Missions*. https://ijfm.org/PDFs_IJFM/03_1-4_PDFs/3_1Wang.pdf.

Wang, Thomas. *The Kingdom Story*. Reprint. Sunnyvale, CA: Great Commission Center International, 2005.

Wang, Thomas. 中華民族最後的轉捩點 [The Last Turning Point of the Chinese Race]. Mountain View, CA: Great Commission Center International, 2004.

Wang, Thomas. "Our Origin and Development: The CCCOWE Movement and World Evangelization." Translated by CCCOWE. *Chinese Church Today*, January 1989. https://www.cccowe.org/pdf/en/cccowe_history.pdf.

Winter, Ralph. "The Mysterious Tension in Missions Today." *Mission Frontiers* (January–February 1992), Editorial Comment, January 1, 1992. https://www.missionfrontiers.org/issue/article/editorial-comment88.

Wood, Rick. "The AD2000 Movement." *Mission Frontiers* (Jan–Feb 1992). https://www.missionfrontiers.org/issue/article/the-ad2000-movement.

Yi, Kevin. "The Temptations of Using Your 'Calling' as an Excuse." Sola Network. https://sola.network/article/temptations-calling-as-excuse.

馮文莊 and 錢志群. "不能忘卻的懷念—追記王永信牧師的事奉人生"

Yi, Kevin. [Unforgettable Memories—Remembering the Life of Rev. Thomas Yung-Hsin Wang]. Chinese Christian Mission, 《傳》 *Bi-Monthly* 179 (July–Aug 2018). https://ccmusa.org/read/read.aspx?id=pro20180401.

Appendix A
Resources and Tools for Diaspora Missions
Annotated Bibliography

The Institute of Diaspora Studies (IDS) began at Western Seminary in Portland, Oregon in May 2007 with this mission statement: "The 'mission' of IDS is to investigate the effective communication of the gospel among the people of diaspora and through their networks to regions beyond."

The following are doctoral dissertations on diaspora missiology/missions available from the Theological Research Exchange Network (https://www.tren.com/).

Chen, Howard. "Marketplace Transformation Motivating and Mobilizing Chinese Churches in the Silicon Valley for Gospel Transformation." DIntSt diss., Western Seminary, 2020.

Choi, Paul. "Towards a Paradigm of Missional Ecclesiology for Korean Diaspora." DMiss diss., Western Seminary, 2014.

Edu-Bekoe, Yaw Attah, and Enoch Wan. *Africans Keep Coming*. Portland, OR: Institute of Diaspora Studies, 2013.

Edu-Bekoe, Yah Attah. "Ghanaian Diaspora: An Integrative Study of the Presbyterian Church of Ghana Congregations in the United States of America." DMiss diss., Western Seminary, 2011.

Hébert, Brian. "An Integrative Model for Sending Exogenous Missionaries to the Middle East and North Africa through Relational Diaspora Missions." DMin diss., Western Seminary, 2015.

Holland, Mike. "Diaspora Mission to Hispanics in the USA." DMiss diss., Western Seminary, 2013.

Isham, Phillip. "An Ethnography of the Tibetan Diaspora: A Multi-Sited Missiological Study." Doctoral diss., Western Seminary, 2020.

Khaing, Thet. "Ethnographic Study on Leadership in the Congregation of Selected Diaspora Burmese Churches in the Greater Chicago Metropolitan Area." DIntSt diss., Western Seminary, 2021.

Lai, James Mook Sum. "An Ethnography of the Contextual Approach of Community Projects Among the Yunnanese Chinese Community in Lashio, Myanmar." DMiss diss., Western Seminary, 2013.

Lau, Susanna. "Participation of Lay Leaders in Global Missions: An Ethnographic Study of Chinese Congregations in San Francisco Bay Area." Doctoral diss., Western Seminary, 2017.

Le, Thanh. "A Missiological Study of Vietnamese Diaspora." DMiss diss., Western Seminary, 2013.

Lopez, David. "An Ethnographic Study of the Hispanic Hybrid Identity in Miami." DIntSt diss., Western Seminary, 2019.

Martin, Ria. "From the Philippines to the Global North: A Participatory Action Research on Intercultural Campus Ministry." DIntSt diss, Western Seminary, 2021.

Nguyen, Tin. "An Intercultural Vocational Training Program for Kingdom Workers in Northern Vietnam." DIntSt diss., Western Seminary, 2022.

Tira, Sadiri Joy. "Filipino Kingdom Workers: An Ethnographic Study." DMiss diss., Western Seminary, 2008.

Tira, Sadiri Joy. *Filipino Kingdom Workers: An Ethnographic Study*. Spring 2008. EMS Dissertation Series. Pasadena, CA: William Carey International University Press, 2011.

Wan, Enoch, and Tuvya Zaretsky. *Jewish-Gentile Couples: Trends, Challenges, and Hopes*. Pasadena, CA: William Carey Library, 2004.

Wang, Juno. "A Phenomenological Study of an Intercultural Outreach Training Program for Multi-Ethnic Community Outreach Workers in Cupertino and Sunnyvale, California." DIntSt diss., Western Seminary, 2020.

Zaretsky, Tuvya. "The Challenges of Jewish-Gentile Couples: A Pre-evangelistic Ethnographic Study." DMiss diss., Western Seminary, 2004.

Institute of Diaspora Studies (IDS) at Western Seminary

In addition to developing leaders in the field of diaspora missiology (e.g., Joy Sidiri Tira of LCWE, Tuvya Zaretsky of Jews for Jesus, Thanh Trung Le of Vietnamese diaspora), IDS (Institute of Diaspora Studies) at Western Seminary has, since 2008, been publishing resources and tools for researchers and practitioners who are engaging in the diaspora missions, and international students ministries.

Center of Diaspora and Relational Research (CDRR) and Western Seminary Press

On April 26, 2018, the CDRR was created during a meeting with Randy Roberts, Enoch Wan, and Bonnie Ekholm. Its mission is "to conduct research and produce publications on diaspora missiology (the *IDS Series*) and relational paradigm (*IRR Series*) for the practice of Christian mission."

There are two branches of CDRR:

1. The Institute of Diaspora Studies (IDS) with publications in the *IDS Series*

2. The Institute of Relational Research (IRR) with publications in the *IRR Series*

The Western Seminary Press was created by and is administratively under the direction of Enoch Wan. It is formed and directed by Enoch Wan solely for the purpose of conducting research and producing publication of CDRR and is managed by Enoch Wan with no financial and legal liability to Western Seminary. Books published by Western Seminary Press (WSP) are mostly about diaspora missiology.

Besides resources produced by LCWE (the Lausanne Congress on World Evangelization) since Cape Town 2010, the following are some of the resources from CDRR.

Edu-Bekoe, Yaw Attah, and Enoch Wan. *Scattered Africans Keep Coming: A Case Study of Diaspora Missiology on Ghanaian Diaspora and Congregations in the USA*. Portland, OR: CreateSpace Independent Publishing Platform, 2013.

Wan, Enoch. *Diaspora Missiology: Theory, Methodology, and Practice*. 2nd ed. Portland, OR: Institute of Diaspora Studies at Western Seminary, 2014.

Wan, Enoch. *Diaspora Missions to International Students*. Portland, OR: Western Seminary Press, 2019.

Wan, Enoch, and Anthony Casey. *Church Planting among Immigrants in US Urban Centers (Second Edition): The "Where", "Why", And "How" of Diaspora*. 2nd ed. Portland, OR: CreateSpace Independent Publishing Platform, 2016.

Wan, Enoch, and Elton S. L. Law. *The 2011 Triple Disaster in Japan and the Diaspora: Lessons Learned and Ways Forward*. Portland, OR: CreateSpace Independent Publishing Platform, 2014.

Wan, Enoch, and Howard Shauhau Chen. *Marketplace Transformation: Motivating and Mobilizing Chinese Churches in the Silicon Valley for Gospel Transformation*. Portland, OR: Western Academic Publishers, 2021.

Wan, Enoch, and Jacky Lau. *Chinese Diaspora Kingdom Workers: In Action and With Guidance*. Portland, OR: Western Seminary Press, 2019.

Wan, Enoch, and J. David Lopez. *The Hispanic Hybrid Identity in Miami: Ethnographic Description and Missiological Implications*. Portland, OR: Western Academic Publishers, 2021.

Wan, Enoch, and Jeremiah Chung. *Engaging Chinese Diaspora in the Ministry of Bible Translation*. Portland, OR: Western Seminary Press, 2019.

Wan, Enoch, and John Kuo. *Multiethnic Ministry and Diaspora Missions in Action: A Case Study of the Wu Chang Church of Kaohsiung, Taiwan*. Portland, OR: Western Seminary Press, 2019.

Wan, Enoch, and Mike Hung Lei. *Missions beyond the Diaspora: Local Cross-Cultural Ministry of Chinese Congregations in the San Francisco Bay Area*. Portland, OR: Western Seminary Press, 2019.

Wan, Enoch, and Ted Rubesh. *Wandering Jews and Scattered Sri Lankans: Viewing Sri Lankans of the Gulf Cooperation Council through the Lens of the Old Testament Jewish Diaspora*. Portland, OR: CreateSpace Independent Publishing Platform, 2014.

Wan, Enoch, and Thanh Trung Le. *Mobilizing Vietnamese Diaspora for the Kingdom*. Portland, OR: CreateSpace Independent Publishing Platform, 2014.

Wan, Enoch, and Tin Nguyen. *A Holistic and Contextualized Mission Training Program: Equipping Lay Leaders for Local Mission in Vietnam*. Portland, OR: Western Academic Publishers, 2022.

PUBLICATIONS by the CENTER of DIASPORA and RELATIONAL RESEARCH (CDRR)
Western Seminary Press—Relational Series

Marketplace Transformation: Motivating and Mobilizing Chinese Churches in the Silicon Valley for Gospel Transformation

By Enoch Wan & Howard Sahuhau Chen

In this book, you will find (1) an ethnographic description of marketplace professionals in the Silicon Valley; (2) practical suggestions for motivating and mobilizing local Chinese churches in the Silicon Valley to engage marketplace professionals for marketplace transformation.

Publication date: August 12, 2021   List Price: $6.99

Covenant Transformative Learning: Theory and Practice for Mission

By Ryan Gimple & Enoch Wan

This book is a representation of covenant transformative learning theory and its application to basic tasks of cross-cultural missions. Covenant transformative learning theory is a derivative of Mezirow's transformative learning theory, but is reformed by the application of Meek's epistemological framework and practical in the use of "relational realism" paradigm.

Publication Date: August 19, 2021   List Price: $8.99

Engaging the Secular World through Life-On-Life Disciple-Making in the British Context: Relational Paradigm in Action

By Enoch Wan & Shane Mikeska

As the first volume in the "Relational Series," this book is a contemporary approach to engage the secular world through relational "life on life disciple-making" in the British context as a way to illustrate relational paradigm in action.

Publication Date: January 14, 2020   List Price: $6.97

The Hispanic Hybrid Identity in Miami: Ethnographic Description and Missiological Implications
By Enoch Wan & J. David Lopez

The purpose of this book is twofold: providing an ethnographic description of the Hispanic hybrid (HH) identity found in Miami-Dade County and deriving missiological implications from the ethnographic data.

Publication Date: January 14, 2020   List Price: $6.97

A Theology of Spirit-anointed Witness in Holistic Christian Mission Framed in the Relational Paradigm
By Enoch Wan & Mathew Karimpanamannil

In this book, a theology of spirit-anointed witness in holistic Christian mission is articulated with an emphasis on "relational paradigm." The thesis is that the church be authorized, enlightened, enriched, equipped and empowered to proclaim, practice and demonstrate the power of God's kingdom.

Publication Date: December 20, 2019   List Price $5.99

Missionary Preparation in the Gospel of Matthew in Light of 28:16–20
By Enoch Wan & Rob Penner

In this book, the authors propose an alternative to the popular understanding that Matthew 28:18–20 is the "Great Commission" passage.

Publication Date: February 18, 2022   List Price: $9.50

Holistic Mission through Mission Partnership
By Enoch Wan & John Jay Flinn

This book is about mission partnership, between Total Health (US based) with the La Ceiba GCLA church in Honduras that offers unique opportunities to transformation in both patients at the clinic and the mission workers at the same time. In this case study of holistic mission through mutuality and reciprocity, God is at work spiritually and physically among both patients in the clinic and the mission workers.

Publication Date: August 19, 2021   List Price: $9.99

The Cross and the Kaleidoscope
By Alex Early & Enoch Wan

The purpose of this book is to integrate the doctrine of Penal substitutionary atonement with the relational paradigm for Christian ministry in the 21st century employing a kaleidoscopic perspective.

Publication Date: November 2, 2021   List Price: $9.99

Doxological Missiology: Theory, Motivation and Practice
By Enoch Wan & Jace Cloud

This book makes the case that the imago Dei can only be properly understood in connection with the mission Dei and the gloria Dei, "Glorifying God" is accomplished as the image bearers of God are sent on the mission Dei in order to spread the glory of God throughout the earth as they live out God's truth, goodness, and beauty in the world. In this sense, the integration of the image of God, mission of God, and glory of God are combined into the new paradigm of "Doxological Missiology" and applied in theory, motivation and practice.

Publication Date: February 29, 2022   List Price: $8.50

Establishing Frontline LGBTQ Outreach
By Noel Chiu & Enoch Wan

This book is an exploratory study dedicated in searching for key parameters which can be systematically followed as guidelines and will positively contribute to Christian leaders seeking to establish Frontline LGBTQ Outreach, in order to witness to those within LGBTQ communities.

Publication Date: February 21, 2022   List Price: $11.75

A Holistic Contextualized Mission Training Program
By Enoch Wan & Tin Nguyen

In this book, the readers will find a detailed presentation of mission training programs for contemporary Vietnam that is contextually appropriate in terms of their cultural background and contemporary living surroundings. The design of the mission training program is based on an educational and anthropological understanding of Vietnamese lay leaders with the goal of motivating and mobilizing them for Christian mission.

Publication Date: March 22, 2022   List Price: $7.50

Relational Leadership Development: An Ethnological Study in Inuit Contexts

By Enoch Wan & John Ferch

By using existing ethnographic data on the Inuit, the authors in this book propose a relational, orality-based model for ministry leadership development that is "glocalized" to Inuit contexts.

Publication Date: February 19, 2022   List Price: $7.50

Appendix B
The Seoul Declaration on Diaspora Missiology

November 14, 2009

Convening as missions leaders, mobilizers, educators, trainers, and kingdom workers in the diaspora at the Lausanne Diaspora Educators Consultation on November 11–14, 2009 in Seoul, Korea—in partnership with and an extension of the Lausanne Diaspora Strategy Consultation held in Manila, Philippines on May 4–8, 2009.

We Acknowledge

1. That the sovereign work of the Father, Son, and Holy Spirit in the gathering and scattering of peoples across the earth is a central part of God's mission and redemptive purposes for the world.
2. That the church, which is the body of Christ, is the principal means through which God is at work in different ways around the globe. We honor the uniqueness, dignity, and beauty in each person and culture, celebrating the collaboration of the church with the broader society.
3. That "diaspora missiology" has emerged as a biblical and strategic field of missiology and is defined as: a missiological framework for understanding and participating in God's redemptive mission among people living outside their place of origin.

We Affirm

1. That our missional focus and ministry integrates and cooperates with the mission and vision of the Lausanne movement for world evangelization as published in The Lausanne Covenant and The Manila Manifesto.
2. That although we draw from various disciplines, our understanding and practice of the mission of God must be informed by, integrated with, and conformed to biblical and theological foundations.

We Appeal

1. To the whole people of God in local churches and church movements, mission agencies, the academy, and the marketplace to mobilize, train, deploy, support, work together with, and empower "diaspora kingdom workers" for the diaspora fields ripe for harvest.

2. To church and mission leaders to recognize and respond to opportunities in world evangelization presented by the realities of the global diaspora.

3. To missions leaders and educators to give strategic priority in the funding and training of personnel and to provide space for the development of "diaspora missiology" in training systems and curricula.

4. To the Lord of the harvest to send forth laborers into the harvest and raise up worldwide intercession for an unprecedented move of the Holy Spirit so that *the Whole Church takes the Whole Gospel to the Whole World.*

LCWE Diaspora Educators Consultation 2009
Torch Trinity Graduate School of Theology
Seoul, South Korea
November 11–14, 2009

Acknowledgments

This volume is the product of collaboration and partnership with like-minded kingdom workers:

- Roberto Bolivar, the Executive Director of PALM Ministry Association, friend, brother, and my encourager.
- Pastor Teck Uy, Pastor Junn Lagud, and their Filipino congregations in Greater Toronto Area (GTA: Friends of Jesus and Hallelujah Fellowship Baptist Church respectively), and the Togade Family, former members of the First Filipino Alliance Church in Edmonton. All of them prayed and shared their financial resources because they saw the potential global impact of this publication.
- All the missiologists, researchers, reflective-practitioners, book endorsers, and the team at William Carey Publishing who contributed their time and professional expertise to this project are all appreciated.

All these partners are like the children of Issachar who understood the time and knew what Israel (the global church) should do (1 Chr 12:32) with the *Tides of Opportunity*.

In the words of the apostle Paul: *Thank you for your partnership in the gospel* (Phil 1:3–5).

SADIRI JOY TIRA, Editor

About the Editors and Contributors

Senior Editor

DR. SADIRI "JOY" TIRA is diaspora missiology specialist at the Jaffray Centre for Global Initiatives at Ambrose University in Canada. A reflective-practitioner, Sadiri Joy Tira served as catalyst for diasporas (formerly, senior associate for diasporas) for the Lausanne Movement from 2007–2019, as founding chairperson of the Global Diaspora Network (2010–2015), and for over two decades, as senior pastor of First Filipino Alliance Church in Edmonton, Alberta—Canada's "Gateway to the North." He is also a blogger for Outreach Canada.

Associate Editors

DAMPLES DULCERO-BACLAGON is the managing editor of *Asian Missions Advance* and secretary of Asia Missions Association. She obtained a master's degree in Asian Studies from the University of the Philippines. Prior to that, she was trained as a missionary at the East West Center for Missions Research and Development, Korea where she also served for six years under the late Dr. David J. Cho. In the Philippines where she now lives, she serves as the national discipleship coordinator of Operation Christmas Child, a ministry of Samaritan's Purse.

LORAJOY TIRA-DIMANGONDAYAO is an MTS student at St. Stephen's College at the University of Alberta (Canada). She has a bachelor's of theology from Ambrose University (formerly Canadian Bible College). Lorajoy serves as a press editor for the Jaffray Centre for Global Initiatives at Ambrose University and serves on the Lausanne Movement Canada's Board of Directors. With diaspora missiology close to her heart, she served as Dr. Sadiri Joy Tira's administrative assistant for two decades. She is co-editor of *Beyond Hospitality: Migration, Multiculturalism, and the Church.*

Contributors

DR. CHRIS CARR and his wife EILEEN have served as executive director and co-director, respectively, of Global Gates Network of Canada since arriving in the Greater Toronto Area in September of 2017. They previously served in Russia and Ukraine from 1999–2015 with the International Mission Board. Chris earned a master of divinity in biblical languages in 1997 from Southwestern Baptist Theological Seminary in Fort Worth, Texas, a doctor of ministry in international church planting leadership in 2010 from Midwestern Baptist Theological Seminary in Kansas City, Missouri, and a PhD in biblical missiology in 2021 from Midwestern Baptist Theological Seminary in Kansas City, Missouri.

MARION L. S. CARSON is a theologian, teacher, and trainer who lives in Glasgow, Scotland. A former psychiatric nurse, she currently serves as chaplain to Glasgow City Mission, where she works with people affected by homelessness and addictions, as well as with asylum seekers and refugees. She is a senior research fellow at International Baptist Theological Study Centre in Amsterdam, Netherlands. She is the author of *Setting the Captives Free: The Bible and Human Trafficking*, and *Human Trafficking, the Bible and the Church: An Interdisciplinary Study*.

REBEKAH CLAPP has spent the past decade working in Hispanic/Latino ministries in the US within the United Methodist Church (UMC) at local and regional levels and more recently in theological education. She is ordained in the UMC and has served in a variety of capacities in Spanish-speaking communities and offered opportunities for theological education at the seminary level to this community in the US and in Latin America. She received her BA in Spanish language and literature, international communications, and philosophy from Asbury College in 2011. She received her MDiv from United Theological Seminary in 2015. Currently, she is a PhD candidate in intercultural studies at Asbury Theological Seminary and a John Wesley Fellow, focusing on contextual theology and diaspora missiology among the US Hispanic/Latino community.

MATT COOK is the Assistant Professor of Bible, Global Missions, and World Religions at Freed-Hardeman University and is the Program Coordinator of the Doctor of Ministry program. Prior to his role at FHU, Matt and his wife Charla were church planters in Cusco, Peru. Matt received a Master of Arts in New Testament and a Master of Divinity (2007) from Freed-Hardeman University, and also received a ThM and a PhD (2019) in Missions and World Religions from The Southern Baptist Theological Seminary. His dissertation was focused on diaspora missiology, specifically diaspora missiology in rural areas of Tennessee. He is proud to be from rural West Virginia and in addition to his professor duties, he serves in ministry with a nearby rural church.

VALERIE GEER is the founder and visionary of the House of Ezer, a trauma-informed ministry for survivors of sex trafficking. While she waits on the Lord to release a property to the ministry, she engages in grassroots advocacy for women experiencing sexual trauma and gender-based marginalization. Prior to this work, her ministry career was focused primarily in mainland China, teaching English (Beijing) and training Chinese teachers (Zhuhai City, Guangdong), as well as establishing TESOL certification and coursework at Christian universities. In 1999 she earned her BA in missions and biblical studies at Northwest University, Kirkland, WA (USA). In 2004 she received her MA in intercultural studies & TESOL from Wheaton College, Wheaton, IL (USA). And in 2017, she obtained her doctor of intercultural studies from Western Seminary, Portland, OR (USA).

THOMAS ALAN HARVEY serves as the academic dean of the Oxford Centre for Mission Studies. He received his training from Asbury Theological Seminary (MDiv), University of Notre Dame (ThM), and Duke University (PhD). Previously he was the senior lecturer at Trinity Theological College in systematic theology and Christian ethics for eleven years. He also worked with the Singaporean Presbyterian Church as a partner in mission from the Presbyterian Church (USA). The Reverend Dr. Harvey is an ordained Minister with the Presbyterian Church (USA), Presbytery of Hope.

CRAIG CLINTON KRAFT and his family joined Outreach Canada Ministries (OC) in 2003 with the goal of serving as missionaries in Africa. Since returning from Africa, Craig has been significantly involved in the development of the OC Global Alliance (OCGA), a partnership of fifteen mission sending organizations around the world. Craig has served in various capacities on the OCGA Guidance Team, where he is currently the moderator. Dr. Craig completed doctor of intercultural studies program at Asia Graduate School of Theology, Philippines. Craig's dissertation is entitled, "Welcoming Strangers: Church Revitalization through the Practice of Biblical Hospitality Toward Syrian Refugees in Canada." Craig is also the author of *New Life in the Church*, and several articles and blogs on biblical hospitality. Dr. Craig C. Kraft (ckraft@outreach.ca) is the executive director of Outreach Canada Ministries. Craig has over thirty years of ministry experience as a Canadian pastor and cross-cultural missionary.

DR. JASON RICHARD TAN serves as a mentor and coach for pastoral leaders, church planters, and pastoral trainers in the Philippines. He has over twenty years of experience in ministry, serving in various capacities as a pastor, missionary, and professor. He is the president of the Great Commission Missionary Training Center in Antipolo City. He also serves as a ministry strategist for the GProCommission for Pastoral Trainers. As a missiologist, he serves on the faculty of the Asia Graduate School of Theology (AGST) and as a visiting professor of Intercultural Studies at Biblical Seminary of the Philippines (BSOP). He holds a PhD in intercultural studies from Trinity Evangelical Divinity School in Illinois, a ThM in systematic theology from Asia Graduate School of Theology in the Philippines, and an MDiv in missions from Alliance Graduate School (AGS). He is available by email at profjtan!@gmail.com.

DR. JUNO WANG is focusing her ministry on glocal missions, relational intercultural training, and publication. She served at the Great Commission Center International under the leadership of the late Dr. Thomas Wang for almost eighteen years before pursuing her seminary training. She graduated from the Western Seminary with an intercultural studies doctorate degree and the Golden Gate Baptist Theological Seminary with an intercultural ministry master's degree. Juno has been involved in the multi-ethnic community outreach in Sunnyvale and Cupertino of California since 2009, and in intercultural training since 2016.

DR. STEVEN YBARROLA is dean of the E. Stanley Jones School of Mission and Ministry, and professor of cultural anthropology, at Asbury Theological Seminary. He earned his BA from Bethel University, and his MA and PhD of Anthropology from Brown University. Prior to his academic career, Steve served for nearly four years with the mission organization Operation Mobilization in Europe and Latin America. He taught at Central College in Pella, Iowa, for fifteen years prior to coming to Asbury in 2006. Steve's areas of specialty in anthropology have been migration, ethnicity/race, intergroup relations, and identity. He has conducted ethnographic research in the Basque Country of Spain, among the Basque diaspora in California, among the Hispanic diaspora in Iowa, and among Cajuns in Louisiana. He is currently studying the Latin American diaspora in the Basque Country of Spain, and the impact they are having on the relatively small evangelical churches there.

TUVYA ZARETSKY is one of the founders of the Jews for Jesus Ministry. He is currently director of staff training and board chair of Jews for Jesus Israel. Raised in the institutions of American Judaism, Zaretsky came to faith in Messiah Jesus in 1970. He attended the first Lausanne Congress in 1974 and has served the Lausanne consultation on Jewish evangelism since 1999. His doctor of missiology in intercultural studies is from Western Seminary, in Portland, Oregon. Dr. Zaretsky's ministry specialization is now helping the Jewish-Gentile couples discover spiritual harmony in Jesus. For two decades, he served as president of the Lausanne Consultation in Jewish Evangelism, the longest standing Lausanne issue network.

WILLIAM CAREY PUBLISHING

visit us at missionbooks.org

A Hybrid World: Diaspora, Hybridity, and Missio Dei

Sadiri Joy Tira and Juliet Lee Uytanlet, editors

A Hybrid World is the product of a global consultation of church and mission leaders who discussed the implications of hybridity in the mission of God. The contributors draw from their collective experiences and perspectives, explore emerging concepts and initiatives, and ground them in authoritative Scripture for application to the challenges that hybridity presents to global missions. This book honestly wrestles with the challenges of ethnic hybridity and ultimately encourages the global church to celebrate the opportunities that our sovereign and loving God provides for the world's scattered people to be gathered to himself.

Refugee Diaspora: Missions amid the Greatest Humanitarian Crisis of the World

Miriam Adeney and Sam George, editors

Refugee Diaspora is a contemporary account of the global refugee situation and how the light of the gospel of Jesus Christ is shining brightly in the darkest corners of the greatest crisis on our planet. These hope-filled pages of refugees encountering Jesus Christ presents models of Christian ministry from the front lines of the refugee crisis and the real challenges of ministering to today's refugees. It includes biblical, theological, and practical reflections on mission in diverse diaspora contexts from leading scholars as well as practitioners in all major regions of the world.

A Better Country (Second Edition): Embracing the Refugees in Our Midst

Cindy M. Wu

A Better Country aims to help Christians—specifically Christians in the United States—think theologically and practically about the ongoing and changing refugee needs. This workbook is divided into six lessons followed by a personal action plan as your application. The second edition includes additional questions for discussion, along with spiritual practices at the end of each chapter for transformation of mind, heart, and soul in our posture toward refugee welcome. This resource balances information and reflection that will stimulate excellent group discussions and individual study.

www.ingramcontent.com/pod-product-compliance
Lightning Source LLC
Chambersburg PA
CBHW052138070526
44585CB00017B/1879